RENEWING
NEIGHBOURH~~OODS~~

Work, enterprise

Stephen Syrett and David

This edition published in Great Britain in 2008 by

The Policy Press
University of Bristol
Fourth Floor
Beacon House
Queen's Road
Bristol BS8 1QU
UK

Tel +44 (0)117 331 4054
Fax +44 (0)117 331 4093
e-mail tpp-info@bristol.ac.uk
www.policypress.org.uk

British Library Cataloguing in Publication Data
A catalogue record for this book is available from the British Library.

Library of Congress Cataloging-in-Publication Data
A catalog record for this book has been requested.

ISBN 978 1 86134 861 6 paperback
ISBN 978 1 86134 862 3 hardcover

The right of Stephen Syrett and David North to be identified as authors of
this work has been asserted by them in accordance with the 1988 Copyright,
Designs and Patents Act.

The statements and opinions contained within this publication are solely those
of the authors and not of The University of Bristol or The Policy Press. The
University of Bristol and The Policy Press disclaim responsibility for any injury
to persons or property resulting from any material published in this publication.

The Policy Press works to counter discrimination on grounds of gender, race,
disability, age and sexuality.

Cover design by Qube Design Associates, Bristol
Front cover: image kindly supplied by www.alamy.com
Printed and bound in Great Britain by Hobbs the Printers, Southampton

For my parents, Pam and Arthur

For Margaret

Contents

List of tables, figures and boxes

Tables

Figures

Boxes

Acknowledgements

While we have been involved in researching and teaching in the field of local economic development and urban policy for many years, the inspiration for this book largely stemmed from our involvement in two particular pieces of research over the last five years, which have focused on policy developments under New Labour. The first of these comprised a series of evidence-based reviews for the government's Neighbourhood Renewal Unit (NRU) on the changes affecting the economies of deprived neighbourhoods. As well as a review of the literature relating to business and regeneration, worklessness and the informal economy, the research also involved a closer examination of what was happening in five deprived localities within England. The second was a study funded by the Joseph Rowntree Foundation as part of its 'Transforming the Prospects of Places' programme on the implications of devolution and regional governance throughout the UK for policies concerned with addressing the economic needs of those living within deprived neighbourhoods. We are most grateful to the many individuals who made these research projects possible including the many policy makers, regeneration professionals, community activists and local residents who gave their time to answer our questions and share their experiences and insights with us. Although these are too many to mention, we would particularly like to thank the two research project managers, Andrew Maginn (of the Department for Communities and Local Government) and Katharine Knox (of the Joseph Rowntree Foundation), for their support and interest in discussing the issues raised by the research, as well as Mel Evans, Ian Sanderson and Colin Williams for their work on the original reports produced for the NRU. Special thanks are due to our colleagues Rob Baldock, Ian Vickers, Stacey Clift and David Etherington in the Centre for Enterprise and Economic Development Research (CEEDR) at Middlesex University for their assistance with carrying out many of the interviews and analysis of secondary sources on which the book is based. We also need to say a special thank you to Sue Engelbert and Pamela Macaulay, also of CEEDR, for their painstaking work in putting the typescript together. And finally, as always with such endeavours, this work could not have been completed without the unending support and understanding of our families, to whom we owe our biggest debt of gratitude.

Stephen Syrett and David North
CEEDR, Middlesex University

List of abbreviations

A8	Accession 8
ABG	Area–Based Grant
ABI	area–based initiative
ATJ	Action Teams for Jobs
BIC	Business in the Community
BL	Business Link
BME	black and minority ethnic
BMEB	black and minority ethnic businesses
CBI	Confederation of British Industries
CDC	City Development Company
CEEDR	Centre for Enterprise and Economic Development Research
CGS	City Growth Strategy
CLG	Communities and Local Government
DBERR	Department for Business, Enterprise and Regulatory Reform
DCLG	Department of Communities and Local Government
DCSF	Department for Children, Schools and Families
DDEP	Derby and Derbyshire Economic Partnership
DfES	Department for Education and Skills
DIUS	Department for Innovation, Universities and Skills
DoT	Department of Transport
DTI	Department for Trade and Industry
DWP	Department for Work and Pensions
eb4u	East Brighton for You
ebbs	East Brighton Business Support
EC	European Commission
emda	East Midlands Development Agency
EMRA	East Midlands Regional Assembly
ERDF	European Regional Development Fund
ESF	European Social Fund
ESRC	Economic and Social Research Council
EU	European Union
EZ	Enterprise Zone
GDP	Gross Domestic Product
GEM	Global Entrepreneurship Monitor
GO	Government Office
GOEM	Government Office for the East Midlands

IB	Incapacity Benefit
ICIC	Initiative for a Competitive Inner City
IDBR	Inter-Departmental Business Register
ILM	intermediate labour market
ILO	International Labour Organisation
IMD	Index of Multiple Deprivation
JCP	Jobcentre Plus
JSA	Jobseeker's Allowance
LA	local authority
LAA	Local Area Agreement
LAD	local authority district
LEGI	Local Enterprise Growth Initiative
LETS	Local Exchange Trading Systems
LFS	Labour Force Survey
LSC	Learning and Skills Council
LSEP	Leicester Shire Economic Partnership
LSP	Local Strategic Partnership
MANSKEP	Mansfield, Sutton and Kirkby Enterprise Partnership
MASP	Mansfield Area Strategic Partnership
NDC	New Deal for Communities
NDLP	New Deal for Lone Parents
NDU	New Deal for the Unemployed
NDYP	New Deal for Young People
NEET	not in education, employment or training
NHS	National Health Service
NRF	Neighbourhood Renewal Fund
NRU	Neighbourhood Renewal Unit
NVQ	National Vocational Qualification
ODPM	Office of the Deputy Prime Minister
PDF	Phoenix Development Fund
PSA	Public Service Agreement
PtW	Pathways to Work
RDA	Regional Development Agency
REF	Regional Employability Framework
RES	Regional Economic Strategy
SDC	Sheffield Development Corporation
SES	Social Enterprise Sunderland
SEU	Social Exclusion Unit
SIMD	Scottish Index of Multiple Deprivation
SME	small and medium-sized enterprise
SOA	Super Output Area

SRB	Single Regeneration Budget
SRBCF	Single Regeneration Budget Challenge Fund
SRP	subregional partnership
TTWA	Travel to Work Area
TUC	Trade Union Congress
UDC	Urban Development Corporation
USM	Under-Served Markets
VAT	Value Added Tax
WIMD	Welsh Index of Multiple Deprivation
WNF	Working Neighbourhoods Fund
WNP	Working Neighbourhoods Pilot

ONE

In search of economic revival

Introduction

The persistence of poverty, social inequality and social exclusion spatially concentrated in certain localities and neighbourhoods is a longstanding and prominent feature of urban landscapes. Such spatially concentrated deprivation is largely tolerated and ignored on a day-to-day basis, yet comes into political focus during periods of social unrest, whether in the form of riots, gangland activity, terrorism or more everyday antisocial behaviour. These events revive, albeit often only temporarily, well-rehearsed debates concerning the dangers of concentrated deprivation in undermining social and community cohesion and creating political instability, as well as the moral issues of permitting the existence of severe social inequalities and the costs of spatial inequalities to wider economic performance.

The shift towards a liberalised global economy has been characterised by not only the persistence but also the entrenchment of concentrated urban deprivation within the advanced Western economies. The contemporary presence of spatially focused poverty is not just an issue for cities and regions experiencing economic decline and readjustment, but also for those that are economically competitive and prosperous. In recent years London, Paris and Los Angeles – cities that are commonly seen as central hubs of the global economy – have all had their own traumatic experiences of high-profile social unrest within deprived inner or outer urban neighbourhoods.

It is against this background that policy makers have been formulating and implementing an array of policy interventions that seek to address the 'problem' of these so-called disadvantaged neighbourhoods. In Britain, the link between social exclusion, community cohesion and spatially concentrated deprivation has given rise to a plethora of policy initiatives. Since 1997, the New Labour governments have placed area-based initiatives (ABIs), such as the National Strategy for Neighbourhood Renewal and the New Deal for Communities (NDC), at the centre of their social exclusion agenda. Yet despite considerable investment in policy development and experimentation there is no sign that localised deprivation is set to disappear. Poor areas persist and new areas of deprivation emerge. Even when areas do undergo regeneration or gentrification, the evidence demonstrates that the majority of local residents of such areas fail to benefit.

The problems of deprived areas are multifaceted, with residents commonly experiencing higher levels of crime, poorer health, environmental degradation and poorer housing than those in less deprived areas. However, it is the failure of the residents of such areas to benefit from processes of economic development that remains at the core of the problem. Within liberal, market economies, labour market exclusion remains central to issues of poverty and deprivation and entering employment remains the most effective route out of poverty. Issues of high levels of unemployment and low economic participation rates, along with low levels of investment, are consequently defining features of deprived neighbourhoods.

Yet tackling the economic basis of this problem remains problematic. Despite an array of approaches that have centred upon varying combinations of interventions related to physical redevelopment, enterprise promotion and labour market integration, success has been largely elusive. In this regard a feature of the high-profile neighbourhood renewal and NDC initiatives in England has been their relative failure to address the economic dimension of the problems besetting deprived neighbourhoods. These area-based approaches have emphasised an integrated and holistic approach to neighbourhood renewal – including issues of employment and economic development – but the evidence suggests that the economic dimension of such policy interventions has been weak and governance arrangements have been poorly positioned to deliver effective economic development to deprived areas. Recognition of this fact has led to recent changes in policy, funding and institutional arrangements, which have moved the economic aspects of neighbourhood renewal centre-stage.

The failure to date to address the economic needs of deprived neighbourhoods suggests that a number of questions remain to be answered if this most recent shift in policy direction is to be successful. What are the lessons from the last 40 years of intervention and have they been learnt? Is there an adequate understanding of the differences between deprived neighbourhoods and how they are linked into the wider economies in which they are embedded? Are the relative merits and limitations of various place-based and people-based interventions fully understood? Is there clarity over the rationale for intervention within deprived neighbourhoods and what is trying to be achieved? What are the most appropriate governance arrangements for delivering effective intervention in these areas and at what spatial scales should they operate? Are there other models of sustainable local development that offer effective alternative paths to the current neoliberal informed policy agenda?

This book seeks to address these questions through critically analysing the economic nature of the problems of deprived neighbourhoods and the policy responses that have developed to this within Britain. The analysis centres upon understanding contemporary economic change and the post-1997 period of the New Labour government, but is placed within a wider context of longer-term processes of economic restructuring and a history of policy intervention that dates back for well over 40 years. The arguments advanced draw upon both findings from recent academic research and policy practice combined with empirical evidence from five case study local areas within England, selected to demonstrate different economic contexts within which deprived neighbourhoods are embedded in the contemporary socioeconomic landscape.

The book focuses on three elements that have dominated policy development and implementation in relation to tackling concentrated deprivation in recent years: work, enterprise and governance. The other major element relating to the economic development of deprived areas – the physical redevelopment of such areas – is here considered in relation to the wider policy agenda and the issues of work, enterprise and governance, but is not pursued as a separate theme. In terms of the element of work, intervention aimed at reducing high levels of worklessness and shifting residents of deprived areas in receipt of welfare benefits into paid employment has been a predominant focus of activity. Alongside this, the promotion of enterprise and an entrepreneurial culture within deprived areas, through both attracting in businesses and developing indigenous businesses and self-employment, has been pursued as a means of developing the economic base and competitiveness of such areas. With respect to governance, repeated changes in institutional frameworks and governance arrangements have attempted to improve the effectiveness of strategy development and policy delivery of economic activity in deprived neighbourhoods. Although strongly interrelated and potentially mutually reinforcing, the pursuit of these different elements also reveals tensions between them, rooted within the wider dominant discourse of urban development that has informed recent policy development.

The rest of this chapter sets out the scope and terms of debate for the rest of the book. The chapter first locates the nature of the problem of deprivation concentrated in particular neighbourhoods within wider trends evident in spatial patterns of deprivation within

—

advanced Western economies generally and the UK in particular. The chapter then outlines what constitutes a 'deprived neighbourhood' and the issues involved in mapping localised concentrations of deprivation. Arguments for different styles of response, whether through the delivery of mainstream policies or via area-based interventions, are introduced and an overview presented of how UK urban policy has addressed the issue of neighbourhood deprivation in the post-Second World War period. The final part of the chapter focuses on policy development under successive New Labour governments and the varying rationales that have informed policy intervention, to identify a number of key themes to be explored throughout the remainder of the book.

Identifying the problem: spatial concentrations of deprivation

The spatial concentrations of deprivation that are such a highly visible component of contemporary urban landscapes in advanced industrial economies are by no means new. Concentrated disadvantage has been a feature of urban capitalist development throughout its history, not least in the cities that grew out of the early phase of industrial capitalism in the late 17th century. In the 20th century, expectations that economic growth might remove such concentrated poverty, either on its own or in concert with a variety of state interventions, were seen to be largely misplaced. Indeed what is impressive is the persistence of poverty in certain neighbourhoods over decades and in some cases centuries. That low-income, disadvantaged neighbourhoods persist through successive periods of economic development indicates the structural role they perform within the operation of the wider urban economy via the production and reproduction of low-cost labour to provide cheap services to businesses and residents (Fainstein et al, 1993; Sassen, 2001). Indeed the original rationale for the building of many low-income neighbourhoods was specifically to provide low-cost labour to particular industries or urban areas (Lupton, 2003).

Yet these patterns of spatial deprivation are not fixed. Alongside neighbourhoods of longstanding deprivation are other narratives of change, of formerly prosperous areas spiralling into dereliction, or the much-vaunted gentrification and regeneration of previously deprived neighbourhoods. This process of capitalist uneven development is memorably described by Harvey (1985, p 150):

> Capitalist development must negotiate a knife-edge between preserving the value of past commitments made at

a particular place and time, or devaluing them to open up
fresh room for accumulation…. The inner contradictions
of capitalism are expressed through the restless formation
and re-formation of geographical landscapes.

Historically different phases of economic development produce
particular spatial and temporal fixes with their own geographic patterns
of growth and deprivation. In the current era of an increasingly
globalised economic arena, processes of structural and technological
change have interacted with state-sponsored processes of deregulation
and reregulation to create new landscapes. Significantly, the current
phase of neoliberal, global economic development is characterised by
the continuation and, in certain cases, intensification of concentrated
deprivation. Indeed a prominent and repeated feature of the economic
heartlands of the global economy, the major global cities and economic
motor regions, is the close proximity of areas of great wealth to areas
of intense deprivation (Sassen, 2001).

Current landscapes of deprivation and social exclusion within
advanced industrial countries are rooted within, and constitutive
of, an increasingly apparent widening of social inequalities. This is
a particular characteristic of those countries that have aggressively
pursued neoliberal economic agendas. In Britain, successive studies have
demonstrated the trend towards increased levels of social inequality,
whether in terms of incomes, skills, education or health. Dorling et
al (2007), in their major study of changing area patterns of poverty
and wealth in Britain, conclude that, since 1970, area rates of poverty
and wealth have changed significantly, with Britain moving back
towards levels of inequality in wealth and poverty last seen more
than 40 years ago. Green and Owen (2006), in their comprehensive
analysis of the changing landscape of work and skills in England and
Wales over the period 1991-2001, similarly conclude that the picture
is one of increasing polarisation in skills demand and supply across
the country.

In policy terms the pursuit of a competitive position within a
liberalised global economy has seen fundamental shifts in the role
of nation states towards a policy emphasis on supporting economic
competitiveness and away from more traditional concerns with welfare
and social justice. This transition has been characterised as a shift from
a Keynesian welfare state to a Schumpeterian workfare state that
dates from 1970s and intensified from the early 1980s (Peck, 2001). In
Britain, this shift has been characterised by a major deregulation and
reregulation of state activity to promote economic competitiveness,

innovation and flexibility. Such an emphasis has remained a defining feature of economic, urban and welfare policy under the New Labour governments that came to power from 1997, despite their introduction of a range of high-profile policies related to poverty and social exclusion that have struggled to promote a more 'equal society' (Hills and Stewart, 2005).

Against this background of economic liberalisation, rising social inequalities and state activity increasingly focused on promoting economic competitiveness, it is perhaps not surprising that spatial divergence has been evident. Recent years have seen the UK's regional and local economies become more divergent, with divides evident not only at the regional level between the fast-growing South East and a few other major cities, and the rest of the country, but also within cities and regions. At the level of major English cities, there is a consistent pattern of better-performing cities, measured on the basis of indices such as education, low worklessness, low poverty, average house prices and life expectancy, being located within the South and particularly South East of England, and only a limited number of northern cities showing similar levels of performance (Dorling, 2006; Parkinson et al, 2006).

In terms of levels of deprivation, this is generally a larger problem in cities, rather than in towns and rural areas, with the metropolitan, larger and smaller cities of the North and West consistently demonstrating the highest levels of deprivation (Parkinson et al, 2006, p 111). Levels of deprivation across English cities show considerable disparities from the highest levels of deprivation in Liverpool through to the lowest levels in southern cities such as Reading, Crawley and Aldershot (see Figure 1.1).

Within cities themselves, research findings demonstrate the persistence of patterns of poverty and deprivation, and in certain cases indications of increasing concentration, which are present even within cities enjoying strong economic growth (Buck et al, 2002; Boddy, 2003; Boddy and Parkinson, 2004; Turok et al, 2004; Parkinson et al, 2006). Overall, the evidence across UK cities is, as Boddy and Parkinson (2004, p 416) conclude, one of 'major variations in levels of social and economic advantage and the concentration in particular neighbourhoods of high levels of persistent disadvantage'. Furthermore, the evidence also suggests that these trends towards increasing geographical inequalities in wealth, which started under the Thatcher period, have in fact intensified under the New Labour government (Dorling, 2006).

Central to understanding the differing trajectories of the UK's regional and local economies is an awareness of how processes of

Figure 1.1: Level of deprivation by individual city in England, 2004

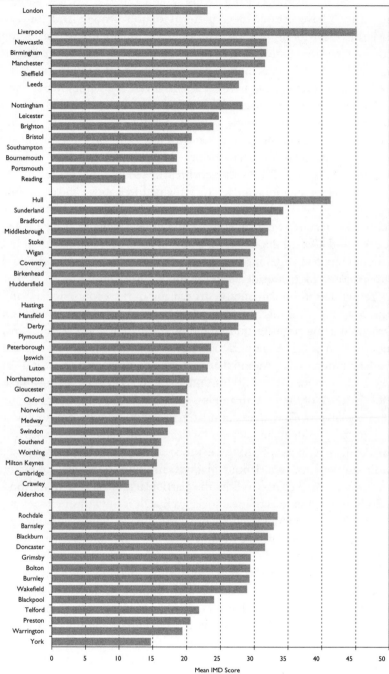

Mean IMD Score

Source: Parkinson et al (2006, p 113)

economic restructuring and sectoral change, most notably the decline of traditional manufacturing industry and the rise of new service industries, have created new patterns of job growth and job loss (Martin and Morrison, 2003). Although nationally the period of job loss and mass unemployment of the 1980s was replaced by rising levels of employment and declining unemployment in the 1990s, processes of labour market change have seen high levels of unemployment and inactivity becoming entrenched within certain groups and certain areas. Groups such as single parents, people from minority ethnic communities, older men and those with low skills are much less likely to be in work. Spatially it has been the large cities in northern Britain, Inner London, as well as former coalfield areas and some seaside towns where levels of unemployment have remained well above, and economic activity rates well below, the national average (Beatty and Fothergill, 1996; Green and Owen, 1998; Turok and Edge, 1999; Beatty et al, 2000; Green and Owen, 2006). These relationships between sectoral and labour market change and the performance of selected local economies are explored in greater detail in the following chapter.

Yet while this fundamental restructuring of the economic base and the resulting winning and losing local and regional economies is a crucial starting point to understanding the extent and nature of area deprivation, it is not enough to explain the patterns of intense spatial concentration of deprivation that are evident within prosperous and less prosperous regions alike. For this, understanding is required of how these new patterns of job growth and loss interact with a range of economic and social processes that cumulatively act to reduce employment prospects of residents and depress local economic activity. As is discussed in detail in Chapter Two, these processes include the operation of housing markets, local labour markets, and public and private sector investment markets, as well as the particularities of neighbourhood effects and formations of local social capital. It is only through seeking to understand how these diverse processes interact within and through specific places that we can begin to understand the particularities, patterns and dynamics of concentrations of deprivation.

It is for these reasons that the policy challenge presented by deprived neighbourhoods is particularly difficult. Conceptually, policy intervention requires understanding of how deep-seated economic processes of change interrelate with a range of economic and social processes across spatial scales operating from the neighbourhood to the global. Translating this into policy practice consequently requires an integration and coordination of policy development and delivery across spheres, sectors and levels of the political and policy-making system; a means of working that the state apparatus has traditionally found difficult to achieve.

Recognising deprived neighbourhoods

In the UK over the past 10 years, 'deprived neighbourhoods' have become a well-established and central notion within the policy agenda. This idea rose to particular prominence as a result of the work of New Labour's Social Exclusion Unit (SEU) in the late 1990s, which identified concentrations of deprivation at the neighbourhood level as a defining feature of the contemporary landscape of social exclusion. The subsequent response to this analysis through the creation of the National Strategy for Neighbourhood Renewal ensured that prominence was given to the identification and targeting of deprived neighbourhoods. Such an approach is not unique to the UK. In the US, where polarisation between prosperous and deprived neighbourhoods in urban conurbations is particularly stark, there has been a longstanding identification of 'poor neighbourhoods' as a focus for policy intervention (Galster et al, 2003). In Europe too, there has been a range of programmes within member states and at the level of the European Union (EU) oriented towards concentrated deprivation within urban areas (Madanipour et al, 1998; Atkinson and Carmichael, 2007).

Common to these agendas is the recognition that social exclusion is concentrated in relatively small 'pockets', predominantly within urban areas, not only within cities and regions undergoing economic decline and readjustment, but also within those experiencing strong economic growth. These highly localised concentrations of various groups at risk of exclusion – migrants, people from minority ethnic communities, the long-term unemployed, one-parent families, older people and young people – are characterised by an intensity of mutually reinforcing processes of social exclusion that produce marked spatial polarisation. In the most extreme examples, social and spatial deprivation can come together to form 'ghettos' of intense exclusion and an associated 'underclass', as identified within many US cities (Massey and Denton, 1993; Wilson, 1996). However, the intensity of deprivation and racial segregation that characterises US cities is not readily apparent within European cities, where different social-spatial formations mean that the circumstances of spatially concentrated deprivation are qualitatively different (Wacquant, 1996; Marcuse and Van Kempen, 2000). Studies of poor areas within the UK, for example, have shown that despite a high presence of excluded people within poor neighbourhoods, overall labour and housing markets are less divided, particularly in terms of race. In addition, the continuing role for the welfare state and family and community relations further prevents the formation of a 'ghetto underclass' (Buck et al, 2002; Watt, 2003; see also Chapter Two).

In the European context, the analysis of spatially concentrated deprivation, particularly informed by the experiences of inner-city areas and peripheral housing estates, has centred on the multiple dimensions of deprivation and social exclusion. The focus here is how different elements of deprivation come together, in specific areas, to produce a mutually reinforcing process. The difficulties that arise from having a large number of deprived individuals concentrated in a particular area are compounded by associated area-based effects (for example, lack of information about jobs, lack of contact with the world of work, area-based discrimination and stigma) and the particularities of any given locality (for example, peripheral location, poor infrastructure, poor-quality local services and lack of transport). Together these factors produce processes that act to maintain existing poor areas in a state of relative deprivation or create a cycle of decline in formerly more prosperous areas (see Chapter Two for a more detailed discussion). The resulting policy emphasis is on how low levels of economic activity, and poor housing, local environment, and public services combined with the characteristics of the local populations, produce relative deprivation in terms of income, health, safety and quality of life. It is also one that recognises important differences between areas and neighbourhoods and the need for place-based interventions that are 'place' sensitive.

What is a deprived neighbourhood?

Although the term 'deprived' or 'disadvantaged' neighbourhood acts as a useful descriptor of what is an important feature of the urban landscape, as an analytical term, what constitutes a deprived neighbourhood is considerably more problematic. Conceptually, there are difficulties here both in defining what constitutes a neighbourhood as well as how the relationship between deprivation and its spatial expression is conceived.

The notion of neighbourhood is heavily contested (Galster, 2001; Kearns and Parkinson, 2001). There is no single, accepted and generalisable definition as to what constitutes a neighbourhood; rather, what emerges from academic debate is a view of neighbourhoods as 'complex, dynamic, multidimensional and subjective constructs with identities and governance capacities that go beyond preconceived geographical or administrative boundaries' (Lepine et al, 2007, p 2).

Beneath this complexity, two key themes are apparent. First is the idea of a neighbourhood as a bounded physical entity, existing at a particular localised scale. In this respect a neighbourhood is normally seen as a small district pitched between a wider local area and the narrower confines of a particular street or housing block. Yet there is no clear agreement as to what constitutes the scale of a neighbourhood. In practice it may range from an area that is little more than a street, to a much larger area based around shops or a school that may comprise several thousand people. While some neighbourhoods may be distinct physical places clearly bounded by roads or rivers, more generally there is an absence of obvious boundary lines, with those living in an area likely to have strongly varying perceptions of the physical extent of 'their neighbourhood'.

A second theme is the neighbourhood as a socially constructed space. Here the neighbourhood is significant as an everyday lived space of social interaction and reproduction and a source of attachment and identity, experienced differently by individuals depending on their particular characteristics (Sullivan and Taylor, 2007). As a socially constructed place, the notion of neighbourhood is frequently conflated with that of community, through the existence of common identities, practices and interests within a small shared space (Forrest and Kearns, 2001). Yet although examples of strong place-based communities do exist, more commonly areas are characterised by the existence of multiple communities of interest and fragmented populations. This makes any neat and tidy relationship between neighbourhoods and community deeply problematic, instead pointing to a messy, complex and dynamic relationship between individuals, communities and the neighbourhoods in which they live.

These problems in defining what constitutes a neighbourhood lead some to prefer to talk only in terms of 'concentrated deprivation'. But this too is problematic, as it removes entirely the very sense of 'place' that is a critical element to the phenomenon under consideration. Importantly, whether localised spatial patterns of deprivation are discussed in terms of 'neighbourhoods' or 'concentrations', they need to be understood in terms of the spectrum of social processes that are constituted in and through particular places rather than being in any sense separate or isolated. These social processes distinguish themselves in deprived neighbourhoods principally by the *extent* and *degree* of their impact and the problems that result, rather than being different by nature.

As a result, there are no simple cut-off points between deprived neighbourhoods and others. Although a significant proportion of individuals experiencing deprivation is resident in what may be classified as disadvantaged neighbourhoods, the majority is not. Spatial scales are not fixed. When considering the operation of socioeconomic processes attention should be focused on the relations between places and scales, rather than seeking to delimit and place borders around them (Massey, 2005). A relational concept of both space and deprivation is critical for any meaningful understanding of spatial concentrations of deprivation and how policy should respond to them. The considerable danger of an analytical and policy focus on deprived localities or neighbourhoods is the 'fetishisation' of a particular spatial scale; seeing it as a distinct and separate entity, when in fact problems of concentrated deprivation need to be viewed as part of a particular expression of the operation of socioeconomic processes over space and through time.

Within such a relational view of places and spaces, looking at deprivation at different spatial scales – whether internationally, nationally, regionally, locally or at the neighbourhood level – is important because it produces different patterns and interpretations of the extent and nature of the problem. A fine-grained neighbourhood focus, for example, brings into focus particular issues (for example, housing type and environmental quality), while a broader analysis at the subregional/local levels brings insight into the operation of labour markets and the interaction between labour supply and demand, as well as the relationships between Travel to Work Areas (TTWAs) and housing markets that predominantly operate at these levels.

Analysis at the level of individual English cities, for example, demonstrates high levels of city-wide deprivation (measured in terms of a mean score on the Index of Multiple Deprivation; IMD) in cities such as Liverpool (45%), Hull (42%), Sunderland (34%) and Rochdale (33%) (Parkinson et al, 2006, p 113) (see Figure 1.1). Similarly, in the city of Glasgow in Scotland, 48% of the population live within the most deprived areas. When examined at the regional level, every city or town in the South and East of England has less than its share of poorest areas (Parkinson et al, 2006, p 114). In contrast, regions such as the North East and North West of England have high proportions of their population, 38% and 33% respectively, living in deprived neighbourhoods, demonstrating the importance of a regional dimension to understanding the location of deprived neighbourhoods (see Table 1.1). When regions, subregions or cities have such a large proportion of their population living within a large number of deprived neighbourhoods, the issue is rather less about the neighbourhoods per se and rather more about the economic conditions at the level of the city or wider region in which they are situated.

Table 1.1: Super Output Areas (SOAs) in the most deprived 20% of SOAs in England, by region, 2004

	Number of SOAs in most deprived 20% of SOAs in England	Number of SOAs in the region	% of SOAs in each region falling in most deprived 20% of SOAs in England
East	220	3,550	6.2
East Midlands	482	2,732	17.6
London	1,260	4,765	26.4
North East	631	1,656	38.1
North West	1,461	4,459	32.8
South East	271	5,319	5.1
South West	278	3,226	8.6
West Midlands	917	3,482	26.3
Yorkshire and the Humber	976	3,293	29.6
Total	6,496	32,482	20.0

Source: Department for Communities and Local Government, Neighbourhood Statistics

The appropriate scale for analysis and policy intervention is a particularly important issue with regard to the economic dimension of deprived areas and is discussed further in Chapter Five. The roots of the economic problems that affect such areas, and the economic processes that are manifest within them, stretch far beyond a highly localised area, pointing to a policy response that needs to be sensitive to, and coordinated across, a range of different scales. In this context, the deprived neighbourhood needs to be conceptualised as a particular socially constructed place embedded in various economic and social processes operating within and between different scales.

Mapping deprivation at the neighbourhood scale

The lack of definitional clarity relating to deprived neighbourhoods ensures that its operationalisation for policy terms is problematic. Definitions from the British government focus on deprived areas, and the people who live within them, as disadvantaged relative to other more prosperous areas:

> People living in deprived areas are more likely to be worse off than similar people living in more prosperous areas ...

[they] ... are less likely to work, more likely to be poor and have lower life expectancy, more likely to live in poorer housing in unattractive local environments with high levels of anti-social behaviour and lawlessness and more likely to receive poorer education and health services. Living in a deprived area adversely affects individuals' life chances over and above what would be predicted by their personal circumstance and characteristics. (PMSU, 2005, p 10)

The more general challenges in identifying and measuring poverty and deprivation are well recognised. The geographical mapping of national patterns of relative deprivation can be conducted at a range of spatial scales from the regional through to the neighbourhood level. Within the current UK policy discourse, the strong emphasis on 'pockets' of localised deprivation has produced a focus on the small-scale, 'neighbourhood', level.

The Index of Multiple Deprivation

In order both to capture the multiple dimensions of deprivation and how these come together at the small-area level, and as a means of operationalising the National Strategy for Neighbourhood Renewal in England, the UK government produced the Index of Multiple Deprivation (IMD), initially published in 2000 (DTLR, 2000) and subsequently in revised form in 2004 (ODPM, 2004) and further updated for 2007 (DCLG, 2008a).

The IMD is based on the concept of distinct dimensions of deprivation that can be recognised and measured separately, and are experienced by individuals living in an area. The overall IMD is conceptualised as a weighted area-level aggregation of the specific dimensions of deprivation. The Index is made up of seven distinct dimensions of deprivation, called domains. Each domain contains a number of indicators (37 in total), which comprise (with their relative weighting indicated in brackets):

- income deprivation (22.5%);
- employment deprivation (22.5%);
- education, training and skills deprivation (13.5%);
- health deprivation and disability (13.5%);
- barriers to housing and services (9.3%);
- living environment deprivation (9.3%); and
- crime (9.3%).

Both Scotland and Wales have developed their own modified versions of the IMD – the Scottish Index of Multiple Deprivation (SIMD) and the Welsh Index of Multiple Deprivation (WIMD).[1] Across all three indices of multiple deprivation, the three domains of employment, income, and education, training and skills are weighted as the most important dimensions, together accounting for between 58.5% to 70% of the aggregate weighting.

In identifying 'deprived areas' the IMD uses a relative measure of deprivation, commonly defining them in terms of the 10% most deprived wards in the 2000 IMD, and the 10% or 20% most deprived Super Output Areas (SOAs) in the 2004 IMD. If deprived areas in England are defined in terms of the 20% most deprived SOAs, 9.8 million people live in these areas, just under 20% of the population. However, not all people living in deprived areas experience deprivation individually. On average just under a third of those people living in deprived areas are likely to be income deprived.

Figure 1.2 displays the distribution of the 20% most deprived SOAs in England in 2004. Concentrations of deprivation reflect the processes of economic restructuring experienced over the last 30 years, with job losses in manufacturing and coal-mining sectors having had major impacts on inner cities, large metropolitan cities, 'one-industry' towns and coalfield areas. As a result, deprived neighbourhoods in the UK are disproportionally found in inner-city areas, mining, industrial and seaside towns, and outer urban areas of industrial and residential expansion. Most such neighbourhoods are located within deprived urban wards, but within England, at least 16 of the 88 most deprived districts also contain substantial rural areas (SEU, 2001).

Severely deprived areas are found in all regions, as are areas among the least deprived. However, as Table 1.1 demonstrates, the localised distribution of the most deprived 20% of SOAs within England does show strong regional variation. The North East has the highest percentage of its SOAs in the most deprived 20% (38.1%), compared with only 8.6% in the South West. London has a high number of SOAs in the most deprived 20% of SOAs (1,260) accounting for a large population of 1,934,000 people.

Constraints of the IMD

Identification of area-based deprivation using the IMD and its use as a means of targeting resources raises a number of issues related to the manner in which it identifies and prioritises certain types of deprived areas.

Figure 1.2: Local concentration district level summary of the IMD (England) 2004

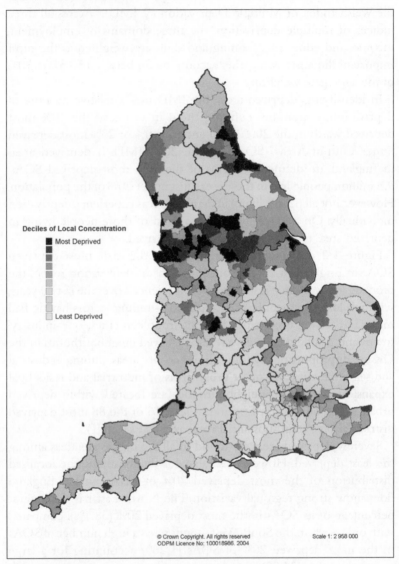

Deciles of Local Concentration

Most Deprived

Least Deprived

Scale 1: 2 958 000

Source: ODPM, 2004

First, such indices are constrained by the statistics routinely available at the lowest spatial scales. In the UK, initially the electoral ward level was used simply because it was the only unit at the sublocal authority level for which there were adequate small-area statistics available nationally with which to construct an IMD. Wards were ranked using the IMD and the 10% most deprived wards, a total of 841, were then designated as the poorest neighbourhoods, 82% of which were concentrated in 88 local authority districts (LADs). From the outset there was a recognition that electoral wards – relatively large, variable in size and subject to constant boundary changes – were a poor proxy for the neighbourhood scale and as a means for reporting small-area statistics. Given that wards, particularly in urban areas, could be large (containing populations of up to 30,000 people), small pockets of deprivation (or indeed wealth) remained hidden within the Index. Such problems were a major factor in the creation from 2004 of a new means for reporting small-area statistics in England and Wales – SOAs – which were first used in the revised IMD in 2004. Super Output Areas have a consistent size, with lower-level SOAs having an average population of 1,800 people, making them more amenable to capturing the 'neighbourhood' scale.[2] However, such statistics still remain only a proxy; they are a statistical geography that makes no attempt to capture or delimit neighbourhoods.

In terms of economic change at the neighbourhood scale, there also remain severe limitations on available economic statistics. There is a notable lack of data related to key issues such as levels of private and public investment, enterprise start-ups and certain aspects of the labour market, and no statistics at all related to the important arena of informal activity. In fact, in relation to the economic dimension of neighbourhood deprivation, much of the focus has related to patterns of worklessness.

Second, the manner in which the different elements of deprivation are weighted within a composite index produces different outcomes. The manner in which the IMD is constructed makes it relatively strong in identifying multiple deprivation in urban areas, where the vast majority of the population reside. However, it is less effective in identifying deprivation dispersed across more geographically sparse populations as occurs in rural areas, and where the basis of deprivation is also different, especially with regard to problems of accessibility to jobs and services. Consequently, in areas with larger rural populations there has been concern over the underreporting of rural deprivation and both Scotland and Wales have revised their indices to include a greater recognition of this issue.

Third, the focus on identifying small-area-based deprivation illustrates the tensions over the choice of scale at which the issue of deprivation is looked at, the indicators used and the nature of the problem subsequently identified. In a region such as the South West of England there is only a relatively small number of SOAs in the worst 20% nationally (8.6%). However, analysis at a higher spatial scale can capture wider structural problems, related to processes of economic development and labour market supply and demand in the subregional/ regional economy. In this regard, for the South West, the EU, using cruder and more restricted criterion (Gross Domestic Product [GDP] per head of population at 75% or less of the European average) applied at the subregional/regional level, identifies Cornwall as a priority area (Objective One) for assistance, even though relatively few localities are highlighted within the IMD.

Finally, although the IMD identifies deprivation at the small scale it is unable to say anything about the nature of the problem. For example, an SEU report (SEU, 2004) pursued the issue of worklessness through small-area analysis down to the level of the street and the housing block. While such an analysis permitted the identification of small-scale 'pockets' of labour market deprivation, it also amply demonstrated the limitations of such an approach. Such maps of localised worklessness were in fact little more than maps of the distribution of public/social housing.

Merely mapping localised economic deprivation provides only very limited insights into the nature of the phenomena and how it is embedded within the wider economic development process. Across England, Scotland and Wales the IMD identifies former coalfield areas, older industrial areas, urban centres, one-industry towns and some seaside towns, as particular foci of concentrated deprivation. However, the nature of the problems of deprived neighbourhoods is in practice very different. The labour market challenges posed by a highly stable, largely homogenous white population that has experienced intergenerational unemployment in a former coalfield area, such as Easington in the North East or Mansfield in the East Midlands, are quite different from those of an ethnically diverse, younger and more transient population living in inner-city areas, such as Newham or Tower Hamlets, within the economically thriving London region. Generalisation across localities may obscure more than it reveals. The differences between deprived neighbourhoods are explored in further detail in the next chapter.

Tackling localised deprivation

People versus place

A central policy concern in relation to tackling concentrated deprivation is whether deprived neighbourhoods should be seen either as a problem in their own right, and therefore in need of 'place'-based interventions, or as a manifestation of wider problems that should be dealt with by 'people'-oriented mainstream employment, education, training and business support policies (among others) focused on individuals, households or firms. Given that the economic problems experienced within deprived neighbourhoods reflect wider socioeconomic processes (for example in terms of deindustrialisation, rising inequality, labour market segmentation and so on), it might seem appropriate that the problems of such areas are addressed through mainstream programmes and policies. But deprived neighbourhoods are not merely empty spaces within which these wider processes are played out, but partially constitute these processes of change. Therefore the particular characteristics of a given place and the manner in which they are embedded within wider local/regional economies matter and policy responses must therefore be responsive to such local difference.

The argument for a place-based element to tackle the problems of deprived areas is rooted within two factors. The first relates to the extent to which place-based factors, or what are commonly referred to as 'area' or 'neighbourhood' effects, exacerbate problems of deprivation and social exclusion. There is considerable disagreement between academics on the importance of neighbourhood effects in perpetuating social exclusion. There are those who argue that they are of minor importance in relation to other factors, while others argue that they play an important role in compounding the effects of multiple dimensions of deprivation concentrated within a given locality. These arguments are explored in further detail in Chapter Two. Although the problems of deprived neighbourhoods are in the main the same in nature as those suffered elsewhere, the degree of poverty and deprivation concentrated in particular places and its persistence over time and across multiple dimensions, clearly produces a set of additional problems that justifies a place-sensitive approach.

The second is rooted in the fact that a whole range of mainstream policies consistently find it difficult to address effectively the problems of residents concentrated in deprived neighbourhoods. There are a number of related reasons for this. First, mainstream policies generally target on the basis of population characteristics and find it difficult to take account of the particular needs of areas facing concentrated deprivation. Second, there is a generally poor take-up of mainstream programmes by residents living within deprived neighbourhoods, whether this is in terms of training schemes, business support or employment services. This reflects both a lack of trust and engagement with such services and often also the absence of opportunities or incentives to seek employment or develop entrepreneurial activity. Third, levels of public spending rarely effectively compensate for the high unit cost involved in tackling social exclusion within deprived areas, while prosperous areas frequently exert pressure to maintain their relatively high level of service provision. Although expenditure within deprived areas may be higher on a per capita basis, such spending is concentrated on benefit regimes, operating to maintain the status quo, rather than on education and training, which might lead to individuals competing more successfully in the labour market and attaining higher levels of earnings. Finally, the poor coordination of mainstream programmes at national and regional levels makes it difficult to integrate these effectively at the local or neighbourhood level.

The role of area-based initiatives

The combination of the particular problems of deprived neighbourhoods and the inability of mainstream programmes to address them effectively has led to the development of a variety of area-based initiatives (ABIs). In the UK there is a long history of such interventions, ranging from the Community Programme of the 1960s, to the Enterprise Zones of the 1980s, to the National Strategy for Neighbourhood Renewal introduced in the late 1990s (see Table 1.2).

As a policy response, ABIs have a number of common features. Central is an emphasis on partnership working. Since the 1980s this has broadened from an emphasis on working in partnership with the private sector to include the community and different public bodies and government departments, to try to ensure the engagement of a broad base of expertise and resources better directed to the needs of deprived areas. Also crucial to ABIs is the encouragement of greater flexibility in local delivery, sensitivity to local needs and autonomy in the management and delivery of local schemes. This element is particularly important within the UK context of a historically highly centralised state system with limited devolution of power to regional, local and neighbourhood levels. An additional feature of ABIs in the UK context is that, since the early 1990s, funds have normally been allocated on a competitive basis, with the intention of providing an incentive for actors to engage in partnership working and to pursue more innovative solutions.

Despite the established history of ABIs and the proliferation of this approach under the New Labour governments, there remains considerable debate over their relative effectiveness (Griggs et al, 2008). Criticisms of ABIs are of two broad types. The first focuses on the fact that such initiatives are seeking to address wider social and economic processes of change. Given that the problems of social inequality and

Table 1.2: Evolution of British urban policy

Period	Policies	Key features	Main actors/partners	Spatial levels of intervention
1940s–1960s	New Towns Urban clearance	Reconstruction and physical regeneration Improvement of housing and living standards	National and local government Public sector-led investment Private sector developers and contractors	Replacement of run-down inner-city areas with development of suburban areas and New Towns Some attempts to rehabilitate deprived neighbourhoods Emphasis on regional policy to decentralise and relocate industry away from the South East
Late 1960s–1970s	Urban Programmes Community Development Projects	In situ renewal and community-based action and greater empowerment Extensive renewal of older urban areas Resource constraints on public sector and growth of private investment	Local authorities Some decentralisation and community involvement Growing role of private sector	Focus on neighbourhood schemes within local level policies Ongoing regional policy

Table 1.2: Evolution of British urban policy (continued)

Period	Policies	Key features	Main actors/ partners	Spatial levels of intervention
Late 1970s	Urban Partnerships	Recognition of structural problems; rising unemployment and social unrest Radical alternatives from Right (free market) and Left (public ownership and modernisation)	National and local government	Shift towards more localised focus Decentralisation and New Towns policies halted
1980s	Urban Development Corporations Enterprise Zones	Major schemes of physical replacement and new development of 'flagship' projects and out of town developments Emphasis upon laissez-faire approach, stimulation of enterprise and dominant role for private sector	Private sector led Selective support from national government Marginalisation of local government Limited community involvement	Emphasis upon major regeneration projects in inner-city and former industrial areas Local-level interventions particularly from Labour-controlled authorities Major weakening of regional policy
Late 1980s	Action for Cities City Action Teams Task Forces	Focus on coordination of policies within cities and subregions	National government and private sector Recognition of role of local authorities	Local/city level Subregional activity related to programmes funded by EU Structural Funds

Table 1.2: Evolution of British urban policy (continued)

Period	Policies	Key features	Main actors/partners	Spatial levels of intervention
1990s	City Challenge Single Regeneration Budget	Partnership dominant with greater balance between public, private and voluntary and community sectors Shift to more integrated and comprehensive response Competition for funding More emphasis upon community engagement, less upon physical redevelopment	Partnership between all key actors, widened to include local authorities and community, voluntary sectors	Primarily locally based interventions Some reintroduction of strategic perspective and growth of regional activity (eg via creation of Government Offices for the Regions)
Late 1990s–early 2000s	New Deal for Communities (NDCs)/National Strategy for Neighbourhood Renewal Multiple examples of ABIs Sustainable Communities Plan Working Neighbourhood Fund/City Strategy Pathfinders	Central focus on social exclusion and concentrated deprivation, particularly worklessness Experimentation with new approaches via multiple ABIs Emphasis upon city competitiveness, innovation and enterprise Some devolution of power and attempts to increase local-level flexibility	Partnership approach central (eg via Local Strategic Partnerships) Increased community involvement and participation Key role for Regional Development Agencies (RDAs) and development of subregional partnerships Increased role for local authorities in economic development	Strong focus on neighbourhood level Reconfigured local-level role via Local Strategic Partnerships and Local Area Agreements Variable devolution and decentralisation of power to nations and regions and cities, Attempt to strengthen subregional level via Multi Area Agreements

Source: Expanded and adapted from Atkinson and Moon (1994); Audit Commission (1999, p 95); Roberts and Sykes, (2000;, p 14)

deprivation in deprived neighbourhoods are manifestations of patterns of inequality set nationally and internationally, the impacts of area-based policies are likely at best to be marginal (Townsend, 1979). Thus Kleinman (1998) argues that in tackling poverty and deprivation the focus should not be on place per se, as the problems of poverty are only in limited instances localised in character. Rather, such problems are more generally widely distributed in relation to national and international economic and social factors and hence require more than local action as a solution. In fact a danger with area-based policy is that problems are mis-specified, with the risk of making the particular locality appear to be responsible for its particular economic problems and hence absolving national governments from taking action.

The second criticism focuses on the significant challenges related to the implementation and evaluation of area-based policy. Of particular importance here are issues of displacement and substitution, such that the economic gains to certain firms and individuals as a result of a policy intervention are offset by losses to others. This is particularly important with regard to jobs, but also applies to service provision, money within the local economy, and community participation. Similarly, the issues of 'deadweight' and non-additionality concern the problems of separating out the impact of a particular policy intervention from other influences and of estimating what would have happened in the local economy without any intervention.

While such arguments provide for some a basis for the rejection of ABIs *tout court*, in fact they do not counter the rationale for ABIs previously outlined. Rather, they point to the need for careful design of such policies: for greater clarity about what can be achieved at the local level, and greater emphasis on their coordination with interventions at the national level and other spatial scales. As Kleinman (1998, p 3) states, ABIs are highly important in terms of their role in providing the appropriate level to organise effective partnerships operating with a clear understanding of local conditions: 'But local initiatives cannot alone provide solutions to problems whose causes are national or even international. Local initiatives must be supported by the right kind of policies at regional and national level.'

Critically, the rationale for the use of ABIs is for them to *add* to the positive impacts of mainstream policies and market mechanisms, not to substitute them, in order to provide a more strategic and coordinated approach to meeting the needs of deprived areas. For example, as has been demonstrated within evaluations of the City Challenge and Single Regeneration Budget (SRB) programmes (DETR, 2000b; Rhodes et al, 2002), the effectiveness of local employment and training initiatives is related to demand conditions in the wider labour market. So the challenge for ABIs is to ensure that maximum labour market benefits accrue to residents of deprived neighbourhoods who face additional problems in the labour market and/or are poorly served by mainstream provision. Similarly, as Moore and Begg (2004) conclude with regard to their study on the competitiveness of urban areas, policy that simply focuses on the regeneration of specific areas is unlikely to be successful. Rather, they argue, attention needs to be given to the wider urban system, and policy should primarily focus on the engagement of mainstream government programmes and how these impact on different parts of the urban system, rather than a narrowly defined urban policy focused only on areas of deprivation.

In practice, this interface between mainstream programmes and ABIs is a problematic one, with considerable difficulties in seeking to ensure that mainstream provision meets the needs of specific places alongside ongoing problems over the design and implementation of ABIs. The debate over 'people' or 'place' remains central to current policy agendas and subsequent chapters will consider these issues in greater detail in relation to enterprise and employment interventions and the system of governance and delivery of policies aimed at tackling the problems of deprived neighbourhoods.

The evolution of policy practice

The 'problem neighbourhood' in the evolution of urban policy

The recognition of 'problems' associated with intense spatial concentrations of poverty within urban areas can be traced back to the 19th century. Since Engels' writings first provided vivid descriptions of the terrible living conditions of workers in Britain's northern industrial cities in 1844 (Engels, 1987), rationales for intervention in deprived urban neighbourhoods have reflected various combinations of political, social and economic anxieties rooted within the dominant ideologies of the time (see, for example, Stedmen Jones, 1971, and White, 2003). While such disquiet has manifested itself in a variety of forms, most commonly it has related to the destabilising impacts of spatially concentrated deprivation on wider society, the negative impacts and economic wastefulness of spatial inequality on processes of urban economic development, and the morality of accepting intense socio-spatial inequalities. The specific constitution of the rationales informing intervention within dominant policy discourses under the New Labour governments is considered in more detail later in this chapter.

Responses to the problems associated with poor neighbourhoods have resulted in a long and varied history of policy intervention in the post-Second World War period (see Table 1.2). In reviewing the development of urban and regional policy across this period it is readily apparent that the nature of the 'problem' of deprived neighbourhoods has been conceived of and approached quite differently and pursued through a variety of different policy instruments. Yet underlying such differences there is also considerable continuity in terms of the basic types of activity that have been pursued in relation to tackling the economic dimension of the neighbourhood problem.

The first of these relates to the physical redevelopment of deprived areas; the so-called 'hard'-based element of regeneration. Here the emphasis is on land and property development and the improvement of the physical environment: the demolition, rebuilding and renovation of housing, industrial and commercial property, alongside improvements in transport infrastructures to reduce marginality and increase access. With respect to the non-physical or 'softer' side of regeneration and renewal, two main types of activity are apparent. First, an array of instruments have focused on the development of enterprise activity related to such areas. These comprise both attracting inward investment to the area and/or the stimulation of indigenous enterprise, either in the form of traditional business forms or through community and socially based enterprise activity. Second, a variety of policy activities related to the labour market have been developed. These have sought to improve the employability of residents and better connect them to available employment opportunities either through enhanced labour mobility to jobs outside of the immediate vicinity, or through better training and linkages to jobs available locally.

The balance between these different types of activity has shifted continuously over the last 60 years. In the immediate post-Second World War period the reconstruction of towns and cities was the priority emphasis. This focus on the physical redevelopment of deprived neighbourhoods, often through the physical demolition of areas of run-down housing and the decanting of residents in such areas to new suburban developments or New Towns, continued throughout the 1950s and 1960s as part of an era of city rebuilding, modernisation and economic growth.

However, by the mid-1960s the limitations of this approach were increasingly recognised. Rather than 'solving' urban problems, such approaches often merely transferred and reconstituted them in other locations, such as in more peripheral housing estates. The emphasis on slum clearance and relocation of inner-city populations was increasingly questioned, as communities were fractured and inner-urban areas left redundant, and immigrant populations became concentrated in certain inner-city areas. Greater engagement with the emerging realities of inner-city areas led to the Urban Programme launched by the Home Office in 1968, followed by a number of other policy initiatives, notably the Community Development Projects. These marked a shift in emphasis towards the renewal of inner-city areas through attempts to integrate the previously separate element of physical, economic and social policy, through an approach that involved greater community participation and state decentralisation.

During the 1970s, the problem of 'inner-city' areas became increasingly apparent. The impacts of long-term economic restructuring, particularly through processes of deindustrialisation, resulted in high levels of unemployment concentrated in particular inner-city and former manufacturing areas and there was increasing concern in relation to social breakdown and unrest. This culminated in a series of urban riots in 1981, initially in Brixton, but subsequently in Handsworth, Southall, Toxteth, Moss Side and smaller incidents across a number of other towns and cities.

While the approach of the Urban Programme and Community Development Projects was more sensitive to local and community differences, the programmes were increasingly criticised for their tendency towards social pathology; the blaming of the 'victims' for their problems rather than looking for the wider economic and social causes. The shift of control of urban policy to the Department of the Environment in 1975 marked a move towards greater recognition of the structural economic causes of inner-city problems. The 1978 Inner Urban Areas Act saw urban policy for the first time becoming a mainstream element of the national government agenda, with a lead role for local authorities in tackling inner-city problems in a number of selected areas.

Yet the increasing scope, scale and ongoing nature of inner-city problems led to a search for more radical alternatives and the redefinition of the focus of urban policy on the structural problem of economic decline (Eisenschitz and Gough, 1993; Cochrane, 2007). From the Right, the dominant argument was that tackling the economic decline of cities required a shift in emphasis towards a market-based, private sector-led approach in order to strengthen the economic competitiveness of cities. The election of the Thatcher-led Conservative government in 1979 marked the beginning of a major shift in direction towards such a neoliberal approach. Predominant local authority public sector ways of working gave way to a lead role for the private sector working through private–public partnerships, alongside the promotion of enterprise and large-scale physical redevelopment in tackling urban problems. While the Urban Programme continued, the early 1980s saw the introduction of the first two Urban Development Corporations (UDCs) in 1981, characterised by a key role for private sector developers and the marginalised position of local authorities and communities, and Enterprise Zones, introduced in 1980, which sought to encourage entrepreneurial activity in deprived areas through removing restrictions to enterprise activity. The urban regeneration agenda of the Thatcher government was characterised by reductions in planning and regulatory controls combined with tax breaks and public subsidies in order to encourage large-scale investment by developers and corporate interests in cities. At the same time, on the Left, Labour-controlled local authorities in the large cities attempted to develop an alternative agenda towards tackling economic decline: one that focused on a programme of greater public control, workplace democracy and economic modernisation.

The limitations of an approach based around large-scale land and property flagship projects and the working of the market to inner-city renewal became quickly apparent (Turok, 1992; Atkinson and Moon, 1994). There was increasing recognition of the need for greater coordination of policies across urban areas, an early response to which was the creation of City Action Teams in the late 1980s. More fundamentally, the notable absence of the 'trickle-down' of wealth to deprived areas, which was supposed to characterise this development model, removed local credibility and engagement, a situation further exacerbated by the exclusion of key partners. Recognition of the need for a wider range and better balance of actors in the urban regeneration process, particularly the need for a key role for local authorities and greater participation of community and voluntary groups, led to a significant change of policy direction. This was exemplified by the introduction of City Challenge (1991) and the SRB (1993), policies that marked a shift towards a more integrated and comprehensive approach, and a move away from a sole emphasis on physical and property development, towards greater attention to economic, social and environmental issues. In addition, these policies also marked the introduction of a system of competitive bidding for resources, with cities and deprived areas invited to compete for funds by demonstrating strong partnership working and innovative approaches to problems.

New Labour, urban policy and the neighbourhood renewal agenda

The incoming New Labour government in 1997 came to power with a clear commitment to the regeneration of Britain's cities and the devolution and decentralisation of power to Scotland and Wales and the English regions. While much continuity with past policy was evident, the period under New Labour has been characterised by notable developments in the scope of the agenda and by the sheer proliferation of initiatives and activities (see Table 1.3).

In terms of continuity, the emerging New Labour agenda was characterised by a strong market-based emphasis on the pursuit of competitive advantage within a global economy through the development of strong city and regional economies within which the private sector was to take a lead role. The physical development element also remained strong, albeit with the recommendations of the Urban Task Force focusing on the need for higher-quality design, and higher-density development of brownfield sites. Yet alongside these was a central commitment to issues of social exclusion, as was evident in the early creation of the SEU (in 1997), and to greater community involvement and participation (Imrie and Raco, 2003).

One aspect that emerged from this agenda was a particular focus on the neighbourhood, albeit in different ways under different policy discourses (Lepine et al, 2007). The 'neighbourhood' was seen as a site to tackle disadvantage and social exclusion as part of the neighbourhood renewal agenda, as well as a space to engage with citizens and communities and revitalise citizenship and political engagement within the local governance and civil renewal agendas. In addition, the neighbourhood was also seen as a desirable place to be 'produced' – in the form of areas characterised by a good quality of life and cohesive mixed communities – under housing development policies such as the 'Sustainable Communities' programme. One important result of the use of the neighbourhood in different ways within different policies has been the resulting confusion as to whether policy is aimed at the neighbourhood itself, the communities and citizens who live within the neighbourhood, or a mixture of both (Atkinson, 2007).

The development of neighbourhood-oriented policy to tackle disadvantage was pursued initially through an explosion of ABIs – including a whole array of Action Zones for Education, Health and Employment and the NDC programme – which sought to pilot new ways of working. The high-profile NDC programme launched in 1998 was targeted at turning around the poorest neighbourhoods through the creation of local partnerships in 39 locations in England. It was followed

Table 1.3: Major developments in urban policy and governance since 1997

Social Exclusion Unit created (1997)	Focus on tackling problems of marginalised groups and areas
Action Zones for Education/Health/Employment and New Deal for Communities (1998)	Emphasis upon area-based initiatives. Shift away from competitive bidding to resource allocation based on need
Regional Development Agencies (1998)	To promote economic development within regions and coordinate regional regeneration plans
Commission for Architecture and the Built Environment (1998)	To champion better architecture, urban design, and parks and open spaces
Urban Task Force (1999)	Remit was to identify how best to tackle urban decline. Recommended better design, higher-density development, use of brownfield sites and greater use of public transport
Urban White Paper (2000)	Endorsed most of the Urban Task Force recommendations
Local Government Act (2000)	Introduced new power of well-being requiring community strategies for localities and new political structures (eg mayors and cabinets)
National Strategy for Neighbourhood Renewal (2001)	Major policy intended to narrow gap between most deprived neighbourhoods and the rest through reshaping of mainstream programmes
Local Strategic Partnerships (2001)	Designed to encourage public, private, community and voluntary sectors to work together in an integrated way
Sustainable Communities Plan (2003)	Set out growth plans for South East, measures for tackling low housing demand and the creation of so-called sustainable communities
The Northern Way (2004)	Growth strategy and action plan for the North designed to narrow the prosperity gap between the eight constituent city-regions in the North and the rest of the UK
Planning and Compulsory Purchase Act (2004)	New planning system replacing Unitary Development Plans with Local Development Frameworks which must incorporating community strategy provisions and introduces regional spatial strategies

Table 1.3: Major developments in urban policy and governance since 1997 (continued)

Egan Review (2004)	Review of skills needed to deliver sustainable communities agenda
Local Area Agreement pilots (2004)	Mechanisms to improved local services through better joint working between central and local partners and more locally tailored policy making
Sustainable Communities: Homes for All (2005)	Plan for delivering new homes, enhancing residential environments and promoting market renewal in low demand areas to make houses more affordable and to extend choice
Local Government White Paper (2006)	Sets out intended reforms for local government, to strengthen leadership and devolve more power to local and neighbourhood levels so it can, with local partners, respond more flexibly to local needs
Leitch Review (2006)	Put forward proposal for reform of skills and training system so it is more demand led and better able to increase productivity and reduce the skills deficit relative to other OECD countries
Sub-national Economic Development and Regeneration Renewal Review (2007)	HM Treasury-led review of policies related to regional economic performance, social exclusion and neighbourhood renewal. Recommendations for increased devolution of powers to sub/city regions (via Multi Area Agreements) and more central role for local authorities in economic development
Local Area Agreements (LAAs) (2007)	LAAs rolled out to all eligible NRF areas and their LSPs to include mandatory outcomes related to neighbourhood renewal
Homes and Community Agency (2007)	Proposed creation of Homes and Communities Agency (operational in 2009) bringing together functions of English Partnerships, the Housing Corporation and CLG, to join up delivery of housing and regeneration
Area-Based Grant (ABG) and Working Neighbourhoods Fund (2008)	General grant to local authorities to provide increased flexibility in their use of mainstream resources. As part of ABG, Working Neighbourhoods Fund replaces the NRF to target worklessness in deprived areas.

Source: Adapted and expanded from Parkinson et al (2006, pp 18-19)

closely by the introduction of the National Strategy for Neighbourhood Renewal in 2001, which aimed to ensure that mainstream resources were better directed and resourced towards meeting the needs of the poorest neighbourhoods. What characterised this profusion of initiatives was a desire to tackle the problems of deprived areas in an integrated and holistic manner with the active engagement of the local community over a longer time period.

The National Strategy for Neighbourhood Renewal lay at the centre of this policy development; a long-term strategy that set out to narrow the gap between outcomes in deprived neighbourhoods and other areas by focusing action on the 88 most severely deprived LADs (SEU, 2001). Within these areas it aimed to integrate policy actions on housing and the physical fabric of neighbourhoods with those on work and enterprise, crime, education and skills, and health. Importantly, the strategy sought to mainstream funding for regeneration by focusing spending from across government departments on deprived areas, rather than the traditional reliance on one-off regeneration funding.

The need within this agenda for effective multi-agency working in order to coordinate the delivery of services and encourage active community participation, involved the development of new governance structures at the local level in the form of Local Strategic Partnerships (LSPs), and at smaller scales via neighbourhood management. The formation of LSPs was a direct response to the evident lack of joint working between the public, private, voluntary and community sectors in the delivery of regeneration and public services. Initially created in the 88 most deprived local authorities as a key element in helping to deliver the National Strategy for Neighbourhood Renewal agenda, these non-statutory, multi-agency partnerships aimed to promote more integrated working between the public, private, community and voluntary sectors at the local level, as well as to change ways of working, and to reallocate resources and 'bend' mainstream programmes towards locally defined priorities. The inability of LSPs to realise these objectives within a highly inflexible, centralised governance system led to the piloting from 2004 of Local Area Agreements (LAAs). LAAs provided a mechanism to improve joint working through setting out the priorities for a local area agreed by central government, the local authority, LSP and other key local partners. From 2007 all eligible Neighbourhood Renewal Fund (NRF) areas and their LSPs began to operate in the context of LAAs, and were required to have mandatory outcomes demonstrating how the gap between the most deprived areas and the less deprived areas was being narrowed.

A refocusing of overall government priorities to emphasise work as the route out of poverty, allied to a recognition of the relative lack of success of neighbourhood renewal policy and active labour market policies to make a significant impact on the scale of persistent worklessness within deprived areas, led to the introduction in 2008 of the Working Neighbourhoods Fund (WNF), to replace the NRF and integrate funding from the Department for Work and Pensions' (DWP's) Deprived Areas Fund. Although again allocated on a spatial basis using the IMD, in contrast to the NRF, the central emphasis of the WNF is on moving people from welfare and into work within deprived areas (DCLG and DWP, 2007). The WNF also forms a distinct element of the Area-Based Grant (ABG), a non-ring-fenced general grant allocated directly to local authorities as additional revenue funding, also introduced in 2008. The ABG aims to provide greater flexibility to local authorities in their use of mainstream resources, by bringing a wide range of existing grants together to enable the design of local programmes to meet local priorities.

The introduction of the WNF marks a significant shift towards a greater economic focus within neighbourhood renewal policy and an attempt to mainstream such activity. Areas receiving funding from the WNF will be expected to include LAA targets on tackling worklessness and boosting enterprise. As a result, these targets become key priorities for the LSPs and their partners in the private, voluntary and community sectors. In conjunction with the development of LAAs, the introduction of the ABG also marks a further attempt to increase local authority flexibility in determining local priorities within the constraints of the existing highly centralised governance arrangements that continue to fundamentally limit the scope for autonomous local governance.

Alongside the pursuit of neighbourhood-focused interventions has been the development of a strengthened regional agenda, notably through the creation of Regional Development Agencies (RDAs), and more latterly through the development of sub/city-region partnerships. While a primary focus of the work of the RDAs is the improvement of regional/city economic performance, they are also charged with reducing disparities both between and within regions (Robson et al, 2000), For economic development and regeneration these developments at multiple spatial levels have resulted in an ever more complex set of governance arrangements, which extend both horizontally and vertically, and across a range of actors from the private, public, voluntary and community sectors (North et al, 2007). The nature and complexity of these arrangements has led to a range of criticisms related to their efficiency, effectiveness, legitimacy and accountability (Robson et al, 2000; Fuller et al, 2004; Goodwin et al, 2005).

In response, a major review of subnational economic development and regeneration policy was concluded in 2007 (HM Treasury et al, 2007). This led to a range of recommendations that sought to build on devolutionary changes and improve coordination between different spatial levels, improve strategy and delivery at the level of subregional partnerships (SRPs) (for example through the mechanism of Multi Area Agreements); and move towards a more central role for local authorities in economic development (for example through a proposed duty to undertake local economic assessments). In addition, with regard to the key sphere of housing and regeneration, local authorities will also have a new delivery partner in the form of the Homes and Communities Agency (to be operational from April 2009), which it is envisaged will help local authorities in the process of strategy formation. In line with the changes in neighbourhood policy, these changes in institutions and governance arrangements provide local authorities and SRPs with a higher-profile role within the subnational economic development process and tackling concentrated worklessness. Against this background, the search for a better understanding of the economic dimension of neighbourhood renewal, and the informing rationale for intervention, is particularly timely.

Rationales for intervention

Under New Labour, the sense in which deprived neighbourhoods constitute a problem, or indeed an 'opportunity', which requires a policy response, reflects the wider discourse relating to urban development and the consequent rationale for urban policy. The major change in the nature of urban policy that took place in the 1980s saw a shift from previous welfarist approaches concerned with issues of social reproduction and collective consumption, towards a central focus on economic regeneration and the promotion of urban competitiveness (Cochrane, 2007). This shift reflected the increased dominance of neoliberal-inspired thinking, which argued that the working of free markets and private sector competition was the best means to create the necessary conditions for personal and community prosperity. Critically, within the development of a liberalised global economy, cities were seen as key sites, which consequently needed to be reimagined and rebuilt accordingly. For cities, the policy agenda that resulted was one increasingly oriented towards competing for economic success, promoting urban entrepreneurialism and rebuilding the urban form, notably through large-scale urban redevelopment projects and the hosting of mega-events (Harvey, 2000; Swyngedouw et al, 2002).

Recognition of a renewed role for cities as drivers of economic growth within a globalising, post-industrial world marked a broad acceptance of a new urban era within the advanced economies. In relation to this a 'new conventional wisdom' emerged across the 1990s, which recognised not only that economic competitiveness was fundamental to city survival in the global economy, but also that this economic role needed to be reinforced by a level of social cohesion, responsive governance and, to a lesser extent, environmental sustainability (Gordon and Buck, 2005). In this model for the development of vital and prosperous cities – a model that informed the development of New Labour urban policy but also has been influential internationally (for example OECD, 2003) – there is consequently a simultaneous attempt to pursue a virtuous circle of economic competitiveness, social inclusion and good governance (Gordon and Buck, 2005).

The emergence of this 'new conventional wisdom' has been characterised by two important elements. First it represents a particular ideological reading of urban development strongly rooted within a neoliberalist agenda, which seeks to develop cities as embodiments of a liberalised market-based approach (Harvey, 2000; Harloe, 2001). Over time and space the nature of this agenda has evolved into diffuse ideological forms (Peck and Tickell, 2007) and its impact on the development of urban policy has been variable and complex, reflecting the contradictions and struggles that have surrounded policy development (Raco, 2005). Second, there is a notable lack of specification of the nature of the assumed positive relationships between the different elements of economic competitiveness, social cohesion and governance, As the findings of the major Economic and Social Research Council (ESRC) Cities research programme demonstrated, there remains only limited evidence in the UK context to support the asserted positive relationships between these three dimensions (Buck et al, 2005). While this model of urban development has been keen to stress the positive synergies between the economic, social and political dimensions of change, this has frequently been at the expense of recognising conflicts and contradictions. The tension between the emergence of increasingly liberalised market-based city economies and the rise in levels of social and spatial inequality, for example, has been largely downplayed, despite the fact that managing the consequences of rising inequality is a major dimension of contemporary urban policy and governance (Jones and Ward, 2002).

Informed by this wider conception of the nature of urban development, three broad sets of rationales for policy intervention in deprived neighbourhoods have been apparent within the policy discourses of New Labour – promoting economic competitiveness, tackling social exclusion, and enhancing community engagement and cohesion. A broader cross-cutting rationale related to the promotion of 'sustainable development' has also been apparent, although notably this dimension has been defined in highly generalised terms and, to date, has played only a restricted role in informing policy intervention in deprived areas. In each of these rationales the economic dimension is variably developed. Furthermore, in practice the extent to which these different rationales are explicitly set out and distinguished from one another varies significantly. To an extent this reflects the reality of the complex interaction of the economic, social and political realms within any given neighbourhood and the adoption of a holistic approach to intervention, yet it also reflects a lack of clarity in the specification of the processes and directions of change and muddled objectives in much policy development.

Economic efficiency and competitiveness

A fundamental justification for intervention into deprived neighbourhoods is that their presence impedes economic competitiveness and efficiency, both in broad national terms and within the cities or regions in which they are located. There are three key arguments advanced here. First, in terms of national competitiveness, concentrated deprivation is economically inefficient in terms of its underutilisation of human and physical capital within these areas. Second, high levels of concentrated deprivation have substantial wider economic costs to the state in terms of welfare benefits, poor health, high levels of crime and a socially and politically disengaged population. Finally, in terms of city competitiveness, it is argued that physically unattractive areas and extreme social deprivation create a negative image, which acts as a disincentive to attracting and retaining investment, business activity and more highly skilled and better-off elements of the population.

Acceptance of a rationale for intervention in deprived neighbourhoods based on improving economic efficiency and more recently competitiveness has been a recurring element in the development of UK urban policy, albeit with differing emphases and approaches. Within the New Labour 'Third Way' agenda this issue has been approached in terms of addressing 'market failures'[3] – for example, those related to externalities, public goods, merit goods, asymmetrical information and imperfect competition – and to a lesser extent 'government failures', such as the unintended consequences of government interventions, political failings and administrative failings (ODPM, 2006; DCLG, 2007b).

Interventions related to market failures have focused on making areas, and the people who live in them, more 'competitive'. Here public sector providers working with the market seek to increase the attractiveness of deprived neighbourhoods so that they are desirable places in which to reside, invest and work, building, where possible, on any comparative advantages such places may have. The focus is on enabling the participation of such areas and their residents within processes of economic growth and in recognising potential economic opportunities. This is pursued through a combination of stimulating urban land and property markets, so that these are more attractive to private sector investment, stimulating entrepreneurial activity and private sector business activity, and making local residents better able to compete in the labour market by improving education and skills and pursuing active labour market policies.

Yet the evidence to support a key notion that informs current policy positions – that concentrated deprivation has a negative impact on economic competitiveness within the wider city, regional and national economy – is not clear cut. Fainstein (2001) concluded her review of the empirical evidence of the relationship between economic competitiveness and social cohesion as 'indeterminate', influenced by a range of contextual factors. Similarly, in research findings from successful urban areas in the UK such as Bristol, London, Leeds and Edinburgh, Boddy and Parkinson (2004, p 428) conclude that 'competitive success is far from incompatible with persistent concentrations of unemployment and social deprivation' and that 'competitive success does not eliminate inequality or concentrated disadvantage'. These studies found only very limited evidence that social cohesion impacted negatively on economic competitiveness (Gordon, 2005). Empirical findings provided little or no support for arguments that low levels of education and skills had had major impacts on employers, or that high levels of crime had discouraged investment and skilled workers from going into large urban areas (Boddy, 2003; Turok et al, 2004).

The lack of strong evidence of the relationships between economic competitiveness and social cohesion may be partly due to the difficulty of identifying them given the complex, indirect and circular nature of such relationships. There are situations where the negative impacts of concentrated deprivation can have damaging economic impacts – for example where this leads to high levels of criminality, social breakdown and unrest, which can have a significant impact on business costs and confidence and can incur significant additional costs (Potts, 2002). In fact, it seems likely that such impacts only become apparent when problems of unrest, criminality or antisocial behaviour reach a particular 'tipping point', and therefore threshold effects may be important, particularly at smaller spatial scales (Buck and Gordon, 2004; Turok et al, 2004).

However, more generally the evidence points to the fact that, despite the economic costs associated with concentrated deprivation, under neoliberal market-based regimes of capital accumulation, localised areas of poverty can exist within cities or regions without substantially impeding economic growth or competitiveness, at least in the short term. In practice, market mechanisms operate to avoid such areas or selectively incorporate them into the economic development process. In the UK, newly emerging sites of employment growth have generally steered clear of deprived inner-urban areas, preferring locations towards the edge of towns or in smaller towns. With regard to the attraction of investment and people, particularly within larger cities, it is evident that investors and skilled workers can largely isolate themselves from areas of deprivation through strategies of segregation. Similarly, the expected inefficiencies and constraints on growth arising from the underutilisation of human capital within areas of concentrated worklessness often never materialise, as the need for low-cost, low-wage labour is met by pulling in migrant workers. This process has been strongly evident in the UK in a period of employment growth from the late 1990s, with cities and regions, including more deprived areas, meeting their low-skilled and unskilled labour needs by attracting in labour, particularly from Eastern Europe (Coombes et al, 2007).

What is also apparent is that certain deprived neighbourhoods can be seen to play a positive role within wider processes of city/regional economic development, providing areas of cheap housing and low living costs for existing workers and acting as 'reception' areas for incoming national and international migrants. In this sense, such areas can be seen as a structural feature of uneven capitalist development providing sites for the production and reproduction of cheap labour power within urban areas (Fainstein et al, 1993; Sassen, 2001).

That market mechanisms operating through the urban system can proceed with little negative impact from the presence of deprived neighbourhoods and can act to persistently reduce the accessibility of residents of deprived areas to employment opportunities, suggests that rather than merely focusing on correcting market failures, alternative urban economic development models may be more appropriate in addressing the economic needs of poor neighbourhoods. One alternative prescription is to seek to insulate deprived areas from the market and processes of economic change; a solution of 'less market' rather than 'more market'. This approach would seek to reduce the openness of local economies, through increasing barriers to trade and migration, while developing indigenous capacities oriented towards meeting local needs, perhaps through the development of community-based enterprises and a social economy.

Within the current context of ever more globally liberalised markets the scope for localities or regions to insulate or detach themselves from the dominant economic paradigm is ever more reduced; however, possibilities do exist for pursuing economic viability through combining a degree of self-reliance with a degree of external openness (Pike et al, 2006a). The work of the New Economics Foundation (NEF, 2002, 2005), for example, has sought to promote ways of increasing the circulation of money within a local economy through attracting in investment and reducing rates of outflow of money and resources. Such approaches also include a central commitment to the longer-term environmental sustainability of the development model, pointing out that locally based self-reliant economies provide a route towards a more environmentally sustainable future through promoting people to live, work, produce and consume more closely together and discouraging longer-distance supply chains for food and other basic resources. However, within the current dominance of neoliberal conceptions of economic development that frame the current policy discourse, successive pro-market governments have shown little or no interest in developing these approaches to local economic development.

Social justice

The lack of strong evidence of negative impacts of areas of poverty and social exclusion on wider city economic competitiveness suggests that the principal justification for policy intervention in deprived areas should be that of social justice, reducing poverty and improving the quality of people's lives, rather than supporting economic efficiency and growth (Turok et al, 2004).

There are a number of differing theories of social justice, which variously emphasise equality of opportunity, outcome and process, but their common starting point is that large inequalities of wealth and opportunity are socially and morally unacceptable, as is the exclusion of certain groups from full participation in society. Under New Labour, the primary emphasis of its approach to social equity is on 'equality of opportunity', so that everyone has the opportunity to use their talents, rather than 'equality of outcome' per se. In terms of outcome, this approach recognises diversity in people's values and preferences about the way they live their lives, as well as the role that society plays in restricting people reaching their full potential, and the need to ensure that people are treated the same in any given situation ('equality of process') (Equalities Review, 2007).

Given a situation where social exclusion is spatially concentrated, with around one third of the UK's socially excluded population living within concentrations of acute multiple deprivation, the rationale for intervention is based in a desire to reduce inequalities between areas, both in terms of relative levels of poverty and deprivation, and in relation to the opportunities for residents to participate within society and realise their potential. Within the New Labour agenda this position is encapsulated in the statement that underpinned the development of the neighbourhood renewal agenda (SEU, 2001, p 5): 'no-one should be seriously disadvantaged by where they live'.

The approach here is principally one of mitigation, recognising that those people who lose from economic change are compensated through benefits and the provision of public services. A large element of such compensation acts as a 'safety net', which ensures certain basic levels of income and quality of life and retains a degree of status quo, largely through the operation of mainstream programmes. However, to actually change structures of opportunity within deprived areas requires interventions that enable people to find routes out of exclusion. In this respect, the New Labour agenda has focused heavily on employment as the principal route out of poverty, seeing tackling worklessness as the single most effective means of achieving this on the basis of available evidence (Harker, 2006; DWP, 2007b; HM Treasury, 2006b).

This focus on employment as the most effective route out of poverty has strong social and economic justifications and has been translated into the UK government's current commitment to achieving nationally an 80% employment rate. Yet this narrow emphasis on formal employment as the only route out of poverty remains problematic, particularly given the quality and pay of many of the jobs on offer to those with few or no skills. In fact, some see this strategy as little more than a means of socialising workers into low-wage labour through impelling them into formal employment or quasi-wage employment in third sector organisations at any cost (Gough, 2002). Alternative approaches have focused on the need to improve state regulation of low-paid employment through improved minimum wages, employment conditions and training opportunities. Others seek to emphasise a wider notion of economic and social well-being rather than one defined entirely in terms of paid employment. This viewpoint recognises the role of work outside of employment, arguing that unpaid work also has an important role to play in encouraging mutuality, social capital development and active citizenship among residents in deprived areas, thus improving their coping capacities and overall quality of life (Williams and Windebank, 2001; Evans et al, 2006).

Community engagement and cohesion

The third major rationale for intervention relates to the development of intense localised deprivation as a site for social and political instability, variously manifested in social unrest, riots, high levels of criminality and antisocial behaviour, and the advance of extremist views. It is argued that concentrated deprivation can have negative impacts in terms of reduced levels of political engagement, active citizenship and social capital formation, and contribute to a rise in social segregation on the basis of income, race, ethnicity and religion. In the UK context, the riots sparked in part by racial tensions in the northern towns of Bradford, Burnley and Oldham in 2001 and the terrorist bombings in London in 2005, set against the wider context of ongoing high levels of international in-migration, have led to increased attention to issues of community cohesion (Home Office, 2001; Cantle, 2005; CIC, 2007).

The relationships between localised deprivation and issues such as instability, segregation, alienation and isolation remain poorly understood – yet despite this have been highly influential within UK policy agendas (SEU, 2001; PMSU, 2005). Much of the academic work on the relative isolation and alienation of populations living in deprived neighbourhoods has been dominated by debates around the extent to which such areas are characterised by the existence of an 'underclass', cut off from mainstream society, with a particular set of cultural traits variously referred to as a 'ghetto culture' or 'culture of poverty' (Massey and Denton, 1993; Murray, 1996). Other work on 'disorganised communities' has sought to relate high population turnover in deprived areas to an erosion of social capital and social networks, leading to lower levels of social control and increased levels of crime, stress and disorder (Sampson, 1988; Sampson and Groves, 1989). And more broadly, the work of Putnam (2000) has been highly influential in seeking to relate falling levels of associational activity and informal ties with reduced levels of political and civic engagement, tolerance and trust. Recently Putnam (2007) has also argued that increasingly diverse communities lead to a withdrawal from collective life and increased levels of distrust of neighbours.

Yet the relationships between these factors are hotly disputed. A number of studies conclude that there is no evidence for a distinct 'underclass' that lies outside mainstream values and norms (Morris, 1993; Wilson, 1996; SEU, 2004), nor that all deprived communities are characterised by instability (Bailey and Livingston, 2007). In fact, as Lupton (2003) observes in her study of 12 deprived areas in England and Wales, what was most remarkable was the extent to which relatively isolated communities endorse, rather than reject, mainstream societal values. Furthermore, as is evident in the work of Murray (1996) when he argues that the problems of deprived areas arise in part from the moral deficiencies of the poor, there is a strong danger that arguments of this type can stigmatise communities that are already in a disadvantaged situation, blaming them for the wider social problems manifested within their neighbourhoods. In seeking to better understand these complex relationships, differences between neighbourhoods are clearly important. As the Commission on Integration and Cohesion (CIC, 2007) report stressed, the challenge of community cohesion is strongly place based, varying significantly in relation to particular histories, local economies and the characteristics of the population.

While much of the policy response to the issue of 'instability' has to date focused on housing policy and the promotion of areas of mixed tenure and income, a key element of the current policy response to issues of segregation and isolation is a focus on 'economic inclusion'. This is again primarily advanced through increased labour market participation as the key means of achieving community cohesion through greater integration, shared experiences and a sense of belonging. Yet, although labour market participation can promote integration and community cohesion, the manner in which low-wage, low-skill labour markets are highly segregated – leading to what May et al (2007) refer to as a new migrant division of labour – combined with the existence of discrimination and negative employer attitudes towards some ethnic groups, indicates that labour market participation can also act to reinforce certain aspects of segregation (Sepulveda, 2007).

Conclusions

The development of a policy focus on the challenges posed by deprivation concentrated at the neighbourhood level in the UK and other advanced Western economies – and especially an increasing prioritisation of the economic dimension to such challenges – has been a notable feature of emergent discourses of urban development and the associated policy terrain in recent years. Given that there has been a long history of policy intervention in relation to deprived neighbourhoods and that problems of concentrated deprivation remain as prevalent as ever within the contemporary urban landscape, analysis of the nature and potential effectiveness of the current policy agenda represents a crucial task. In setting out the broad context for the discussion of contemporary approaches towards the economic dimension of deprived neighbourhoods, this chapter has identified a number of central themes that will be pursued in greater depth throughout subsequent chapters.

The first of these relates to the extent and nature of differences between deprived neighbourhoods. Although there are a number of common economic problems that beset so-called deprived neighbourhoods in contemporary Britain, this chapter has begun to indicate that important differences exist between such neighbourhoods and that these places can only be understood contextually, in terms of the wider local, sub/ city-regional, national and international economies within which they are embedded. Such spatial differences have profound implications not only for the conceptualisation and understanding of how economic change is constituted and experienced within particular deprived areas but also for the nature and delivery of any policy response.

The second concerns the nature of policy intervention and whether this is focused on those living in deprived neighbourhoods, the neighbourhoods themselves, or a mixture of the two. A significant proportion of the UK population currently lives in areas encountering problems of multiple deprivation – yet not all living in such areas are themselves experiencing deprivation and the majority of poor people do not live in such areas. Much recent policy debate has adopted a dichotomous 'people versus place' form. Given this, there is a need for critical analysis of the relative merits of mainstream and area-based approaches and, more fundamentally, interrogation as to whether counterpoising 'people' and 'place' is a useful way to present and understand the problems of poor neighbourhoods.

A third central issue relates to the informing ideologies and rationalities for development and the specific objectives that are being pursued by existing policy initiatives. Policy intervention towards deprived neighbourhoods has historically been informed by an array of different motives and the economic dimension to such initiatives has been variously developed. The current policy agenda, embedded as it is within a particular model of urban development informed by wider discourses of neoliberal economic development, presents a particular (and partial) understanding of the dynamics of contemporary urban deprivation rooted within economic competitiveness, social exclusion, community cohesion and good governance. Achieving a better understanding of what evidence exists to support the various policy objectives that characterise these agendas, the tensions that arise from the pursuit of multiple and often competing objectives, and the possibilities for alternative approaches informed by different conceptions of the development process is a further core theme running through the rest of this book.

A final concern relates to the particular nature of the governance challenge presented to policy interventions that seek to address the economic needs of deprived localities. As an object of policy, the disadvantaged neighbourhood presents particular tests, both in terms of coordinating activities related to the multiple dimensions of deprivation that extend across the economic, social and political spheres, and identifying and integrating the appropriate spatial scales for intervention. Yet the extent to which this governance dimension plays into the socioeconomic challenges evident within deprived neighbourhoods requires far better understanding, not least to confront fears that the high level of attention afforded to institutional structures and governance arrangements acts to obscure rather than enlighten analysis of socioeconomic change in poor neighbourhoods.

In the rest of the book, the following chapter (Chapter Two) focuses on the importance of uneven spatial development by looking in more detail at the economic characteristics of deprived areas, the long-term socioeconomic processes that underpin the economic difficulties of deprived areas and their interaction with particular local circumstances to create the particularities of any given neighbourhood. The analysis of the economic dimensions of deprived neighbourhoods and the various related policy responses are then considered in more detail with regard to work and worklessness (Chapter Three), enterprise (Chapter Four), and the wider governance issues related to coordinating and delivering policy for deprived neighbourhoods (Chapter Five). The final chapter (Chapter Six) returns to the questions and themes identified in the present chapter to consider the potential for more effective policy action in relation to deprived neighbourhoods within existing and alternative models of urban economic development.

Notes

[1] The SIMD and the WIMD adopt the same basic methodology, with relatively small differences relating to the domains and their relative weighting. The major differences relate to them both having a lower

emphasis on crime and including separate domains for housing and geographic access to services. The latter, which includes indicators that relate to public transport travel times, reflects concerns in both nations of the need for greater recognition of the problems of the poor and unemployed in rural areas in accessing distant services.

[2] SOAs are delimited in three layers: lower, middle (average population size 7,200) and upper. A similar process also took place within Scotland and Northern Ireland, but with different delimitations in terms of population size. The advantages of SOAs include a design that avoids the constant boundary changes that beset electoral wards and hence permits better comparison over time, and as different layers have a minimum population, this avoids the risks of releasing data that could be traced to individuals.

[3] Market failures relate to the inability of the market to provide goods and services either at all, or in an economically optimal way.

TWO

In what sense a neighbourhood problem?

Introduction

Fundamental to effective policy responses to the economic challenges posed by deprived neighbourhoods is an understanding of the processes that produce and reproduce contemporary patterns of concentrated deprivation. This chapter sets out an understanding of neighbourhood deprivation rooted in the interface between wider processes of economic change and the particular place-based characteristics of neighbourhoods embedded within wider local and regional economies. Although the economic drivers that underlie the emerging geographies of enterprise and employment provide insights into the causes underlying concentrated deprivation, they cannot explain their particular constitution in a given place at a particular time. For this the nature and interaction of stocks and flows of different forms of capital within a given locality need to be analysed alongside the operation of mutually interdependent and reinforcing processes operating across labour, housing markets and investment flows.

This chapter first analyses the basic economic characteristics of deprived neighbourhoods and the wider processes of economic and spatial change within which they are embedded. Consideration of commonalities and differences in deprived neighbourhoods is pursued through a number of case studies selected to enable examination of the manner in which particular deprived neighbourhoods are rooted within a range of local economies (for example, inner city, coalfield, coastal, industrial) situated within differing regional contexts. These case study areas are used throughout this and subsequent chapters, to develop an analysis of deprived neighbourhoods rooted within wider economic, governance and policy structures.

The chapter then turns to consider wider economic processes of deindustrialisation, labour market change and the changing geographies of employment and enterprise, which provide the wider spatial context within which deprived neighbourhoods are situated. The focus then shifts to identify place-based characteristics related to location and integration in the local economy, population characteristics and area-based effects, and how these come together to produce different economic dynamics within deprived neighbourhoods. The interplay between these factors is then discussed in relation to mutually reinforcing cycles of decline related to labour markets, housing markets and private and public investment and provision. The chapter concludes by considering the policy implications that arise from an understanding of the economic problems of deprived neighbourhoods rooted within the interaction of wider processes of change and the particularities of individual places via a series of complex and mutually reinforcing socioeconomic processes.

The economic features of deprived neighbourhoods

In setting out the key economic characteristics of deprived neighbourhoods, definitions commonly focus on the combination of three core elements: the restricted nature of labour market participation, as demonstrated by high levels of unemployment, low rates of employment activity and low levels of skills and education; low levels of business activity and services; and the degraded physical environment and poor housing stock (PMSU, 2005). However, in seeking to analyse the particular incorporation of these places into wider processes of economic development, a systematic consideration of the characteristics of deprived neighbourhoods in relation to the core elements of the capital accumulation process provides a more useful starting point.

Human capital

Residents of deprived neighbourhoods typically have low levels of education, training and skills, which make it difficult for them to compete successfully for available jobs (Gordon, 2003). If jobs are obtained, these are likely to be low wage, low skill and often insecure. For those in receipt of benefit, low-wage, insecure jobs can limit the incentive to enter formal work. However, there are significant differences in the relations between the human capital present in deprived areas and the operation of the local labour market. In some cases, areas and their workers have been made redundant by the closure of major employment sites (for example, mines, major manufacturing plants) and/or large-scale sectoral restructuring. This results in a lack of jobs and workers with skills, experience and expectations poorly aligned to new employment growth opportunities. This can result in very high levels of unemployment, often concentrated within certain groups, typically older male workers. In other cases, deprived neighbourhoods may be an established source of cheap, flexible and often informal unskilled/low-skilled labour for manufacturing, service and primary sector activities within the wider economy, a role particularly associated with neighbourhoods that act as reception areas for migrant workers.

Physical capital

An ongoing lack of financial investment, often over a long period, combined with problems of crime and antisocial behaviour, mean that deprived neighbourhoods are normally characterised by a degraded physical environment. This is particularly evident in terms of housing, where ageing housing stock has fallen into disrepair and/or more recently built social or private sector housing is of low quality. Even where higher-quality social housing has been built, ongoing lack of investment and poor upkeep means that this can deteriorate rapidly. Deprived areas also often suffer from a lack of investment in transport infrastructures, particularly in the case of deprived neighbourhoods peripherally located on the edge of urban areas although provision of transport infrastructures in inner-city areas is more variable.

The physical capital of deprived areas is also limited in terms of appropriate sites for business investment. Where larger abandoned areas of land exist, for example on former heavy industrial sites, these often require expensive environmental remediation and also substantial investment in transport infrastructure. Given relatively low land prices, these sites remain unattractive to private sector investment unless there is major public sector investment to underwrite such costs. Elsewhere, in more densely populated deprived neighbourhoods, there is often a lack of the larger sites required for many current manufacturing, logistical and distribution activities, which instead prefer more accessible edge-of-city locations.

Financial capital

A principal economic feature of deprived neighbourhoods is the low and declining levels of formal private sector activity and the absence of private sector investment. This is particularly evident with respect to housing and retail markets given the frequent absence of other forms of private sector activity. In general, deprived areas are unattractive sites for investment. Given a limited private sector presence, public sector investment is relatively more important, although patterns of public investment are themselves strongly influenced by those of the private sector.

Private investment in property-related developments seeks profitability via margins on sales and potential rental growth arising from occupier demand and capital appreciation. In consequence, property investment is influenced not only by the development value of the land, but also by factors such as the level of risk and physical quality of the development and the environmental quality of contiguous neighbourhoods (CPP, 1998). Much private sector house building and office and retail development has in recent years been most profitable on the edge of urban areas or in surrounding smaller towns and villages, rather than in deprived inner-city neighbourhoods. In consequence, land in deprived neighbourhoods can remain undeveloped for long periods due to low development values, the high cost of assembly, fragmented ownership and uncertain demand.

These commercial realities mean that deprived neighbourhoods generally provide few attractions to property developers. There are, of course, notable exceptions where major sites within particular deprived neighbourhoods provide attractive investment opportunities, particularly where the state takes a major role in underwriting costs related to land assembly, infrastructure provision and site remediation. Furthermore, the well-established process of gentrification of certain low-cost, physically deteriorated, inner-city neighbourhoods can lead to a physical and social transformation of these areas. In these cases private sector investment is attracted into areas of relatively low property value by a combination of factors, principally the availability of an appropriate housing stock, but also the presence of a good accessible central location, decent transport links and proximity to other wealthier neighbourhoods. However, as has been well documented, while the gentrification process pulls in large-scale private investment to upgrade the physical environment and attract in services to formerly deprived neighbourhoods, the increase in property values and inflow of wealthier residents displaces the former resident population and disperses communities to other low-cost areas of the city (Smith, 1996; Lees et al, 2007).

In terms of attracting businesses into deprived areas, the relatively low levels of spending power and skills available locally, combined with the negative images of such areas in relation to issues of crime and a degraded physical environment, provide strong disincentives to business investment. In areas where property values become very low in relatively accessible inner-city areas and/or where the withdrawal of services (for example, retail, leisure, banking) has been particularly extreme, private sector investment can be attracted into so-called 'underserved markets' (Porter, 1995). However, evidence for this is largely restricted to areas where there has been a very high level of private sector disinvestment, for example in certain US inner-city areas, and where such extreme disparities are less pronounced this process is less apparent.

For indigenous growth via self-employment and business start-ups, those resident in deprived neighbourhoods are themselves capital poor, thus self-finance, the most important source of finance for small firms elsewhere in the economy, is a restricted option. Furthermore, a lack of collateral, notably in the UK context in terms of being owner-occupiers of housing, combined with a fragile local economy, the higher costs of smaller loans, and a lack of approachability and interest from banks, all compound the problems of accessing external sources of finance for entrepreneurs within deprived neighbourhoods (SEU, 1999).

Social capital

At the centre of Putnam's (2000) influential work on social capital is the thesis that declining levels of associational activity and public participation have led to a reduction in the stock of social capital, resulting in the weakened fabric of social, community and family life. This argument is often seen to be particularly resonant within deprived neighbourhoods where, it is argued, a decline of civic engagement, restricted social networks, and reduced levels of shared values and a sense of belonging are often apparent. Thus, the SEU (2000) argues that reduced social capital is a 'key factor' in the decline of deprived neighbourhoods and that the presence of social capital is vital in building social stability and community self-help within such areas.

Yet the wide-ranging nature of the definition of social capital, plus the considerable problems of measuring it, have meant that there has been little systematic attempt to model the direction of change in stocks of social capital within deprived neighbourhoods (Conscise, 2003). In fact, there is evidence that certain deprived neighbourhoods may have levels of certain forms of social capital – notably intra-community 'bonding' social capital, which connects members of a group to each other – that are equal to, or above, that of more affluent districts. In her study of deprived neighbourhoods in the US, Bright (2003) concludes that certain types of low-income neighbourhoods are on a par with, or even superior to, their wealthier neighbours in terms of levels of social capital. Forrest and Kearns (1999) also conclude that social capital survives in many disadvantaged neighbourhoods and that it would be wrong to characterise disadvantaged areas as lacking social cohesion and interaction.

The existence of stronger bonding social capital within certain deprived areas reflects the limited degree of mobility of residents in such neighbourhoods compared with more affluent areas, as well as the importance of informal networks for getting by on low incomes. Traditionally, large-scale employment in particular factories, mines or shipyards contributed to the development over time of shared norms, trust and strong institutional and social ties, although with the closure of many of these large employers this source of 'bonding' is often of declining importance. However, while stocks of bonding social capital may be high in some deprived neighbourhoods with relatively stable populations, there often remains an absence of other forms of social capital. This is particularly notable with regard to the lack of extra-community 'bridging' social capital, which connects different groups and individuals to a wider range of social networks that extend beyond their community. The downside of this imbalance in the social capital mix is that it can lead to an insular and exclusionary local culture, which limits connections to potentially beneficial external networks, including those relating to employment opportunities (de Souza Briggs, 1998; Taylor, 2002).

Concerns relating to declining levels of social capital centre particularly on areas undergoing major changes in their constituent population, where traditionally stable populations have been replaced by more transient incoming populations with fewer local networks and who demonstrate less commitment to the neighbourhood (Lupton, 2003). Many new residents moving into deprived neighbourhoods view this as a temporary arrangement and hence make little effort to invest in developing local ties and networks. Such populations are less likely to take care of the communal environment, while norms and accepted behaviours, and the ability of the community to organise, are likely to weaken (Power, 1996, 1997; Sampson, 1999). Yet the important differences between deprived neighbourhoods indicate that this is only one of a number of different developmental dynamics in relation to the production and reproduction of social capital. Critically, the presence of social capital per se is of limited use, needing to operate alongside other forms of physical, financial and human capital if positive socioeconomic development is to take place (Conscise, 2003; Evans and Syrett, 2007). In deprived neighbourhoods the relative absence of these other forms of capital limits any potential positive benefits that may arise from the presence of certain forms of social capital.

Placing deprived neighbourhoods in context: the case study areas

The discussion so far has demonstrated the importance of recognising the extent of differences between disadvantaged neighbourhoods. In order to analyse in greater depth the differences between deprived neighbourhoods in terms of their relationships with the wider local/ subregional/city economy and related governance structures, five case study local economies, and selected deprived neighbourhoods within them, are examined throughout this book. The case study local economies – Brighton and Hove, Newham, Oldham, Mansfield and Sunderland – were defined at the local authority district scale and selected to cover a range of deprived area types (inner city, coastal, coalfield, manufacturing) within different regional contexts (see Box 2.1). These ranged from the high-growth London and South East region (Brighton and Hove, Newham), to lower-growth areas in northern England (Mansfield, Oldham, Sunderland). All were ranked within the government's 88 most deprived local authority districts in 2004 and included localised concentrations of deprivation (see Table 2.1 later in this chapter).

Box 2.1: Case study local authorities

Sunderland (population 280,807) is an important industrial and business city within the North East region, historically associated with coalmining, shipbuilding, engineering and glassmaking. Since before the end of the 1980s, when the remaining shipyard and coalmine closed, the city has been seeking to attract new industries and sources of employment. It has had several successes, notably Nissan in the 1980s, and more recently it attracted several call/contact centres. However, Sunderland continues to contain some of the most deprived communities within the North East, particularly in the inner-city and riverside areas. The city council has been very active in the area of local economic development for over 20 years and has formed strong partnerships with neighbouring local authorities and, more recently, with the Regional Development Agency (RDA) and various subregional organisations.

Oldham (population 217,273) is part of the Greater Manchester subregion and is a largely working-class town. Traditionally, the Oldham economy was dominated by the cotton textile spinning and textile machinery industry. However, it suffered large-scale mill closures in the 1960s and the residual manufacturing sector continued to lose employment with closures in the defence and electronics industries. However, new service sector jobs have been created in retailing, wholesale and public services. The borough has a significant minority ethnic population (13.9%), mainly Asian/Asian British originally attracted to work in the cotton textile industry. Much of the town's built environment is in poor condition, particularly the areas of Victorian terraced housing and estates built in the 1960s/1970s, which are characteristic of the most deprived areas. Around a third of Oldham's wards are within the 10% most deprived nationally, with multiple deprivation concentrated around the central area. The largely Asian minority ethnic population is strongly concentrated in certain neighbourhoods and this high level of spatial and social segregation has created considerable challenges for community cohesion, as seen in the social unrest that emerged in 2001.

Mansfield (population 98,181) is located at the centre of what is still referred to as the North Nottinghamshire coalfield area and is the major town serving this area to the north of Nottingham. Since the late 1970s, the local economy has witnessed the long-term decline of coalmining and traditional manufacturing industries such as textiles and engineering. The formerly dominant coalmining industry has now all but disappeared, and the decline of the textile industry has been similarly dramatic. Despite ongoing decline, there remains a significant manufacturing sector, although recent job growth has been concentrated in the distribution, retail, hospitality and public sectors. The Mansfield economy is predominantly a low-skill, low-wage economy and this, combined with high levels of worklessness, has meant that average household incomes remain significantly below regional and national averages. In 2001 Mansfield had seven wards within the 10% most deprived wards in England. Deprived neighbourhoods are characterised by relatively high levels of unemployment and worklessness, low rates of economic activity and employment, and low levels of household income and skills and education. Populations in these areas tend to be predominantly white, comprising a high proportion of long-term residents, although there is often an incoming younger population of varying significance.

Brighton and Hove (population 247,817) is a city that has experienced considerable economic growth during the past 10 years. Key growth sectors in the local economy include new media and cultural industries, business and financial services, tourism and hospitality and construction. Despite rising commercial property costs, commercial rents remain well below those in London and the city continues to attract inward investment. Major concerns relate to the potential mobility of a number of larger employers whose headquarters are elsewhere, the growth of low-skill/low-paid jobs in call centres and the lack of brownfield development land and premises to facilitate existing business growth. Despite the city's recent economic growth, Brighton and Hove remains a relatively low-pay economy when compared to average wage rates in the South East region and England as a whole. There are also pockets of deprivation, most notably in the eastern wards. The concentrated poverty that currently afflicts the deprived neighbourhoods of East Brighton is the legacy of manufacturing decline in the 1970s, and the residents in these neighbourhoods, mainly accommodated in social housing, have been largely bypassed by the wider dynamism of the city's economy.

London Borough of Newham (population 243,891) was ranked as the 11th most deprived local authority district in England in 2004. It is characterised by a higher unemployment rate than the London average and has suffered from long-term decline in the traditional port-related and manufacturing industries. However, Newham is also situated in inner East London, geographically close to the capital's expanding financial centre and the London Olympics site and located within the wider Thames Gateway subregion, which is the main focus for brownfield development. Newham has one of the fastest-growing and youngest populations within England. It has a highly diverse ethnic population, with the highest proportion of black and minority ethnic (BME) groups of any local authority in England – 61% of the population being drawn from Mixed, Asian or Asian British, Black or Black British, Chinese or other ethnic groups. Newham has the second highest proportion of people of Asian background in the country, including the second largest proportion of Bangladeshis and the second highest proportion of Black Africans. The various ethnic groups tend to be concentrated in different parts of the borough, with Asian communities particularly concentrated in the north-east of the borough and black communities in the west. A feature of deprivation in Newham is its spread across the borough as a whole, with many neighbourhoods ranked within the 20% most deprived Super Output Areas (SOAs) nationally. The high incidence of unemployment and economic inactivity among Newham residents, together with the fact that those in work tend to be in lower-skilled occupations, means that the average income level in the borough is significantly (23%) below the London average.

The case study areas reveal considerable similarities in their economic characteristics and recent evolution, but also important differences in the nature and scale of deprivation within the most deprived areas, as shown by Table 2.1, which gives various measures from the 2004 and 2007 Index of Multiple Deprivation (IMD). In terms of their overall ranking on the IMD, the case studies range from Newham, ranked as the 11th most deprived local authority district (LAD) within England in 2004 (and the 6th most deprived in 2007), to Brighton and Hove, ranked 83rd in 2004 (and 79th in 2007). Sunderland experienced the greatest improvement of the case study areas in its relative position between 2004 and 2007, moving from being the 22nd to the 35th most deprived LAD. The 'concentration' index enables a comparison of the case study areas in terms of the 10% of each district's population living in the most deprived SOAs. On this measure, Oldham and Mansfield are the most deprived, with Mansfield experiencing a significant worsening in its relative position (falling from being the 38th most deprived in 2004 to the 28th in 2007). This is an indication that deprivation tends to be more concentrated in these two areas than in the other case study areas; Oldham, for example, has some of the most deprived SOAs within England, as well as a large number of affluent neighbourhoods. A different measure is the 'extent' index, based on the proportion of a district's population living in the 10% most deprived SOAs nationally. This highlights the widespread nature of deprivation in Newham, ranked as the 6th worst LAD on this measure in 2004 and 2nd in 2007. In fact 70% of Newham's population lived in SOAs in the 10% most deprived nationally in 2004. This contrasts with Brighton and Hove, ranked 87th in 2004 and 95th in 2007, where a fifth of its population were living in SOAs in the 10% most deprived nationally in 2004.

In addition to analysing changes at the district scale, the research focused on selected deprived wards in each case study area in order to highlight the specificities of deprived neighbourhoods and differences between them in terms of their economic contexts (for example, city-centre fringe locations compared to outer housing estates) and their spatial dynamics (for example, changes in local economic structures and local housing markets). The deprived neighbourhoods selected are introduced in Box 2.2, and Table 2.2 sets out comparative statistics related to levels of deprivation within these selected neighbourhoods.

Table 2.1: Rankings of the five case study local authority districts on the Index of Multiple Deprivation, 2004 and 2007

Location (region)	Area type	LA district score on IMD (worst SOA within district)		LA district rank (i) on IMD (worst SOA rank (ii) out of 32,482 nationally)		LA district rank on 'concentration' index (iii)		LA district rank on 'extent' index (iv)		LA district rank on employment domain (v)		LA district rank on income domain (vi)	
		2004	2007	2004	2007	2004	2007	2004	2007	2004	2007	2004	2007
Sunderland (North East)	Former coalmining/ manufacturing	34.24 (76.34)	31.79 (80.62)	22 (98)	35 (14)	37	43	23	33	7	7	20	24
Oldham (North West)	Manufacturing	30.73 (78.88)	30.82 (76.99)	43 (37)	42 (56)	26	23	36	34	44	49	48	39
Mansfield (East Midlands)	Former coalmining/ manufacturing	32.53 (72.14)	31.80 (77.12)	33 (213)	34 (54)	38	28	30	35	91	105	110	123
Newham (London)	Inner city	40.41 (66.94)	42.95 (64.75)	11 (433)	6 (504)	60	51	6	2	24	26	7	7
Brighton and Hove (South East)	Coastal	25.68 (64.53)	25.56 (64.87)	83 (569)	79 (499)	74	70	87	95	43	46	50	51

Source: Department for Communities and Local Government, Neighbourhood Statistics

Notes: (i) The 354 local authority districts in England are ranked from the most deprived (1) to the least deprived (354)
(ii) The 32,482 Super Output Areas (SOAs) in England are ranked from the most deprived (1) to the least deprived (32,482). The ranking given is that of the most deprived SOA in each of the case study areas.
(iii) The 'concentration' index is a measure of the level of deprivation in those SOAs containing 10 per cent of the district's population.
(iv) The 'extent' index is a measure of the proportion of the district's population living in the 10 per cent most deprived SOAs nationally.
(v) The employment scale is based on the number of people who are employment deprived (as measured by a number of unemployment and worklessness variables).
(vi) The income scale is based on the number of people who are income deprived (as measured by a number of income variables).

Box 2.2: Case study neighbourhoods

East End and Hendon (*Sunderland*) contains around 9,000 residents and is an area bordered by the city centre to the west, the River Wear to the north, the port/docks and North Sea to the east and Grangetown on the southern fringe of the city. The area has been particularly affected by the decline of both the port and its associated activities and manufacturing industry, including some large textiles factories. A number of other large employers have left the area more recently including Littlewoods and some food processing firms. The remaining small industrial area near the docks/seafront is very poor in physical condition and appearance, although there are a number of businesses that continue to operate. This area is largely residential but contains some employment areas (including retail and wholesale distribution), particularly near the docks. The location of the area in relation to the city centre and port is an advantage, but it contains areas of severe deprivation and is a designated New Deal for Communities (NDC) area, with £54 million committed to supporting community regeneration over a 10-year period.

Hathershaw and Fitton Hill (*Oldham*) is a designated NDC area to the south of the town centre, with £87 million of government, European and Lottery funding for regeneration for the 2002–12 period. Fitton Hill is a council housing estate built in the late 1960s/early 1970s. The resident population is characterised by a range of long-established social problems (for example, drugs, crime, low educational achievement and so on) and is predominantly white, with a tradition of support for the British National Party. While parts of this area are characterised by a deeply rooted and stable population, in others the population is highly transient. In Hathershaw a private rented sector in predominantly terraced housing exists, with a higher proportion of minority ethnic (largely Asian) residents, and its very poor quality means that this has been targeted for intervention via Housing Market Renewal.

Northfield (*Mansfield*) is situated to the north-west of Mansfield Woodhouse Town Centre and is the most deprived neighbourhood in Mansfield District. Those receiving Income Support are approximately double the national average and there are also high rates for those receiving incapacity and disability benefits. The neighbourhood has a young population, with 27% aged under 16, well above the district average, and high levels of teenage pregnancies. The area is primarily residential, comprising an interwar estate and older colliery housing, and there are considerable problems with a run-down physical appearance and a significant number of boarded-up vacant properties, as well as with crime, drug abuse and lack of provision for young people.

West Titchfield (*Mansfield*) is located close to Mansfield town centre and has particular problems in terms of low levels of income and health and a resulting reliance on state benefits, and high levels of crime and drug abuse. The area comprises both a residential area of dense terraced housing as well as an area of mixed residential and industrial use, which suffers particular environmental problems. The population comprises both longstanding residents and a more mobile incoming population resident in private sector rented property. The younger incoming population has resulted in a relatively youthful population with a high birth rate and a high rate of teenage pregnancies. There is also a small minority ethnic population.

Saunders Park (*Brighton and Hove*) is an area of social housing operated by a consortium of housing associations. There is good accessibility to Brighton city centre and the area attracts a young, mobile and transient population, with a significant number of single mothers. Those who work are concentrated in low-paid service activities. There are limited local services with no banks or post offices but Saunders Park adjoins a sizeable retail park and also Preston Barracks, a former Ministry of Defence site, where a major redevelopment is planned, which will combine high-quality office space, retail provision, housing and an innovation centre.

North Moulsecoomb (*Brighton and Hove*) is the most deprived area in Brighton and Hove, and is characterised by mainly social housing, containing many long-established families who have lived through several generations of unemployment. Educational attainment is low and local schools have a history of poor performance. Although mainly residential, the recently refurbished Fairways industrial estate contains a wide range of light industrial and service activities. Those who work typically do so in part-time and seasonal low-paid service jobs and there is also a significant number who are self-employed.

Beckton (*Newham, London*) is one of the most deprived neighbourhoods within Newham, but is undergoing change related to the new developments in this former docklands ward. Situated by the Thames, in the south-west corner of the borough, Beckton has a population of 7,255, 27% under 15 years of age, and unlike Newham as a whole, over half of the population is white (62%). The character of the local economy is changing, with the traditional dock-related industries replaced by various 'lifestyle services', including a developing hospitality cluster with a number of hotels and bars, targeting corporate business clients. The large amount of new housing has led to a changing social composition, attracting not only people wanting to buy their own home but also property investors who rent out houses at price levels beyond the reach of most long-term residents.

The new housing estates are commonly criticised for their lack of a sense of community and basic retail facilities. As a result, much of the income brought in by those moving into the area 'leaks out', not just out of the neighbourhood, but also out of the borough.

Green Street (*Newham, London*) is characterised by a large Asian population (65%), primarily families of Indian (30%) and Pakistani (17%) origin, but also a sizeable Bangladeshi (16%) community. Average incomes in Green Street are below those of Newham as a whole and employment rates are very low (41%), reflecting cultural traditions as to the role of women in Asian families, as well as language barriers to obtaining work and the presence of a high proportion of full-time students (25%). The area is a 'close-knit' Asian community with a vibrant but self-contained economy dominated by small independent retailers and wholesalers, specialising in food, textiles and jewellery, principally for the local Asian market. Partly as a result of a number of initiatives to promote the area, Green Street is becoming well known in London as a lively Asian retailing area and is attracting visitors and 'cultural tourists' from elsewhere in London and beyond.

Table 2.2: Levels of deprivation within case study areas, 2001

Local authority district/ neighbourhood	Unemployed (%)	Permanently sick/ disabled (%)	No qualifications (%)
Sunderland	9.9	26.3	36.9
Hendon NDC	16.4	30.1	45.0
Oldham	5.7	21.9	37.7
Hathershaw NDC	11.5	23.7	51.5
Mansfield	7.0	22.9	38.2
Northfield	8.7	23.7	45.8
West Titchfield	12.1	27.9	42.7
Newham	11.4	16.5	33.6
Beckton	11.6	24.0	41.4
Green Street	13.7	14.0	36.2
Brighton and Hove	5.3	16.3	22.1
Saunders Park	6.4	20.4	36.5
North Moulsecoomb	4.4	8.1	24.0
England	**5.4**	**16.0**	**28.9**

Source: Census, 2001

Research into the case study local economies and selected neighbourhoods comprised three elements: the collection and review of locally produced economic development and neighbourhood renewal related reports; analysis of government databases relating to the structure, evolution and key characteristics of the local economies; and a series of interviews with key actors and residents within each case study local economy and neighbourhood to gain insights into processes, trends and governance arrangements at the local and neighbourhood level, their particular characteristics, and the extent and nature of the integration of deprived neighbourhoods. The selection of 'key actors' was specific to each case study, but included: those with responsibility for economic development at the subregional and local levels (within local authorities and subregional units); selected members of Local Strategic Partnerships (LSPs); representatives of private sector organisations (for example, Business in the Community, CBI, Chambers of Commerce); representatives of key public sector organisations; managers of Jobcentre Plus; neighbourhood-based residents, professionals and activists; and other key local stakeholders as appropriate (for example, from sectoral organisations, academia and so on).

Economic change and uneven development

The rescaling of economic activity

Analysis of concentrated deprivation must be rooted within an understanding of wider processes of economic change and uneven development. The current era of increasing global flows of capital, investment, trade and labour, driven by rapid technological change, is characterised by evolving spatial patterns of development and divisions of labour. Former industrial heartlands in the advanced Western economies have experienced often traumatic restructuring, as they have struggled to compete with new manufacturing centres within emerging industrial economies. At the same time a feature of the competitive basis of leading growth sectors such as financial and producer services, hi-technology and the cultural industries is their geographical clustering in certain global cities, city-regions and industrial districts.

The changes in the relative economic relationships between supranational, national, city-region, local and neighbourhood scales has led some to identify a 'rescaling' of economic activity, with a particular focus on new roles for cities and regions as motors within a globalising economy (Storper, 1997). Within a global economy, where many factors of production are increasingly mobile, it is argued that it is territorially rooted, immobile, 'relational assets' – a range of sociocultural factors, like conventions and trust, shared values and norms that underwrite the existence of networks, collaborative relations and institutional capacities – that are increasingly important in providing competitive advantage (Amin and Thrift, 1994; Storper, 1995). Furthermore, the flows and networks that characterise a globalising economy have contributed to new ways of thinking about 'places' – not as bounded spaces of coherent and homogenous communities, but rather as processes tying together social and economic interactions (Massey, 1997). This view challenges us to think about the uniqueness of 'neighbourhoods' in terms of how flows and interactions come together in one place alongside more traditional readings related to a sense of rootedness and fixity.

How emerging patterns of uneven development associated with wider global economic shifts in production, consumption and exchange and a changing territorial basis for economic competitiveness relate to the experiences and trajectories of poorer neighbourhoods is necessarily complex. While, on the one hand, concentrated deprivation is associated with older industrial areas left redundant and in need of reinvention, on the other hand, poor low-income neighbourhoods and pockets of social exclusion are present in prosperous high-growth city-regions, reflecting the need for low-cost workers to service economic growth and rising levels of social inequality. However, two interrelated factors are particularly important in specifying how wider economic processes are shaping the economic contexts within which deprived neighbourhoods are embedded: sectoral restructuring via deindustrialisation and service sector growth, and changes in the nature and types of employment.

Sectoral restructuring and labour market change

The consequences of the long-term decline of manufacturing and coalmining are central to understanding the current economic problems facing deprived neighbourhoods in Britain. The patterns of concentrated disadvantage discussed previously (see Chapter One) illustrate the disproportionate location of deprived neighbourhoods within areas of former manufacturing and coalmining activity within inner-city areas of large metropolitan cities, northern towns and cities, 'one-industry' towns, and outer urban areas. The loss of traditional manufacturing jobs has negatively impacted not only on particular areas but also on specific groups. This is especially apparent in the case of older men, who were employed previously in relatively well-paid skilled or semi-skilled occupations, and who have subsequently often struggled to find a route back into employment either because of a lack of jobs, or an inability to compete for the new types of jobs being created.

In all the case study areas the ongoing consequences of long-term manufacturing decline are readily apparent. These are rooted within particular sectoral decline relating to coalmining, shipbuilding, textiles and light manufacturing industry, which in all cases can only be understood as part of wider processes of global and national industrial restructuring. Given the particular geography of these industries, sectoral decline necessarily has uneven impacts with specialist regional, subregional and local economies suffering dramatic losses in jobs and investment. This structural decline of traditional industries has produced economies within the northern towns of Mansfield, Oldham and Sunderland with common weaknesses in terms of low levels of productivity, economic activity, income, wages, skills and education.

This process of deindustrialisation is still ongoing, lying at the heart of the recent job losses in the case study areas, notably in Mansfield, Oldham and Sunderland (see Table 2.3). Four of the five largest declining sectors in absolute terms in both Oldham and Sunderland over the 1997-2004 period were in manufacturing. In fact, manufacturing employment declined by 32.7% (8,223 jobs) in Oldham and 28% (7,410 jobs) in Sunderland over this seven-year period. Similarly, in Mansfield all five of the largest declining sectors were in manufacturing, resulting in the loss of a third of its manufacturing employment (see Box 2.3).

For the other case study local economies, where the impact of the loss of manufacturing jobs is less apparent in recent years, historically manufacturing decline has been important in shaping local labour market conditions. In Brighton, where manufacturing employment has traditionally been of limited importance to the local economy, the economic difficulties of the East Brighton area relate back to the closure of two large manufacturers in the 1970s. In Newham in Inner London, the loss of manufacturing employment and port-related activity has been a fundamental driver of changes in the local labour market over the last 50 years, although in areas such as Beckton, the dock-related industries have now been largely replaced by services related to the financial and producer services sector and new higher-income residents.

Table 2.3: Sectors experiencing the largest employment decline in the case study areas, 1997–2004

Sectors ranked by absolute decline in job numbers (with percentage decline in parentheses)

Sunderland	Manufacture of wearing apparel −1,747 (−89.5%)	Manufacture of machinery and equipment −1,624 (−61%)	Manufacture of radio, television and communication −1,290 (−78.8%)	Manufacture of food and beverages −1,060 (−56.4%)	Land transport; transport via pipelines −987 (−33.6%)
Oldham	Manufacture of machinery and equipment −1,414 (−48.2%)	Manufacture of textiles −1,408 (−55%)	Hotels and restaurants −1,381 (−26%)	Manufacture of medical instruments −1,061 (−69.4%)	Manufacture of other non-metallic mineral products −751 (−90.6%)
Mansfield	Manufacture of textiles −710 (−66.5%)	Manufacture of food and beverages −630 (−81.4%)	Manufacture of furniture −547 (−60.7%)	Tanning and dressing of leather −414 (−99%)	Manufacture of fabricated metal products −393 (−40.3%)
Newham	Financial intermediation −1,612 (−87%)	Computer and related activities −601 (−55.1%)	Manufacture of food and beverages −466 (−22.7%)	Manufacture of wearing apparel −440 (−64%)	Post and telecommunications −426 (−20.1%)
Brighton and Hove	Post and telecommunications −1,766 (−52.3%)	Insurance and pension funding −1,685 (−46.5%)	Financial intermediation −806 (−14.1%)	Sewage and refuse disposal −641 (−84.1%)	Construction −541 (−18.7%)

Source: Annual Business Inquiry

Box 2.3: Sectoral change in Mansfield

The fundamental restructuring of local economies through processes of sectoral change is readily apparent in the case of Mansfield where the local economy has experienced a dramatic decline in employment in mining and manufacturing. Whereas in 1984 there were 13 pits within the Mansfield Travel to Work Area (TTWA) employing 16,500 people, by 2004 this was reduced to just two pits, employing less than 1,000 people, a change reflecting the wider decline of coalmining within the North Nottinghamshire and North Derbyshire coalfield area. The decline in the coal industry had a major negative impact on employment in a range of ancillary industries as well as on service industries through the loss of a large number of relatively well-paid jobs. In addition, the local economy has experienced a significant loss of employment in its major traditional manufacturing industries of textiles – now only a minimal source of employment – and engineering, as well as in other manufacturing sectors (for example, food, furniture and leather tanning). Despite this dramatic decline, the manufacturing sector still employs above the national average (22.7% compared to 15.7%). However, local employment growth has been concentrated within service sector industries, such as wholesale, retail, hotels and catering, sale and repair of motor vehicles, public sector administration, health and social services and education. These growing service sector activities are generally low 'value added' and generate low-paid jobs, so this recent employment growth has reinforced the low-wage nature of the Mansfield economy.

The problems of concentrated deprivation relate not only to the geography of job loss, but also to the geography of new sources of employment and the nature of the jobs being created. Despite employment growth nationally in the UK, the accessibility of residents of deprived areas to employment opportunities has been limited by the mismatch between the former geography of employment and newly emerging geographies of job growth. In general, new and existing enterprises have favoured locations away from deprived inner-city neighbourhoods, often towards the edge of towns or in smaller towns. Many of the new employment opportunities have developed on the edge of urban areas rather than in the inner cities and much new firm formation, retail activity and many emerging markets have been attracted to accessible areas outside large urban areas. This mismatch between old and new economic geographies has led to population movement as people have moved in search of work. This forms part of a longer-term urban–rural shift within Britain as the population, particularly the more skilled element, has moved out of cities in search of not just employment, but also a better quality of life, especially in terms of housing, schooling and safety (Champion and Fisher, 2004; Moore and Begg, 2004).

Population change in the case study areas shows a strong contrast between the older industrial areas, which have experienced population decline (–3.9% in Sunderland and –2.4% in Mansfield in the 1994–2005 period) or stagnation (0.1% in Oldham), and those areas integrated into the wider South East labour market, which have seen strong above-average population growth (5.9% in Brighton and 9.5% in Newham) (Table 2.4). Important here is the scale and selective nature of population change. Out-migration is dominated by the loss of the most economically active population, leading to reduced levels of skills and a relatively ageing population. This migration process therefore remains a weak means of adjusting residential patterns of the working-age population with employment opportunities, either because for those with few or no skills competing for jobs elsewhere is difficult, or because for many individuals their ties to family, friends and places, and related issues of their overall quality of life, make out-migration an unattractive option. The other means of improving linkages between areas of employment growth is through commuting, but for those on low wages with restricted transport mobility, the possibilities of long-range commuting are limited.

Yet the issue is not only about the new geographies of employment, but also the types of jobs being created within sectors of employment growth. In the case study areas, despite the decline of manufacturing employment, all achieved net job growth over the 1997–2007 period, although the rate of growth varied widely from 20.7% in Newham to just 0.9% in Oldham. The bulk of new employment opportunities were

Table 2.4: Population change in the case study LADs, 1994–2005

	Population 1994	Aged 16–74 1994	Population 2005	Aged 16–74 2005	Total % change	Aged 16–74 % change
Sunderland	295,300	218,800	283,700	215,000	–3.90	–1.70
Oldham	219,400	158,300	219,200	158,600	–0.10	–0.20
Mansfield	101,400	74,500	99,000	73,600	–2.40	–1.20
Newham	224,900	157,500	246,200	181,100	9.50	14.90
Brighton and Hove	240,800	176,600	255,000	196,100	5.90	11.10
England		35,559,800	50,431,700	37,502,800	4.60	5.50

Source: NOMIS Population Estimates

found within various service sectors and especially within consumer and public services, rather than in business and producer services. Table 2.5 ranks the top five largest employment creation sectors in absolute terms in each case study area and highlights the importance of the retail and wholesale trade sectors and public service employment to job growth within these local economies.

A defining feature of recent service sector growth has been the increasing polarisation between relatively well-paid and high-skilled professionals working in the 'knowledge-based' sectors, on the one hand, and the growth of a flexible workforce, including many low-paid workers in insecure and low-grade service sector employment, on the other (Hutton, 1995; Goos and Manning, 2004). One of the consequences of the loss of semi-skilled and skilled jobs in manufacturing has been the disappearance of the kinds of jobs that had previously occupied the 'middle ground' in local labour markets. For residents in less prosperous neighbourhoods, it is the growth of low-skill, low-wage insecure jobs encouraged by sectoral change and the pursuit of greater labour market flexibility that are most likely to provide a route into the labour market. Yet such jobs are often unattractive in terms of their pay, conditions and career development potential and for those in receipt of benefits, the low level of wages may result in a minimal or no increase in overall household income. These issues relating to changes in labour market supply and demand and their interaction mediated by various institutional forms are explored in further detail in Chapter Three.

Differences between neighbourhoods

Although it is possible to identify certain common economic characteristics of deprived neighbourhoods and their experience of wider processes of economic and regional change, they also exhibit fundamental differences. Difference between poor neighbourhoods is emphasised by a range of academics engaged in their analysis from a variety of disciplinary perspectives (McGregor and McConnachie, 1995; Maclennan, 2000; Buck, 2001; Lupton, 2003). Such variation is rooted in the interplay between the characteristics of places, their resident populations and the local operation of key processes, notably housing markets, labour markets and levels of private and public sector investment and provision.

Table 2.5: Sectors experiencing the largest employment growth in the case study areas, 1997–2004

Sectors ranked by absolute growth in job numbers (with percentage growth in parentheses)

Sunderland	Public administration and defence 3,739 (73%)	Retail trade 2,797 (25.8%)	Other business activity 2,207 (27.1%)	Education 2,117 (26.3%)	Health and social work 1,633 (12.7%)
Oldham	Retail trade 5,501 (67.9%)	Health and social work 3,175 (52.5%)	Other business activity 2,973 (92.8%)	Construction 816 (19.8%)	Education 744 (10.7%)
Mansfield	Retail trade 1,630 (34.1%)	Other business activity 863 (35.2%)	Construction 766 (35.6%)	Public administration and defence 546 (29.9%)	Education 369 (11.2%)
Newham	Other business activity 3,847 (84.3%)	Retail trade 2,401 (36.1%)	Education 2,249 (44.2%)	Public administration and defence 2,000 (59%)	Construction 988 (46.5%)
Brighton and Hove	Other business activity 4,786 (39%)	Retail trade 3,259 (28.1%)	Hotels and restaurants 3,109 (37.6%)	Education 3,026 (26.1%)	Health and social work 2,715 (20.2%)

Source: Annual Business Inquiry

Place-based differences

Individual deprived neighbourhoods need to be placed within their historical and geographical setting, sensitive to how such places have evolved over time. While certain locales were designed to be, and have remained, low-cost, low-income areas, other disadvantaged areas were formerly more affluent and have entered a period of decline. While certain place-based characteristics may be more intangible, relating to the particular 'spirit' or atmosphere of a place, others are rooted in the physical location of a neighbourhood and its relation to the wider local economy.

In terms of their physical location in relation to city centres and major transport networks, disadvantaged neighbourhoods range from those where a marginal location and poor accessibility are principal problems – for example in certain outer urban, suburban or rural areas – through to highly accessible inner-city locations. However, even in areas better served by transport links, the low incomes of residents often significantly limit their ability to utilise available transport infrastructures.

As the case study areas demonstrate, the relation of poor neighbourhoods to the wider local or sub/city-regional economy varies significantly (North and Syrett, 2006). These neighbourhoods can be located within a city or subregion experiencing widespread deprivation related to depressed demand for labour and the dominance of low-wage, low-skilled employment, as is the case within certain former coalfield areas and/or industrial cities in the North (for example Sunderland). Yet deprived neighbourhoods also exist as 'pockets' of deprivation within relatively well-performing sub/city-regional economies such as London and the wider South East (for example Brighton and Hove). Such 'pockets' normally relate to the dominance of particular housing tenures, either social housing or cheap rented accommodation, that house socially marginalised groups and/or a reservoir of cheap labour to serve local employment needs related to low-wage, low-skill jobs.

Although there are important relationships between particular neighbourhoods and the wider sub/city-region, the extent and nature of these relationships with regard to sub/city-regional economic performance is less clear. Evidence of change within England indicates some relationship between the improved performance of local authority districts (LADs) and the improved economic performance of seaside towns (for example, Blackpool, Great Yarmouth and Hastings), large freestanding cities (for example, Bristol, Leicester and Nottingham), conurbation cores (for example, Liverpool, Manchester and Newcastle) and the London core (for example, Brent, Camden and Greenwich)

(Amion Consulting, 2007a). In contrast, LADs least likely to experience positive change include dormitory areas of London (for example, Luton, Croydon and Ealing), other cities (for example, Solihull, Trafford and Warrington) and rural areas (for example, Allerdale, Kerrier and Penwith), while those in industrial and mining areas (for example, Blackburn, Burnley, Easington, Mansfield and Stoke), large freestanding towns (for example, Brighton and Hove, Lincoln, Norwich and Preston) and industrial conurbations (for example, Bolton and Derby) show little change.

Yet available data indicate no clear relationship between the performance of the 88 most deprived local authority districts (which in England were those that received support via the Neighbourhood Renewal Fund; NRF) and improved conditions in the most deprived neighbourhoods (Amion Consulting, 2007a). In relation to levels of worklessness in the 2001-05 period, although the gap between the LAD level and national level narrowed, the gap between the LAD and the 10% most deprived neighbourhoods within the LAD remained. While 41% of the most deprived LADs experienced a narrowing of worklessness levels at both local authority and neighbourhood levels, 24% saw improvement at the LAD level but a worsening performance in deprived neighbourhoods, and 19% experienced a widening of the gap at both LAD and deprived neighbourhood levels.

Such evidence demonstrates the difficulties of making easy associations between neighbourhood performance and the wider performance of the city or local authority area. While wider local/city economic performance can provide growth in employment opportunities, what is critical is the manner and processes of labour market integration for those living in deprived neighbourhoods. The evidence demonstrates that certain groups and areas consistently remain marginalised from the labour market even within the most dynamic economic areas. It also points to the importance of understanding the ongoing concentrations of worklessness not only in employment terms but also in relation to other processes related to housing markets and social exclusion.

People-based differences

Population change and turnover

The particular population characteristics and dynamics relating to given deprived neighbourhoods is a further source of differentiation. Alongside the differences in terms of overall levels of population growth and decline in the case study areas previously discussed, there are also important differences in terms of age structure (see Table 2.6). In those areas with stagnant and falling populations there is a notable decline in the population below the age of 24, while in Newham and Brighton this younger element of the population is growing strongly. The population structure of Newham is significantly younger than the other case study areas, a situation reflected in the Beckton and Green Street neighbourhoods, which display higher than average proportions of the population in the 0-15 and 16-24 age groups, and a significantly lower population in the 65+ age group. Oldham also has above-average levels in the 0-15 age group, and as with Newham, this reflects the younger age structure of the resident ethnic populations. In the deprived areas of Northfield and West Titchfield in Mansfield and Hendon in Sunderland, a 0-15 population slightly above the national average reflects the presence of a relatively high level of single parents.

Analysis of change in the numbers and structure of the resident population of deprived neighbourhoods needs to be undertaken with care and knowledge of local conditions. This is particularly important with regard to the nature of inward and outward flows of population as the result of the operation of sorting mechanisms in the local housing market and the ethnic composition of the population. Such changes may result in stability or growth in the aggregate size of the population

Table 2.6: Population age structure in the case study areas, 2001

Area	Total population	Age group (%)				
		0–15	16–24	25–64	65+	All
Sunderland	**280,807**	**20.0**	**12.1**	**52.3**	**15.6**	**100.0**
Hendon NDC	8,591	21.2	13.8	49.7	15.3	100.0
Oldham	**217,273**	**23.0**	**10.7**	**52.1**	**14.3**	**100.0**
Hathershaw NDC	6,089	25.4	14.2	47.7	13.7	100.0
Mansfield	**98,181**	**20.6**	**10.2**	**52.9**	**16.4**	**100.0**
Northfield	6,918	22.7	10.4	49.4	17.5	100.0
West Titchfield	7,324	22.2	12.3	50.3	15.2	100.0
Newham	**243,891**	**26.2**	**14.7**	**50.2**	**8.9**	**100.0**
Beckton	7,255	27.0	12.4	19.8	10.8	100.0
Green Street	6,630	27.3	17.6	47.7	7.4	100.0
Brighton and Hove	**247,817**	**16.6**	**12.9**	**54.1**	**16.3**	**100.0**
Saunders Park	7,459	20.7	14.8	47.4	17.1	100.0
North Moulescoomb	8,907	18.0	41.0	32.4	8.6	100.0
England	**49,138,831**	**20.2**	**10.9**	**53.0**	**15.9**	**100.0**

Source: Census, 2001

but significant changes in its composition. Sensitivity is required to the scale of flows and the selective nature of outflows – often the employed and better-skilled element of the population – and of inflows – often students, young single parents, refugees, asylum seekers and benefit claimants – which result from the operation of public housing policies and the availability of cheap rented housing. Consequently, some deprived areas can be characterised by a relatively long-term, ageing, stable but declining population at one extreme, or a younger, growing and more transient population at the other, while others simultaneously contain elements of both.

The extent and nature of population turnover or 'churn' can play a significant role with regard to the nature of social networks. In relatively isolated deprived neighbourhoods, which may experience relatively low levels of population turnover, there may be problems related to the highly constrained nature of social networks. In contrast, in areas with very high levels of turnover, social networks may be more fluid and outward looking, creating considerable challenges related to the development and maintenance of neighbourhood-based networks. Variation in levels of population turnover in deprived neighbourhoods is influenced by a variety of factors not least the role of the neighbourhood within the wider urban system. Housing tenure is one important factor here, with certain deprived neighbourhoods characterised by social housing stocks that can limit the extent of turnover, while in others low-quality private sector rented accommodation may facilitate rapid turnover.

At an aggregate level the rate of population turnover is not significantly greater in deprived areas than in less deprived areas. As Bailey and Livingston (2007) demonstrate, levels of deprivation explain around 4% of the variance of gross turnover between neighbourhoods in England and none of the variance in Scotland. They argue that it is important to guard against making simple assertions that relate deprived neighbourhoods with high levels of instability and isolation, and pathologise these areas by asserting that instability is a response to living and moral conditions. However, there are important differences between deprived areas in the rate of churn. It is possible to identify different types of deprived areas on this basis of population turnover, ranging from 'escalators', 'gentrifiers', 'isolates' and 'transits' (Amion Consulting, 2007b; Robson et al, 2008, forthcoming) (see Table 2.7). Thus, in 'escalator' neighbourhoods people are moving out to better areas, with consequent issues related to the loss of the most skilled and aspirational element of the population, whereas in well-connected 'transit' areas, residents are likely to have better access to job opportunities than those residing in 'isolated' neighbourhoods.

Table 2.7: Population turnover and deprived areas

Deprived area type	Escalators	Gentrifiers	Isolates (disconnected)	Transits (well-connected)
In-movers	*from similar or poorer areas*	*from better areas*	*from similar or poorer areas*	*from better areas*
Out-movers	*to better areas*	*to similar or poorer areas*	*to similar or poorer areas*	*to better areas*

Source: Amion Consulting (2007b). (Typology developed in conjunction with Professor Brian Robson, Centre for Urban Policy Studies, University of Manchester. See Robson et al, 2008)

Ethnic diversity

The degree of population diversity/homogeneity and the changing nature of their ethnic make-up provide a key dimension of variation in disadvantaged neighbourhoods in relation to processes of labour market integration and community cohesion. Given the rapid growth of in-migration into the UK over recent years, issues of population diversity and community cohesion have become an increasingly important issue, which has extended beyond those neighbourhoods that have traditionally been important reception areas within major cities. In addition to a number of well-established minority ethnic communities, the new wave of migration from the mid-1990s, heightened dramatically by the flow of migrants from Eastern Europe after 2004, has increased the size of immigrant populations, their geography and levels of diversity (Vertovec, 2006; Syrett and Lyons, 2007).

Minority ethnic communities are more likely to live in the poorest neighbourhoods. Analysis of 2001 Census data demonstrates that the non-white population living in deprived neighbourhoods is around twice as high as the percentage living in other urban neighbourhoods (Parkinson et al, 2006). However, there remain substantial differences between deprived neighbourhoods in terms of the size and characteristics of ethnic populations. This is clearly demonstrated within the case study localities (see Table 2.8). The London Borough of Newham is by far the most ethnically diverse local area with 60.6% of the area BME population, with large Asian and Black populations. However, within this context the two neighbourhoods demonstrate marked differences. Green Street has a dominant BME population (83.6%) of largely Asian origin and Beckton has a much smaller BME population (37.8%). Oldham too has a significant BME population (13.9%), which is predominantly Asian and strongly concentrated in particular neighbourhoods, accounting for 38.9% of the population in Hathershaw, and in two other wards forms

Table 2.8: Ethnic composition of the population in case study areas, 2001

Area	% of total population according to ethnic group					
	White	Non-white	Mixed	Asian	Black	Chinese
Sunderland	**98.1**	**1.9**	**0.4**	**1.0**	**0.1**	**0.3**
Hendon NDC	93.4	6.6	0.8	4.9	0.4	0.5
Oldham	**86.1**	**13.9**	**1.1**	**11.9**	**0.6**	**0.3**
Hathershaw NDC	61.1	38.9	2.0	35.5	1.3	0.1
Mansfield	**98.3**	**1.7**	**0.6**	**0.6**	**0.2**	**0.2**
Northfield	99.1	0.9	0.6	0.2	0.1	0.1
West Titchfield	97.8	2.2	0.9	0.7	0.4	0.2
Newham	**39.4**	**60.6**	**3.4**	**32.5**	**21.6**	**3.1**
Beckton	62.2	37.8	3.4	5.1	27.3	2.0
Green Street	16.4	83.6	2.2	65.4	14.2	1.8
Brighton and Hove	**94.3**	**5.7**	**1.9**	**1.8**	**0.8**	**1.2**
Saunders Park	94.2	5.8	1.7	2.3	1.0	0.7
North Moulescoomb	91.1	8.9	2.2	3.2	1.6	1.9
England	**90.9**	**9.1**	**1.3**	**4.6**	**2.3**	**0.9**

Source: Census, 2001

the majority population. In contrast, Sunderland and Mansfield have predominantly White populations (98.1% and 98.3% respectively), a situation reflected within their deprived areas, while Brighton's deprived neighbourhoods have a small (5.7%) mixed BME population.

The precise spatial impacts of the most recent phase of immigration to the UK currently remain poorly understood, not least because of the lack of appropriate data to analyse these recent and rapid flows. However, what is clear is that recent immigration has had an impact across a range of cities and regions, as economic migrants have been pulled to areas of labour market shortage (Coombes et al, 2007). In this respect the Commission on Integration and Cohesion (CIC, 2007, p 58) identifies four broad area types that present particular characteristics and differing types of cohesion challenge:

- *changing less affluent rural areas*: typically areas experiencing complex patterns of immigration for the first time, with Eastern European migrants coming to work in agriculture and/or food processing;
- *stable less affluent urban areas that have experienced manufacturing decline*: prevalent in the North and the Midlands, which have resulted in

major problems of deprivation. Such areas include some of the 'classic cohesion' problem textile-producing areas, where longstanding white and Asian communities live parallel lives, although the report stresses that the majority is not like this;

- *stable less affluent urban areas without manufacturing decline*: these are spread across the country and relate to problems of deprivation. They include areas in the South East where comparatively lower house prices attract newcomers, leading to tensions with the existing community;
- *changing less affluent urban areas*: again spread across the country, where there is a high demand for low-skilled labour – either in manufacturing or tourist industries (for example coastal towns) – resulting in increased numbers of migrant workers and increased competition for jobs.

Area or neighbourhood effects

While it is possible to identify important place- and people-based differences between deprived neighbourhoods, a more controversial issue is the extent to which the spatial concentration of poverty within a neighbourhood produces externalities with an additional effect on the well-being and life chances of the resident population. 'Area effects' or 'neighbourhood effects' refer to the notion that spatial variations in economic and social conditions that produce concentrated deprivation are not reducible to 'compositional effects' (that is, a reflection of the personal and family characteristics of the population that compose the area), but that there is an additional, area-related effect that results from concentrated disadvantage. With respect to disadvantaged neighbourhoods, such area effects are overwhelmingly negative, acting to further compound problems of concentrated disadvantage and social exclusion.

Given the complex and multiple relationships between people and the places they live in and how these evolve through time, separating out and identifying area effects is conceptually and methodologically problematic. A wide range of potential area effects can be identified (Ellen and Turner, 1997; Atkinson and Kintrea, 2001). Conceptually, it is possible to distinguish between effects that flow from the characteristics of the population, and those that flow from the characteristics of the place itself. Population-rooted area effects emanate from the nature of socialisation processes in deprived neighbourhoods, the existence of constraining forms of social capital and restricted social networks, the stigmatisation of residents through the poor reputation of a neighbourhood and a high burden on local service provision. In contrast, intrinsic place-based area effects relate to the poor quality and/or absence of private services, lower standards of public service provision, features of the built environment and high levels of environmental pollution, as well as the physical isolation of a neighbourhood. In addition, it is also important to note the presence of indirect effects. For example, higher levels of criminal behaviour and social disorder (which may result from some of the preceding factors) may impact on all neighbourhood residents, either by constraining behaviour or through the costs of victimisation.

There is considerable dispute within the academic literature as to the existence of population-related area effects and their relative importance (Buck, 2001; McCulloch, 2001). Much of the academic literature on area effects is derived from studies from the US, which have particularly focused on neighbourhoods that are characterised by extreme segregation, predominantly on a racial basis, and high levels of disparity rooted within close connections between employment, income and housing quality. Reviews of the US literature generally conclude that area effects are important in these neighbourhoods (Jencks and Mayer, 1990; Brooks-Gunn et al, 1993; Ellen and Turner, 1997). However, as Ostendorf et al (2001) observe, the European context is significantly different from the US, in that levels of disparity are moderated through the operation of the welfare state and the provision of social housing, while levels of racial segregation are generally much less pronounced. Therefore, neighbourhood effects identified in the US, particularly those related to discourses concerning the identification of a 'ghetto culture' or 'underclass', are less apparent in the European context, particularly if there is an expectation that such effects may only become significant above certain thresholds.

In the UK a number of reviews have concluded that the evidence for neighbourhood effects is weak and that they are of marginal importance in comparison to individual and family characteristics in determining life outcomes (Gordon, 1996; Dickens, 1999; DETR, 2001; Sanderson, 2006). Yet a number of UK studies also provide evidence of the existence of various area effects across the diverse fields of employment, education, crime and health (for example, Atkinson and Kintrea, 2001; Burgess et al, 2001; Forrest and Kearns, 2001; Lupton, 2003; Mumford and Power, 2003). This lack of clear evidence in relation to area effects reflects the difficulties in isolating and demonstrating them empirically given the complexity of disentangling an individual from the context in which they reside, socialise and grow up. As Manski (1993) observed, the central problem is one of 'simultaneity'; people are influenced by their context and at the same time influence their context.

In addition, there are a number of other related methodological problems (Buck, 2001). First, the process by which individuals become resident in different neighbourhoods reflects a degree of selection, which means that individual characteristics will influence choice and outcomes, which may overplay or underplay neighbourhood effects. Second, statistical data available for the neighbourhood level are restricted and often of poor quality and of limited relevance in measuring area effects. Third, in seeking to identify effects there is a need for sensitivity to non-linear relationships, recognising that effects may come into operation at particular thresholds (Galster et al, 2000). Fourth, there is an issue of spatial scale, as different neighbourhood effects will operate at different scales. Finally, the combination of interrelated factors within any given area ensures that there are multiple pathways of cause and effect; the existence, extent and importance of neighbourhood effects will clearly vary in relation to the characteristics of particular areas.

Taken together, the absence of clear evidence that surrounds the identification of neighbourhood effects often says as much about the limitations of methodological approaches that seek to break down and separate out the relationship between people and place as it does about the lived experiences and life chances of those living in deprived neighbourhoods.

Cycles of decline: producing and maintaining localised deprivation

Central to the challenge posed by areas that suffer multiple deprivation is how different dimensions of deprivation (including neighbourhood effects) operate in a mutually reinforcing manner to create and reinforce concentrated deprivation. The interlocking causes of deprivation are often portrayed diagrammatically as 'vicious cycles' or 'cycles of decline' (see Figure 2.1).

The differences between deprived neighbourhoods significantly influence the nature and relative importance of the elements of such cycles. Important too is the role of 'tipping points' or 'thresholds', which when reached can trigger or intensify the operation of such cycles. Economically, particular events, such as the closure of a major employer, can have a dramatic impact, leading to increased levels of unemployment, reduced local incomes and loss of skills, as well as an associated negative multiplier effect on local suppliers and services. Such

Figure 2.1: Cycles of decline in areas of multiple deprivation

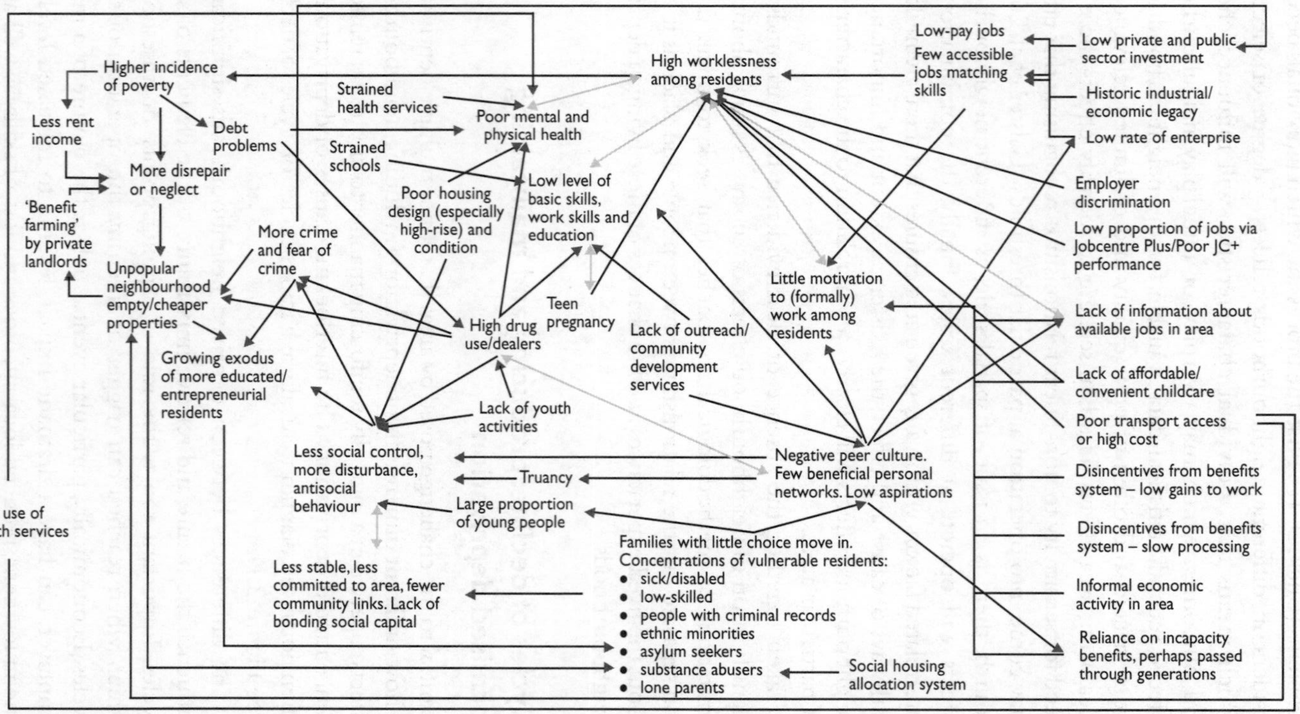

Low private and public sector investment

Historic industrial/economic legacy

Low rate of enterprise

Employer discrimination

Low proportion of jobs via Jobcentre Plus/Poor JC+ performance

Lack of information about available jobs in area

Lack of affordable/convenient childcare

Poor transport access or high cost

Disincentives from benefits system – low gains to work

Disincentives from benefits system – slow processing

Informal economic activity in area

Reliance on incapacity benefits, perhaps passed through generations

Low-pay jobs

Few accessible jobs matching skills

High worklessness among residents

Little motivation to (formally) work among residents

Negative peer culture. Few beneficial personal networks. Low aspirations

Social housing allocation system

Families with little choice move in. Concentrations of vulnerable residents:
- sick/disabled
- low-skilled
- people with criminal records
- ethnic minorities
- asylum seekers
- substance abusers
- lone parents

Strained health services

Strained schools

Poor mental and physical health

Low level of basic skills, work skills and education

Teen pregnancy

Lack of outreach/community development services

High drug use/dealers

Lack of youth activities

Truancy

Large proportion of young people

Poor housing design (especially high-rise) and condition

Less social control, more disturbance, antisocial behaviour

Less stable, less committed to area, fewer community links. Lack of bonding social capital

Higher incidence of poverty

Less rent income

'Benefit farming' by private landlords

Debt problems

More disrepair or neglect

More crime and fear of crime

Unpopular neighbourhood empty/cheaper properties

Growing exodus of more educated/entrepreneurial residents

Low use of health services

Source: PMSU (2005, p 44)

impacts are particularly traumatic where one or two large employers dominate and closure results in the rapid disappearance of not only the economic heart of the local economy, but also the major source of social networks, community cohesion, sense of identity and future prospects. Non-economic events can likewise trigger decline, for example urban redevelopments that provide new housing opportunities outside of the area, civil disturbance and lawlessness, or rapid changes in the ethnic or racial composition of an area.

Operating within such overall cycles of neighbourhood decline are various economic-related cycles, the most important of which relate to labour markets, housing markets, the provision of private and public sector services and the role of social capital.

Labour markets

Cycles that reinforce persistent worklessness are particularly rooted in person and household factors and the overall population mix, and compounded by the operation of housing markets, the failure of employers to address discrimination, and poor access to job information (Kitson et al, 2000; Gordon, 2003). In explaining the persistence of worklessness in particular areas, Gordon (2003) identifies two key factors. First, in certain areas there are recurring patterns of job loss, often sectorally rooted, which continue to affect particular regions and neighbourhoods. Second, some kind of 'hysteresis' effect is evident, whereby past experience of unemployment actively promotes concentration within an area. This hysteresis effect results from a number of interrelated processes. First, a lack of effective equilibrating processes (that is, via migration and commuting) between areas of differential employment reinforces existing concentrations. Second, those with a history of a lack of employment and job loss who are concentrated in particular neighbourhoods are more vulnerable to further unemployment. Third, spatial externalities in the housing market lead to a residential sorting process (Cheshire et al, 2003). Fourth, spatial externalities in the labour market may operate such that residents of areas with fewer employed residents lose out in the competition for jobs due to factors such as postcode discrimination, demotivation from job search or poorer access to job information. The second and the fourth of these factors are particularly important in terms of understanding the significance of localised factors as these illustrate that the chances of an individual gaining or holding a job are directly affected by their past experiences of unemployment and those of their neighbours.

Overall, the geography of concentrated unemployment only partially reflects that of job loss and job growth. Gordon (2003) identifies a series of vicious circles that link local unemployment to local social outcomes, acting to further reduce the employment prospects of residents in the short and longer term. Issues such as access to job information, short-term jobs creating interrupted work histories, health deterioration, family fragmentation, notably the impact of lone parenthood, and educational underachievement are particularly important here and these are discussed further in Chapter Three. Taken together, these largely *social* forces tend to reproduce spatial concentrations of unemployment, even if the original reason for high unemployment was in fact something quite different.

Although most studies of work and worklessness in relation to deprived neighbourhoods conclude that neighbourhood effects have only a minimal additional impact over and above the characteristics and circumstances of individuals and households (for example, Fieldhouse and Tranmer, 2001; Buck and Gordon, 2004; Sanderson, 2006), there is recognition that certain neighbourhood effects compound problems of labour market exclusion, particularly in terms of localised work cultures, restricted social networks, employer discrimination against stigmatised neighbourhoods and a physically isolated location with poor public transport (see Chapter Three for further discussion).

The most debated of these neighbourhood effects relates to whether deprived neighbourhoods develop localised 'cultures of worklessness', that is, a distinctive set of attitudes, norms and values to work that lies outside those of mainstream society. As was argued earlier with regard to more generalised notions of 'cultures of poverty' (see Chapter One), there is only limited evidence to support notions of the existence of 'cultures of worklessness' within deprived neighbourhoods. There is, however, evidence of particular perceptions, attitudes and aspirations towards work that reflect the nature of socialisation that takes place within a particular milieu characterised by prolonged periods of intergenerational worklessness and limited employment opportunities for a high proportion of the resident population (Bauder, 2001). Where cultures of worklessness are said to exist, they are characterised by lowered incentives to work – in a context where peers are also unemployed and the informal economy has a strong pull factor – and a view of joblessness as unproblematic given circumstances of lowered aspirations and short-term horizons (Ritchie et al, 2005). Such attitudes and aspirations may result from peer pressure, a lack of role models (that is, of those in employment, or more importantly still, those in good jobs with career advancement possibilities), low self-esteem and expectations (of individuals themselves and externally from employers), and limited experience, direct or indirect, of the world of work.

Differences in local perceptions and behaviours are often characterised by a narrow, insular and highly localised view of the labour market (Green and White, 2007), often reinforced by local stigma, which produces narrow travel horizons and compounds exclusion through a loose sense of attachment to the mainstream labour market (Fieldhouse, 1999). Certainly in the case study neighbourhoods, attitudes towards work and education were commonly characterised by reduced expectations and aspirations emanating from limited experience of employment extending across generations, and an acceptance of the need to 'get by' on the basis of state benefits supplemented by various paid and unpaid informal work. Yet, such attitudes and expectations did not pervade all residents of deprived neighbourhoods, nor were they confined only to these areas, but were also evident within the broader local economy. The prevalence of such attitudes was therefore different by *degree* rather than *kind*, reinforced by the material circumstances of residents of disadvantaged areas and their more restricted social networks.

Housing markets

The housing market in deprived neighbourhoods has significantly higher proportions of low-cost rented properties and social housing than other areas. Residential sorting associated with the availability of low-cost rented property and the allocation of social housing is the principal factor in explaining why concentrations of deprivation exist where they do. As Maclennan (2000, p 14) observes: 'Ignoring the core role of the housing system in translating local economic change into damaging concentrations of the disadvantaged is a bit like trying to deal with low wages without understanding the labour-market processes that produce them'. The dynamics of housing markets are therefore critical in their own right in understanding the trajectories of deprived neighbourhoods and provide a crucial interface with associated changes in local labour markets and flows of private and public investment (see Box 2.4).

Box 2.4: Housing in Hathershaw and Fitton Hill (Oldham)

The Hathershaw and Fitton Hill area demonstrates the central importance of housing stock and residential sorting mechanisms to processes of concentrated deprivation. In Fitton Hill, the housing stock was controlled by the council for many years, although it has now been transferred to housing association control. Within the long-term, predominantly white, population resident on this housing estate are many deeply entrenched social problems (for example, criminality, drug use, high rates of teenage pregnancy, unemployment and low educational achievement), which often span generations. By way of contrast, in Hathershaw the old and poorly maintained terraced properties house an older population as well as a growing Asian population. As many empty properties are boarded up and unsellable or unlettable, a large number of private landlords in Hathershaw let properties cheaply on an indiscriminate basis, leading to the development of a transient population and concentrations of social groups unable to find affordable housing elsewhere in the area. Many local shops have closed and remain boarded up or are struggling to survive. This contributes to a degraded local environment and an absence of decent-quality local retail service provision, despite its importance to a population with limited mobility due to low levels of car ownership.

Notions of cycles of decline are well developed with respect to housing markets in deprived areas (Power, 1996; Skifter-Anderson, 2003). In terms of private sector housing, processes of neighbourhood decay reflect the interaction between the composition of residents in the neighbourhood, the economic conditions of the properties and the physical condition of buildings and the neighbourhood as a whole (Skifter-Anderson, 2003). These three factors change simultaneously through mutually reinforcing mechanisms. As lower-income residents move into an area, demand for higher rental properties decreases, which makes it less profitable to invest in maintenance and improvements. As a result, the physical condition of buildings declines and certain dwellings become obsolete, reducing the attractiveness of the area. At a certain threshold, when a large proportion of the resident population have social problems, economic losses occur via losses in rental incomes (via non-payment) and increased periods of vacancy (due to higher turnover of residents). Wear and tear on the properties also increases as residents take less care of the dwellings. Figure 2.2 illustrates this negative lettings spiral and its relationship with population turnover, increased instability and higher levels of criminality and antisocial behaviour. Critical here is the falling proportion of those both in employment and in better-paid employment, which further reduces neighbourhood linkages into local labour markets.

Figure 2.2: The residential lettings spiral

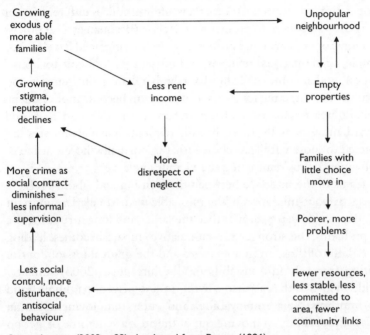

Source: Lupton (2003, p 89), developed from Power (1996)

Of decisive importance to these processes of decline are perceptions by potential residents concerning the trajectory of a particular neighbourhood. Within private sector housing, the long-term nature of housing investment means that householders are highly sensitive to image and expectations about future neighbourhood conditions (for example, schools, property prices and crime) when choosing neighbourhoods (Ellen, 2000). Thus, once negative perceptions of a neighbourhood are in place these become self-reinforcing and difficult to reverse. Models of this kind emphasise the importance of private sector investment into housing either for owner-occupiers or for rent. Loss of investor confidence, which can occur for a variety of real and perceived reasons, leads to reduced maintenance and investment as profits and land values fall. Conversely, in certain deprived neighbourhoods, low property prices can provide a basis for profitable investment and a gentrification process where there exists a combination of a particular type of housing stock and rising expectations for the future of a neighbourhood (Lees et al, 2007).

The operation of sorting mechanisms in public housing allocation is also crucially important given that many deprived areas in the UK are characterised by a high proportion of local authority or social housing stock. The presence of public housing significantly influences the operation of private sector markets and introduces different sets of factors that contribute to processes of decline (Brennan et al, 2000). As concentrations of particular groups most in housing need develop (for example, single parents, refugees, asylum seekers, 'difficult-to-house' families), and incomes fall due to a high reliance on benefits and difficulties in competing for jobs, social problems become more evident. A falling area reputation and population loss leads to an increased outward movement by those in employment, while in-movers are restricted to those with least choice (that is, normally those outside of employment), thus reinforcing the vicious circle.

In terms of the interface between the housing and labour markets, the selective out-migration of the most able is a particularly important issue. Power (2000, p 8) argues that 'the larger and longer running the area problems, the stronger the cumulative impact becomes, leading to the flight of those most able to go and the gradual loss of control resulting from chronic instability'. Cheshire et al (2003) similarly provide evidence that a person living in a deprived neighbourhood who improves their employability and enters employment has an increased probability of moving out of the area; a syndrome of 'get on and get out'. Yet while there is evidence of this process, its nature and impacts are by no means uniform across all areas (for example, Cole et al, 2007; Green and White, 2007). As Maclennan (2000) emphasises, the types of residents who move out of deprived areas and the reasons why they move can vary significantly between neighbourhoods. Hence, care needs to be taken in identifying the causal and reinforcing mechanisms operating in different places and to avoid imposing a 'top-down hypothesis about change on individual neighbourhoods' (Maclennan, 2000, p 17).

Analysis of the interaction between economic processes and the operation of the housing market also emphasises the broader relationships between income inequality, urban segregation and social exclusion. As Cheshire et al (2003, p 101) argue, given

> [T]he existence of locationally fixed amenities in urban
> housing markets (including the socio-economic composition
> of the neighbourhood itself), and the fact that such attributes

of a house are both normal goods and inelastic in supply, as
the distribution of incomes becomes more unequal, social
segregation will tend to become more intense.

Access to locationally fixed amenities (schools, parks and so on), which
are often purely positional goods, appears therefore to depend on a
household's position within the distribution of income within the urban
area, rather than absolute income. Income distribution is therefore an
important driver of residential segregation and social exclusion, a factor
of considerable importance given current UK trends towards increased
levels of income inequality.

Private sector services and investment

Cycles of decline are also evident in the withdrawal of private sector
services from deprived neighbourhoods. Speak and Graham (2000)
identify a negative cycle whereby the nature of the local environment,
low levels of demand and active discrimination become mutually
reinforcing, leading to the further reduction of private sector activity
and investment. Furthermore, low levels of private sector services make
a neighbourhood less attractive to live in, thus further destabilising
communities.

The relative unattractiveness of the local environment, in terms of its
physical characteristics (quality and design of buildings), the degradation
of the environment (in terms of litter, graffiti and vandalism) and the
additional problems and costs that arise from operating in an area
with higher levels of criminal activity contribute to declining levels
of business activity. For retail activity in particular, the appearance and
nature of the local environment is a critical factor that often plays a
key role in its withdrawal from disadvantaged neighbourhoods (Carley
et al, 2001). Derelict precincts and boarded-up shops dispirit the local
community, stigmatise the area and become the focus for antisocial
behaviour. Crime, and the threat of crime, are especially damaging here
in terms of the threat to personal safety discouraging local shop use,
increased costs through crime prevention and dealing with criminal
activity, as well as a high level of security measures creating an unsightly
and off-putting environment (SEU, 1999).

Low and declining levels of demand lead to a fall in the level of
service provision and reduced levels of competition, often resulting in
poorer-quality, higher-cost services. Speak and Graham (2000), in their
study of the withdrawal of private sector services from disadvantaged
neighbourhoods, across four key private sector services – retail

shopping, energy, financial services and telecommunications – in two deprived neighbourhoods located in Liverpool and Newcastle, found that impacts included a lack of competition in terms of price, as well as poorer service availability and quality. For retailing, falling and low demand and the lack of local competition, leading to overpricing and poor goods and service provision, were identified as two of the key reasons in undermining the viability of small independent stores operating in deprived neighbourhoods (SEU, 1999). Studies in Glasgow (Cummins and Macintyre, 2002) and Northern Ireland (Strugnell et al, 2003) demonstrate important spatial differences related to food price and availability within urban areas, with those on lower incomes and without cars needing to shop locally and hence suffering from restricted access to food items in terms of range, quality and price.

Active discrimination against deprived neighbourhoods by the private sector reflects an avoidance of actual and perceived risk of operating within stigmatised neighbourhoods. This takes the form of 'redlining' or 'postcode discrimination' whereby service providers actively exclude the provision of certain services on the basis of geographical location. Such exclusion is evident across a range of activities and sectors, but has traditionally been most evident and damaging with regard to financial products (such as mortgages and insurance), where redlining directly reinforces neighbourhood problems for business and residents. For example, Lupton (2003) reported evidence that residents of deprived neighbourhoods were unable to get credit to buy household goods or purchase items from catalogues on the basis of their postcode, and Speak and Graham (2000) identified a virtual redlining in their study areas in relation to commercial household insurance. However, evidence on the extent and nature of such activity is difficult to obtain given that commercial companies are unwilling to admit to acting in a manner that overtly discriminates against poor areas.

These processes of decline in private sector service provision in deprived neighbourhoods are rooted within wider processes of sectoral change and their related geographies. Carley et al (2001), in their study of retailing in deprived neighbourhoods, stress that problems of retail decline extend beyond deprived areas to many local and district centres as a result of retail and transport trends. For example, the worsening of access to food retail provision in certain poor neighbourhoods in the UK is related to the era of intense food superstore development on edge-of-town sites in the late 1980s and early 1990s (Wrigley, 2002). Such developments led to the closure of many smaller food retailers as well as a shift to lower-quality and more restricted provision for those that survived. This led to the identification of 'food deserts' in more deprived areas and rising concern over the impact of this on the diet and health of residents in these areas (Wrigley et al, 2003). Similarly, the withdrawal of financial services institutions, notably the closure of bank branches, has been part of a wider restructuring of this sector. Again this has had a disproportionately negative impact on deprived areas, as a result of banks and financial institutions preferring to target more affluent groups and areas and the more restricted mobility of those living in disadvantaged neighbourhoods, and has contributed to increased levels of financial exclusion (Leyshon and Thrift, 1995; Speak and Graham, 2000; Sinclair, 2001).

The withdrawal of private sector services from deprived areas has created business opportunities that have attracted some businesses to move back into these areas. The existence of 'unmet local demand' or 'underserved markets' in low-income inner-city areas has been most apparent in the US, and interest in the possibilities of using such markets as a basis for stimulating corporate private capital to reinvest in such areas has been advanced by the work of Porter (1995, 1997). Private investment into deprived areas has focused primarily on the retail sector, particularly grocery chains, but also chemists, clothing retailers and leisure services, and in some cases, banks. Such investments have involved local or regional retail chains as well as high-profile global corporations, such as GAP and Starbucks, which have sought to harness the substantial purchasing power of dense and heavily populated urban areas, despite low average incomes. This strategy often involves catering for the distinct needs of inner-city consumers with products reflecting the particular ethnic mix of a neighbourhood (see Chapter Four for further discussion).

Public sector services and investment

The provision of public services within poor neighbourhoods also displays negative cycles. In disadvantaged areas a higher proportion of residents need to utilise public sector services, while in many cases these residents have complex and multiple problems. This places considerable pressure on the capacities of public services to meet these needs, a pressure further exacerbated by the difficult operating environment within such areas resulting from a low-quality physical environment, fears over personal safety and low levels of trust and differing values (Lupton, 2003). This situation can create operational problems, particularly related to the difficulties of recruiting and retaining good staff while operating under additional budgetary constraints (see Figure 2.3).

Figure 2.3: Pressures on public services in deprived areas

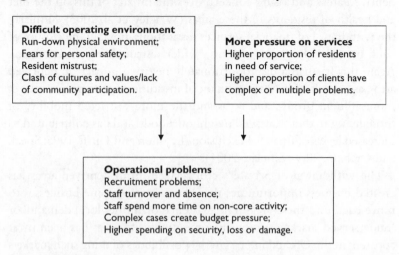

Source: Lupton (2003, p 106)

A range of studies provides evidence for the poor quality and overstretched nature of public sector services in deprived areas (Duffy, 2000). Dean and Hastings (2000), in their study of the regeneration of housing estates, observe that the speed and frequency of public sector services are worse in many deprived neighbourhoods, particularly with regard to repair and maintenance services and regeneration works such as landscaping, refuse collection and street cleansing. Mumford and Power (2003) also stress the problems of public sector services in many key areas including the quality of the environment, particularly with regard to rubbish collection and street cleaning, as well as transport, training and childcare services.

For the economic development process, the problem of maintaining a decent quality of public service provision within deprived areas has a number of important implications. First, lower-quality public service provision and its inability to meet considerable local needs contribute to the stigmatisation of deprived neighbourhoods and their run-down physical appearance. This reduces their attractiveness as residential and business locations. Second, the quality of public service provision has a direct bearing on the ability of residents to gain and retain employment whether this is with respect to educational and health provision, or in terms of the availability and quality of transport and childcare services. Third, the effectiveness of services directly related to employment and economic development (for example, employment services, skills development, careers advice, small business support services and so on) suffer similar pressures, which can reduce their effectiveness. Finally, the difficulties of the operating environment and the quality of staff resources can mean that deprived areas struggle to compete for the public sector resources available to support local economic development and to spend such funds effectively.

Conclusions

The analysis of the economic dimension of disadvantaged neighbourhoods presented in this chapter demonstrates the multiple and reinforcing nature of different dimensions of deprivation. Viewed in this way, any policy response needs to adopt a holistic approach that tackles these problems in an integrated and coordinated manner. Indeed this was the starting point for the New Labour neighbourhood agenda through policies such as the NDC and neighbourhood renewal. However, the relative lack of success of these policies, particularly in relation to promoting effective economic development in disadvantaged neighbourhoods, illustrates a number of the challenges that confront such a policy agenda. These relate not only to the need for a better understanding of how wider socioeconomic processes interrelate with different spatial contexts, but also how best to coordinate interventions within and across spatial scales based on clearly defined objectives and an understanding of the possibilities and constraints for action.

In seeking to better understand how and why localised concentrations of deprivation occur and their differing constitution and dynamics within different places, the evidence presented in this chapter demonstrates the complexity of interaction and the limited understanding of how processes are realised in and through given spatial contexts. The highly complex nature of such contextually embedded interactions creates problems in identifying causal relationships and illustrates the importance of place uniqueness in relation to wider processes of change. The resulting danger is that 'holistic' approaches, in their focus on describing complex interactions, can fail to specify key relationships and drivers of change, leading to a lack of clarity in objectives and implementation. This is well exemplified by the pursuit of much-vaunted 'win-win' solutions in recent regeneration activity that simultaneously seek to meet multiple economic, social and environmental objectives. In practice, such approaches often only serve to obfuscate the development of clear rationales for intervention through failing to address the existence of multiple and conflicting interests and agendas.

In seeking to address economic development issues in relation to deprived neighbourhoods, policy intervention needs to be rooted in an understanding of the different elements of human, physical, financial and social capital within these areas and their wider local economies, and the interrelationship between them. In practice, policy interventions tend to focus only on limited elements of this mix. For example, under urban policy initiatives in the 1980s a narrow focus on the development of certain aspects of physical and financial capital related to property development abjectly failed to address issues related to human and social capital and ensured that local residents saw little benefit from regeneration activity. Conversely, certain aspects of the recent neighbourhood renewal agenda have at times sought to develop elements of social capital at the neighbourhood level without concomitant attention to the development of other forms of capital necessary to realise its benefits. More critically still, the narrow focus on the supply side of human capital development that has predominated over recent years has often failed to understand how labour markets operate and the need to address multiple supply-side issues alongside demand-side and institutional considerations within wider local and urban economic development strategies. These particular issues related to labour market policy are discussed in greater detail in the next chapter.

Beyond the dynamic of economic development per se, many of the relationships between economic processes and other key elements producing and retaining neighbourhood disadvantage remain poorly understood. A central issue here is the crucial interface between housing markets – the single most important factor in producing concentrated deprivation – and labour markets. Within any given deprived area there is often limited understanding as to which sections of the population are moving in and out, on what scale and why, and how this relates to housing and labour market conditions (Cole et al, 2007). While it is possible to recognise generalised processes related to population turnover, such as 'get on and get out', without clear understanding of local processes and conditions it is possible to confuse problems and solutions (Maclennan, 2000). If those in employment are moving out, the reasons for this (for example to attain a bigger house, a change of tenure, better schools, to escape criminality and a poor environment and so on) need to be understood and addressed accordingly. Yet, if those leaving an area are predominantly workless households, this suggests the importance of employment-led responses (Maclennan, 2000). Furthermore, a focus only on developing the skills of individuals within deprived areas is clearly problematic if it promotes selective outward mobility in the absence of complementary housing policies and interventions that build up local communal resources, networks and social capital rooted in the area (Hibbitt et al, 2001; Conscise, 2003). The complexity of these relationships in any given locality indicates the need for clear analysis of local conditions and the importance of developing locally sensitive policies rather than top-down solutions based on generalised assumptions concerning the nature of local change. In the absence of this it is quite possible that inappropriate and uncoordinated housing or employment interventions might exacerbate problems of deprived neighbourhoods rather than solve them.

A focus on the dynamic processes creating spatially concentrated deprivation and the direction and speed of such processes shifts attention away from the status of the area per se and helps identify interventions that can arrest, reverse or indeed stop neighbourhoods entering spirals of decline in the first place (Skifter-Anderson, 2003). Similarly, a better understanding of occasions where deprived neighbourhoods have revived and in what form (for example through gentrification processes) can also provide valuable insights into the inclusionary and exclusionary nature of processes of change at the neighbourhood level.

This approach also requires a better understanding of how processes operate in and through space across different scales. The analysis presented here and the evidence from different studies that describe the interlocking cycles of decline operating within deprived neighbourhoods draw attention to the operation of wider national and regional economic processes and the need for policy responses at that level. Broader macroeconomic conditions and processes of sectoral change and rising inequality are central to understanding problems of social and spatial deprivation. As Townsend (1979) famously argued 30 years ago, area-based policies in themselves cannot solve the problems of poor areas because the pattern of inequality within them is set nationally. Cheshire et al (2003) similarly highlight the importance of income inequality in driving processes of urban segregation and emphasise that policy should focus on wider processes influencing income inequality (for example distribution of earnings, shifts in demand, incidence of unemployment and labour market exclusion), which can be most readily influenced by national level policy. While they recognise that spatial segregation itself does influence the process through the operation of area effects, they argue that these are of relatively minor importance and more difficult to influence via policy.

Yet it is also clear that changes in macroeconomic conditions often leave the problems of deprived areas largely untouched. Processes such as economic restructuring, labour market change and income inequality affect all neighbourhoods, but it is the intensity of impacts and their mutual interaction with the specificities of particular places that creates spatially concentrated decline, as the preceding analysis has demonstrated. As a result, there is broad recognition that the problems of concentrated deprivation cannot be effectively tackled only by macro-level policies due to the inability of such policies to adapt to and address local differences and because of the operation of various area effects (Kleinman, 1998; Lupton, 2003). As Bright (2003, p 4) argues, 'since each neighbourhood is different, no single substantive combination of programs will work in all neighbourhoods. The substantive aspects of revitalisation must be tailored to each area.' To date, there is little evidence that mainstream national economic and social policies are capable of this degree of place-based sensitivity.

With regard to area effects, the choice is not between a situation where, on the one hand, there are no neighbourhood effects – that is, compositional effects and sorting mechanisms are responsible for all neighbourhood differences – or on the other, strong neighbourhood effects determine lifecourses within deprived areas via the production of segregated cultures. Rather, what must be recognised are the incremental effects of the neighbourhood context – different within different neighbourhoods – on individuals and families in a manner that shapes, but does not determine, their subjective opportunity structures and lifecourses. As Buck (2001, p 2275) argues, area effects have a persistent and accumulating effect on various types of capital, which 'will have additional positive or negative effects on life chances throughout the life-course'. Speak and Graham (2000) illustrate this in their study of private sector services in deprived neighbourhoods, arguing that although limited access to services such as telephones, banks and insurance was not decisive in decisions as to whether to enter formal employment, it was an issue in deciding whether employment was beneficial. Exclusion from such services does not occur in isolation but compounds other factors of disadvantage in the everyday lives of those living in poorer neighbourhoods, shaping what Shuttleworth et al (2003) term an individual's 'subjective opportunity structures'.

This analysis indicates that policy needs to focus on tackling problems within deprived areas in an integrated and simultaneous manner, through the complementary development of mainstream programmes and bottom-up neighbourhood policies. While there is a central role for national-level policies, whether in promoting increased social equality, better pay and working conditions for low-grade employment or improved access to education and training provision, there is also a need for other interventions at different spatial scales. This issue of intervention at different scales and the challenges of coordinating policy across and within spatial levels while also integrating diverse economic, social and political agendas is examined in further detail in Chapter Five. Prior to this, the next two chapters analyse in greater detail two key arenas for policy action related to the economic development of deprived neighbourhood – work and enterprise – to detail changing rationales for intervention, the nature of policy development and the effectiveness of policy actions.

THREE

Work and worklessness

Introduction

A defining characteristic of deprived neighbourhoods is the relatively high levels of unemployment and worklessness experienced by their resident populations. This has fundamental implications as involuntary exclusion from the labour market is the principal cause of social exclusion in a society where paid work is the main source of income, social status and identity, and social interaction outside the family (Gordon and Turok, 2005, p 254). It follows therefore that the regeneration and renewal of deprived neighbourhoods is closely linked to increasing the proportion of the working-age population who are in work and, in so doing, overcoming the various barriers that stand in the way of them entering the labour market. It has certainly been the view of successive New Labour governments that getting more people living in deprived neighbourhoods into work is one of the best ways of overcoming multiple deprivation, with labour market inclusion being one of the principal ways of achieving social inclusion (McQuaid and Lindsay, 2005, p 204). To quote from New Labour's manifesto at the time of the 2001 General Election, 'work is the best anti-poverty, anti-crime and pro-family policy yet invented' ('Ambitions for Britain', Labour Party Manifesto 2001, p 24).

Despite the government's claim that there are now record numbers of people within the UK in employment, exclusion from the labour market remains a major problem within society, albeit perhaps less obvious than in the early 1980s when the unemployment rate exceeded three million people. One of the striking trends of the last decade has been the increase in the numbers of people of working age who are classified as being economically inactive and not *actively* seeking employment at a time when the numbers of registered unemployed have been falling. Thus, whereas there were half a million fewer people of working age in the UK who were unemployed in 2005 than in 1997 (down from 1.9 million to 1.4 million), the number who were economically inactive increased by more than a quarter of a million (from 7.6 million to 7.9 million), indicating a move of unemployed people into other statuses, such as sickness, Incapacity Benefit (IB), and early retirement (Webster, 2000). In Glasgow, Liverpool and Manchester almost one in five of the working-age population in 2003 claimed sickness and disability benefits, which is between three and four times their rates of registered unemployment (Gordon and Turok, 2005, p 255). Beatty and Fothergill (2002, 2003) have drawn attention to the growth of 'hidden unemployment', resulting in much higher levels of unemployment than the official figures indicate; for example, in Mansfield they calculated that the official rate of 4.5% in 2002 rose dramatically to 15.7% when working-age people in other statuses were included.

Another distinctive trend has been for those people who are excluded from the labour market to become more geographically concentrated at the neighbourhood scale and particularly in the most deprived neighbourhoods. Thus, Green and Owen (1998) found that between 1981 and 1991 there had been an increasing polarisation of unemployment at the ward scale, with the largest increases being in those wards already experiencing the highest levels of unemployment. More recent evidence for England relating to 2001 shows that worklessness was 23 times higher in the most deprived areas than in the least deprived, with 30% of adults being out of work and on benefits in the most deprived 10th of Census output areas compared with just 1.3% in the least deprived 10th. Moreover, 60% of concentrations of worklessness were within the 10% most deprived wards and over three quarters within the 15% most deprived wards (SEU, 2004). While these localised concentrations of worklessness are to be found in all regions, there are marked differences between regions in the extent of worklessness. At one extreme, more than a quarter of streets in the North East are classified as concentrations of worklessness, compared with just 1 in 40 streets within the South East at the other extreme (SEU, 2004, p 19). The largest numbers of localised concentrations of worklessness are to be found in the biggest cities outside London: Birmingham, Liverpool and Manchester.

The need to address the problems associated with localised concentrations of unemployment and worklessness has become an increasingly prominent feature of employment and spatial policy in Britain. Within the context of national policies that are seeking to shift from welfare to workfare regimes (Haughton et al, 2000), policy responses have been characterised by an emphasis on employability programmes. The dominant preoccupation of these has been with supply-side measures (McQuaid and Lindsay, 2005) aimed at enhancing the ability of individuals to compete for and access available jobs through tackling the various barriers to work that they face. Yet the difficulties of mainstream national-level programmes to reach marginalised groups and areas have led to a number of area-based interventions that seek to target resources on localised concentrations of worklessness. Despite a wide range of government programmes and pilot projects since 1997 aimed at grappling with the problem, significant localised concentrations of worklessness remain in a diverse range of geographical contexts, as this chapter will demonstrate.

After presenting data relating to levels and trends in employment, unemployment and worklessness in the five case study areas, this chapter considers the various factors that help explain these localised concentrations of worklessness and the kinds of barriers that those who are not working face in entering the labour market. This leads on to a review of the various policies introduced by New Labour governments aimed at getting more people into work and increasing employment rates among those living in deprived neighbourhoods.

Employment and unemployment in the case study areas

The five case study areas serve to illustrate the various trends that have been occurring in the local labour markets of various types of deprived area in different regional contexts over the last decade. As shown in Table 3.1, four out of the five case study areas, including the two in former coalfield areas (Sunderland and Mansfield), have experienced a significant growth in employment in terms of the numbers of jobs located within the local authority districts (LADs) since 1997. In fact, in all four cases the growth in employment has been greater than the national average (10.3% over the 1997-2006 period), with Newham achieving the fastest growth (20.7%). This suggests that job growth, per se, is not the central issue affecting levels of worklessness in these four localities, whereas it does appear to be more of a problem within Oldham where there has been little overall change in the number of jobs within the local economy over the last 11 years (0.9% growth). Table 3.1 also shows that jobs filled by men have been increasing faster than those filled by women in three of the localities (Mansfield, Oldham, and Brighton and Hove), whereas the other two (Sunderland and Newham) are in line with the national trend of a bigger increase in jobs filled by women.

Despite the significant growth in the numbers of jobs within the case study areas, the proportion of the working-age population who are in employment has continued to fall well below the national average in four of the areas, the exception being Brighton and Hove

Table 3.1: Employment change in the case study areas, 1997–2006

Area	1997 Total	2006 Total	1997–2006 % change
Sunderland	103,558	118,730	14.7
Oldham	76,584	77,269	0.9
Mansfield	33,959	38,415	13.1
Newham	58,630	70,751	20.7
Brighton and Hove	102,243	115,642	13.1
England	20,640,103	22,766,568	10.3
Male			
Sunderland	52,925	59,132	11.7
Oldham	38,879	39,846	2.5
Mansfield	16,176	18,626	15.1
Newham	30,322	35,353	16.6
Brighton and Hove	46,898	54,588	16.4
England	10,472,183	11,487,326	9.7
Female			
Sunderland	50,618	59,598	17.7
Oldham	37,706	37,423	−0.8
Mansfield	17,775	19,779	11.3
Newham	28,308	35,398	25.0
Brighton and Hove	55,275	61,043	10.4
England	10,167,918	11,279,210	10.9
Full time			
Sunderland	74,237	80,581	8.5
Oldham	55,117	53,096	−3.7
Mansfield	22,486	24,565	9.2
Newham	43,644	48,719	11.6
Brighton and Hove	67,289	74,183	10.2
England	14,691,616	15,721,510	7.0
Part time			
Sunderland	29,306	38,148	30.2
Oldham	21,467	24,173	12.6
Mansfield	11,465	13,841	20.7
Newham	14,986	22,032	47.0
Brighton and Hove	34,885	41,448	18.8
England	5,948,486	7,045,026	18.4

Source: Office for National Statistics, Annual Business Inquiry

where the employment rate has been close to the national average over the 2000-07 period (see Table 3.2). It is striking that the average employment rate in Newham over this period is some 20 percentage points below the national average, in spite of the rapid job growth that this London borough has experienced. Similarly, the job growth experienced by both Sunderland and Mansfield appears to have led to only marginal improvements in their employment rates. The conclusion to be drawn from the failure of employment rates to improve significantly as a result of job growth is that many of the additional jobs generated in these local economies must have drawn in their workforces from elsewhere, particularly via workers commuting in from other areas or from in-migrants.

Table 3.2: Employment rates for those of working age in the case study areas, 2000–07 (%)

	2000/ 01	2001/ 02	2002/ 03	2003/ 04	2004/ 05	2005/ 06	2006/ 07	Average
Sunderland	65.8	65.9	67.0	66.0	68.5	69.7	68.3	67.3
Oldham	68.6	72.2	73.5	73.4	71.9	74.7	69.2	71.9
Mansfield	68.0	71.3	68.5	64.9	72.7	65.8	68.7	68.5
Newham	50.5	54.0	52.7	52.4	55.6	59.4	57.4	54.6
Brighton and Hove	71.3	75.1	76.8	78.1	75.9	74.3	73.1	74.9
England	75.2	75.1	75.0	75.0	74.8	74.4	74.3	74.8

Source: Department for Work and Pensions

Low employment rates are an indication of high levels of unemployment and other forms of worklessness within the working-age population. Table 3.3 shows the levels and rates of unemployment, using both the official claimant count data as well as the International Labour Organisation (ILO) measure of unemployment,[1] and also the numbers and rate of IB claimants. While the unemployment rate (measured by the claimant count) in all the study areas remained above the national average in 2006, in some areas, notably Sunderland and Mansfield, there has been a significant fall in the unemployment rate since 2001 when it was 4.3% in Sunderland and 3.3% in Mansfield (compared with 2.5% nationally). In fact, the numbers of unemployed people fell by 20.5% in Sunderland and 14.7% in Mansfield over the 2001-06 period (compared with an increase of 4.8% nationally). However, a rather different picture emerges from using the ILO measure instead, as the unemployment rate in Mansfield appears to have increased although the decline in unemployment in Sunderland is confirmed. Whichever measure is used, Newham again stands out as the study area with an unemployment rate that is well above the national average (more than double if the claimant count is used), with little sign of any convergence towards the national average rate taking place, despite the major expansion of employment within the borough and surrounding parts of London.

Table 3.3: Unemployment and Incapacity Benefit claimants in the case study areas, 2006

		Unemployment (claimant count)[1]	Long-term (12 months) unemployment (claimant count)[1]	Unemployment (ILO)[2]	IB claimants[3]
Sunderland	number	6,048	920	7,600	19,360
	rate	3.4	0.5	6.0	10.9
Oldham	number	4,224	390	4,200	12,530
	rate	3.2	0.3	4.1	9.5
Mansfield	number	1,693	175	5,500	6,200
	rate	2.8	0.3	12.5	10.1
Newham	number	8,712	1,525	9,000	12,450
	rate	5.4	0.9	8.8	7.6
Brighton and Hove	number	5,171	1,205	8,800	11,500
	rate	3.0	0.7	6.6	6.8
England	number	791,890	125,325	1,219,800	1,939,870
	rate	2.5	0.4	5.1	6.1

Sources: [1] DWP Claimant Count and Rates. Rates are percentages of working-age population (16–74) in June 2006.
[2] LFS (ILO) Unemployment Rates. Rates are percentages of working-age population (16–74), from LFS population estimates, in March 2006.
[3] DWP Benefit Claimant Rates. Rates are percentages of working-age population (16–74) in June 2006.

Turning to the data on those receiving IB, there are some notable differences between the five case study areas. While the number receiving IB far exceeds the number claiming unemployment benefit (that is, Jobseeker's Allowance; JSA) in all five case study areas, it is the three areas with a history of coalmining and heavy industry (that is, Mansfield, Oldham and Sunderland) that have the highest proportions of their working-age population drawing IB (around 1 in 10 compared with 1 in 16 nationally). However, Sunderland and Mansfield in particular both experienced a significant fall in the numbers on IB between 2001 and 2006 (14.0% and 10.9% respectively compared with a national fall of 7.1%), possibly indicating a movement into retirement rather than work. Although Newham's unemployment rate is one of the highest in the UK, its IB claimant rate is closer to the national average, although still high by London standards. Similarly, Brighton's

IB claimant rate is just above the national rate, although one of the highest in the South East region.

A summary measure of employment deprivation is provided by the composite employment index of the 2007 Index of Multiple Deprivation (IMD), comprising the number of unemployed claimants, IB and severe disablement claimants, and New Deal participants. Table 3.4 shows the rankings of the five case study areas in terms of their level of employment deprivation in 2007, together with the proportion of Super Output Areas (SOAs) within each LAD that fall within the 10% and 20% most deprived SOAs nationally. Despite its recent employment growth and above-average reduction in unemployment, Sunderland continues to be the most employment deprived of the study areas, being the 7th worst LAD nationally due primarily to its large numbers of IB and severe disablement claimants and New Deal participants. Over a third of Sunderland's SOAs were among the 10% most employment deprived nationally in 2007 and over half within the 20% most employment deprived. This contrasts with Brighton and Hove, where employment deprivation was concentrated in a smaller number of pockets, with just under a fifth of SOAs falling within the 20% most employment deprived nationally in 2007.

Table 3.4: Employment deprivation in the case study areas: 2007 IMD employment domain index

	LAD national ranking (lowest ranked SOA)	Proportion of SOAs in most deprived 10% nationally (%)	Proportion of SOAs in most deprived 20% nationally (%)
Sunderland	7 (14)	35.8	57.8
Oldham	49 (10)	27.3	41.3
Mansfield	105 (170)	20.0	53.8
Newham	26 (1,403)	5.7	28.5
Brighton and Hove	46 (65)	9.8	19.0

Note: Employment deprivation is defined in the IMD as involuntary exclusion from the world of work, and the employment domain index comprises unemployed claimants, iB and severe disablement claimants, and New Deal participants.

Source: Department for Communities and Local Government, Index of Multiple Deprivation (2007)

To summarise, therefore, this statistical comparison between the five case study areas points to some of the differences between them with regard to the underlying causes of high levels of worklessness and employment deprivation. The lack of job growth would appear to have been a significant contributor to high levels of worklessness in Oldham, but less so in the other four study areas, which have experienced above-average job growth over the last decade. The industrial legacy of coalmining and heavy industry still accounts for the large numbers of people on sickness and incapacity benefits in Sunderland and Mansfield. However, explanations for the localised concentrations of employment deprivation found in both Newham and Brighton and Hove, which are located in buoyant regional economies, are not so readily apparent from the statistics themselves, indicating that a greater depth of analysis is needed to identify the interplay of causal factors that apply to specific local circumstances.

Conceptualising local labour markets

In order to understand the various causal processes leading to concentrations of worklessness, this chapter follows the work of Sanderson (2006) in identifying three sets of factors that influence the opportunities available to individuals in the labour market and their ability to realise these opportunities (see Figure 3.1). This incorporates an 'institutional' perspective, which sees the local labour market as 'a *set of social institutions* embedded in local networks and systems of formal and informal conventions, routines, customs and practices, including those institutionalised practices that produce and reproduce patterns

Figure 3.1: Influences on levels of unemployment and worklessness

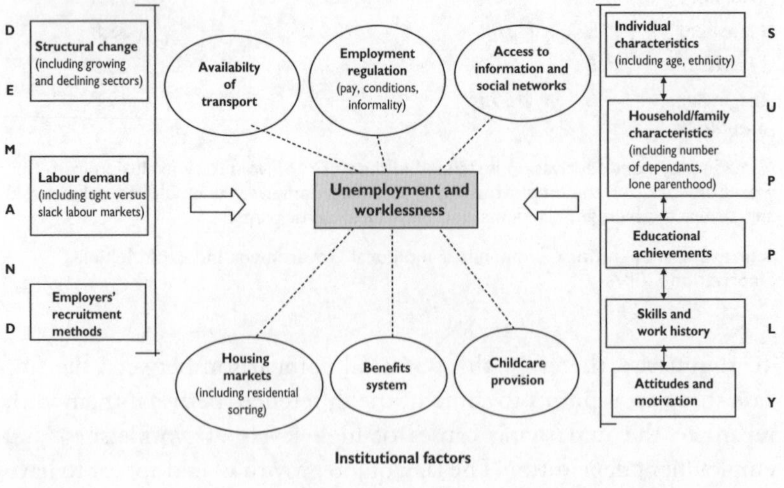

102

of discrimination and stratification' (Martin and Morrison, 2003, p 10; emphasis in original).

* *Demand-side factors*: these affect the quantity and quality of jobs in the local labour market, the nature and extent of segmentation of the job market, and hence the opportunities for disadvantaged groups. At the macro level they include the occupational and spatial pattern of employment growth and decline of different sectors as well as the cyclical influences on the strength of demand within a local labour market. At the micro level, they include the characteristics of employers, their attitudes and perceptions about different groups of workers, and their recruitment practices.
* *Supply-side factors*: various processes operate at the individual and household/family levels to structure the labour force, including access to education and training, educational achievement, skills, previous work history and parental responsibilities. At the community level, the nature of social contacts and networks condition 'peer influences' on attitudes and motivation towards work as well as access to information about job opportunities.
* *Institutional factors*: the interaction between the various supply-side and demand-side factors is mediated by various institutional forms principally generated by the state. Many of the most influential are the product of state policy responses to market failures within the labour market, relating to the need for regulation in relation to pay, conditions and irregular working as well as the provision of various employment services concerned with matching the unemployed to job vacancies and providing various kinds of training and advice. However, other important factors relate to other 'markets' that influence people's capability to function effectively in the labour market, such as the housing market, public transport, and the availability and cost of childcare. The local as well as the national institutional context can have an important influence on the scale and nature of worklessness and on the effectiveness of policies to tackle the problem.

It is the nature of the interaction between these three sets of factors that creates and reinforces inequalities in the labour market prospects of different groups, creating 'vicious cycles of deprivation' such that those individuals and households with poor resource endowments have fewer capabilities and opportunities to gain access to the kind of education, training and jobs that will enable them to escape the 'poverty trap' (Kitson et al, 2000). Intimately connected to the workings of the formal labour market is a range of informal economic activity, which includes informal paid work, illegal economic activity, mutual aid and self-provisioning. While the scale of such informal economic activity is limited by the lack of dynamism and wealth in the overall local economy, informal working plays a key role within low-income areas in terms of developing coping strategies, meeting basic needs and generating additional household income (Evans et al, 2006).

A spatial dimension is central to the way in which these factors operate and interact. Processes of mobility (that is, migration and commuting) between occupations and places act to reinforce socio-spatial inequalities in employment opportunities, which can result in the increased concentration of unemployment among unskilled groups and in the areas where they live (Gordon, 2003). By adopting a holistic perspective based on demand, supply and institutional factors, their relative importance and the nature of the interplay between them can be shown to vary between local labour markets. This enables the identification and differentiation of the processes that result in concentrations of worklessness in different geographical contexts.

Demand-side considerations

Jobs gap

At the heart of the policy debate about tackling high levels of worklessness in deprived neighbourhoods is the question of whether there is a shortfall in the quantity of jobs that are accessible to the working-age residents of deprived neighbourhoods. On the basis of analysing employment change data relating to the 1980s and 1990s, a number of writers have shown the existence of a jobs gap, particularly affecting industrial cities in northern England and Scotland (for example, Turok and Edge, 1999; Webster, 1999). It is argued that occupational and spatial changes in employment within the UK over recent decades have reduced access to employment for many living in deprived neighbourhoods, particularly in former coalfields and industrial cities, and that by themselves supply-side adjustments have been inadequate in solving the problems of unemployment and economic inactivity in these areas. Consequently, the geographical concentrations of unemployment and worklessness created or enlarged during the recessions of the early 1980s and early 1990s have largely persisted since then and relate to the structural weaknesses that are still found at the regional and subregional scales.

In criticising the government's New Deal for the Unemployed (NDU) for failing to take account of the structural causes of unemployment and demand deficiency in many local labour markets, Peck (1999, p 360) writes: 'unemployment is not five times higher in the Yorkshire coalfields than in the Surrey suburbs because of some local deficiency in the northern work ethic, it is a straightforward reflection of job availability'. Similarly Webster (2000) maintains that the basic problem is that the New Deal is attempting to place the largest number of people into jobs in exactly the places where jobs are scarcest. Because spatial labour market adjustments through migration and commuting have been too weak to prevent concentrations of unemployment and worklessness developing, Webster argues that more needs to be done on the demand side of the labour market to increase job growth near deprived communities: 'unless new jobs are located within about 3 miles of the target unemployment blackspots, their residents will not get any significant share of them. Leaving the local development entirely to the market is, therefore, not a realistic option' (Webster, 2000, p 126).

The government has consistently maintained that as a result of employment growth in the UK economy over the last decade – with a record 31.6 million jobs in 2007 – there is no shortage of job opportunities in most places. The evidence on job growth at the district level in the case study areas discussed earlier (see Table 3.1) would seem to support the view that while there may not be job growth within or close to deprived neighbourhoods themselves, there are often areas of significant job growth within commuting distance of them. However, various researchers have disputed this. For example, analysis of data from the 2001 Census showed that there were in fact very few instances of areas with low job growth being near to areas of high job growth and where these were found, the areas of job growth tended to be significantly smaller than the areas of job shortfalls (Coombes and Raybould, 2004). The implication is that in many areas, especially those previously dominated by mining, manufacturing and port activities, the only options available to those seeking work are long-distance commuting, which is likely to be too costly for those lacking skills and qualifications, or out-migration.

It would appear from the evidence therefore that there remains a significant demand-side deficiency in those areas where deindustrialisation resulted in the loss of thousands of jobs over recent decades and that this continues to be a major reason for the concentrations of worklessness in these areas. Yet, even in those areas where significant job growth has occurred, such as Brighton and Hove, pockets of high unemployment and economic inactivity remain that can be traced back to previous industrial closures (see Box 3.1). Nor can it be guaranteed that the new jobs will be taken by local people, as jobs 'leak out' as a result of migration and commuting, especially in very open and permeable labour markets such as that found in the London region. Thus, in Newham, which has experienced substantial employment growth over the last decade, its employment rate continues to be one of the lowest in the UK and its unemployment rate remains stubbornly high (see Tables 3.2 and 3.3).

Box 3.1 Economic restructuring and inactivity in East Brighton

The East Brighton case study shows that even within a buoyant local economy, there are still pockets of deprivation including high levels of economic inactivity that cannot be understood without considering the economic restructuring and the associated employment changes of the last three decades (Ambrose, 2003). During the 1950s and 1960s, East Brighton grew rapidly with the development of two large local manufacturing companies – Creed Teleprinters and Gross Cash Registers – and a great deal of low-cost housing, including local authority housing, was built to house the expanding workforce locally. However, in the mid-1970s both companies closed, resulting in the loss of around 7,000 jobs. Today, some wards within East Brighton are still ranked within the 5% most deprived in England and the residents of these neighbourhoods appear not to have benefited from the successes of the city's economy, particularly the growth of financial services and knowledge-based services. A labour-flow analysis carried out by Brighton and Hove City Council shows that the area has become a net exporter of low-paid and low-skilled labour such as retail sales and elementary service occupations. According to the East Brighton New Deal for Communities (NDC) Director, finding work for the large numbers of unemployed and economically inactive has been problematic because there is a 'locked-in culture' whereby people do not consider work outside of their locality.

Despite the strong demand for labour in London, the levels of unemployment and economic inactivity in boroughs such as Newham, which abut the major employment area of Central London, remain considerably above the London average. Much of the job growth there has been met at the top end by drawing on the national and international labour market, by commuters in the middle-skill range, and for low-skill jobs, increasingly by foreign workers (Kleinman, 1998). Increased competition from migrant workers, such as those from the European Union (EU) 'Accession 8' (A8) countries of Central and Eastern Europe, is now making it even more difficult for local people to compete for local jobs. For these reasons there is no guarantee that efforts to create jobs in areas close to high unemployment neighbourhoods will make it any easier for their residents to compete successfully for them unless they are in appropriate occupations (generally lower skilled) and ways are found of overcoming the multiple barriers that prevent those living in deprived neighbourhoods reconnecting with the London labour market.

Type and quality of jobs

Another strand to this debate focuses as much on the quality as on the quantity of the jobs that are available. The problem is seen as being a lack of suitable jobs that are attractive to those who are out of work in terms of pay, working conditions and future prospects, whereas many of the additional jobs, especially those in the low value-added services, are temporary and part time and perceived as being insecure and low paid. As Table 3.1 shows, the growth of part-time jobs has outpaced that of full-time jobs in all five case study areas. For example, in Sunderland part-time jobs increased by 30.2% over the 1997-2006 period compared with an 8.5% increase for full-time jobs. Similarly, in Newham more than half (58%) of the additional jobs were part time. This places the job growth that has taken place over the last decade in a rather different light since structural changes are resulting in a shift away from full-time jobs. Part-time jobs are unlikely to attract those seeking full-time work, on the one hand, and are unlikely to provide sufficient income to support those households where there is a single wage earner (for example lone-parent households), on the other.

Tackling worklessness is therefore going to be most difficult in those local labour markets where there are insufficient entry-level jobs of a quality and remuneration that makes work pay. To quote from an interviewed community worker in the Hendon NDC area of Sunderland: 'there is a difficulty in convincing young people that there is a realistic level of reward for the right kind of effort – not just financial reward but also around job security'. The 'new' jobs are either not the kind of jobs that those out of work want or have done previously, or are beyond their reach because they require high-level skills and qualifications (McQuaid and Lindsay, 2005). The disappearance of many semi-skilled and 'heavy' industrial jobs has resulted in an increasing polarisation between high-paid skilled service jobs and low-paid unskilled service employment that has adversely affected employment prospects especially for men in former industrial regions. And whereas those responsible for producing economic development strategies see the future in terms of the growth of the 'knowledge economy' and 'knowledge jobs', these are far removed from the expectations of people living in deprived communities who are seeking work. As a community worker in Sunderland observed,

> 'The "visions" to be found in strategy and policy documents are miles away from the realistic economic expectations of people living in the deprived neighbourhoods – they are not skilled, they don't have the mindset to effectively engage with a knowledge-driven economy unless there is significant capacity building, and that is not happening.'

In their study of the long-term unemployed in Scotland, McQuaid and Lindsay (2002) illustrate that the problem is not simply a matter of low demand, but rather a problem of jobseekers' perceptions of, and attitudes towards, the jobs that are available in the local labour market. It was found that many of the long-term unemployed had restricted job search strategies because they perceived that there were few jobs available in the local labour market. Research has also found that many older male jobseekers have continued to look for work in traditional sectors that are in decline and are reluctant to consider occupations in rapidly expanding areas of the service economy such as retailing, hospitality and teleservicing, not least because of the fear of becoming trapped in low-status, low-paid work (Lindsay and McQuaid, 2004). Moreover, the 'new jobs' invariably require very different skill sets to those held by the unemployed. Some evidence from the North East indicates that employers, especially those running small and medium-sized enterprises, are looking for a range of 'enterprising and flexible skills' (that is, being innovative, acting autonomously, taking risks, being proactive and competing intensively) whereas many of the unemployed who worked in the traditional industries have a more functional skill set related to job-specific competencies (Hartshorn and Sear, 2005).

The evidence indicates therefore that it is not a case of there being an insufficient number of jobs in many local labour markets, but rather an insufficient number of the kinds of jobs that those seeking work are prepared to accept, on the one hand, or have the skills for, on the other. Although in most local economies there has been at least a modest growth in the numbers of jobs in recent years, the jobs may not be sufficiently well paid or attractive in terms of hours, security and work practices to make movement off welfare benefits a rational choice (Beatty et al, 2007).

Employers' recruitment practices

As well as the issue of job creation in deprived neighbourhoods, the call for greater attention to be paid to demand-side considerations also relates to employers' recruitment practices and the question of whether the recruitment practices of employers disadvantage particular groups. There are various aspects to this issue. First, it has been suggested that there is a mismatch between the informal recruitment methods of employers, particularly smaller employers who tend to rely on 'word-of-mouth' methods, and the job search routes of residents, especially in deprived communities where the networks and contacts for obtaining information about job vacancies are poor (Hasluck, 1999). This implies that those seeking work may encounter particular difficulties in those local labour markets dominated by small and medium-sized enterprises. In addition, a reliance on word-of-mouth recruitment can also result in ethnic segregation between workplaces. This was a feature of workplaces in the Hathershaw NDC area in Oldham, where people from minority ethnic groups relied on word of mouth from family or extended family members for finding employment opportunities, which resulted in one large employer having a predominantly Bangladeshi workforce and another a largely Pakistani one. In addition, some employers or agencies operating in low-wage sectors of the economy actively recruit from vulnerable groups, particularly undocumented migrants but also women, lone parents and others, via informal networks or agents, in order for them to work irregularly and cut employer costs.

Second, employers tend to be averse to employing someone who has been out of work for a long time. Drawing on evidence from the Employers Skill Survey (2001) in Birmingham, East London, Lancashire and Solihull, Devins and Hogarth (2005) found that many aspects of the recruitment process made it difficult for the long-term unemployed to obtain employment: 'many employers would rather not take on a new recruit than take on someone who might disrupt the work-place ... generally, the more hurdles a prospective candidate has to clear, the more likely those susceptible to unemployment would be to fall by the wayside' (Devins and Hogarth, 2005, p 254). Employers look for people with relevant experience and who are in groups deemed to be 'low risk', thereby discriminating consciously or unconsciously against the unemployed and workless, being most averse to employing those with criminal records, language problems and mental health problems (Sanderson, 2006). Research undertaken as part of the evaluation of the government's Working Neighbourhoods Pilots (WNPs) found that the jobs remaining in deprived neighbourhoods were often with small employers who sought immediate employability in terms of generic and vocational skills, thereby disadvantaging those applicants suffering from disability, poor health and a history of worklessness (Dewson et al, 2007). Moreover, it has been found that employers prefer in-migrants from the A8 countries rather than British workers because the former are perceived as having a stronger work ethic (Green, 2007, p 357). The co-existence of high levels of unemployment with hard-to-fill vacancies in central Scotland led Adams et al (2002) to conclude that employer specification and recruitment practices may be as important as skill shortages themselves in leading to a mismatch between labour supply and labour demand.

Third, it has been suggested that some employers discriminate against jobseekers from deprived neighbourhoods, although the evidence to support this is fairly limited. Lawless (1995) found some evidence of implicit discrimination by employers against long-term unemployed residents of a deprived neighbourhood in Sheffield that had a poor reputation. Similarly, Speak (2000) presents evidence of postcode discrimination against lone parents from stigmatised areas in Newcastle. It would appear that those seeking work often think that they are disadvantaged by where they live; for example, in a study of the young unemployed in Newham, Roberts (1999) found that almost a third of the interviewed young people from the most deprived parts of the borough thought that employers were put off by the area in which they lived.

From the existing literature it is difficult to know the extent of various forms of racial discrimination within the labour market. Because there tend to be local concentrations of particular minority ethnic groups, often living in the most deprived neighbourhoods, it is likely that racial and area discrimination are closely associated with each other so that redlining certain areas is, in the minds of some employers, tantamount to shutting out certain groups of people. Indirect discrimination can also result from the reliance of many employers on informal recruitment methods as well as the relatively low numbers of senior positions held by black and minority ethnic people. The fact that people from certain ethnic groups do not obtain employment that is commensurate with their qualifications is often taken to indicate that there is discrimination in the labour market (for example DfEE, 1999). A major study of multiple disadvantage in employment concluded that there was a significant 'ethnic penalty' even after controlling for education, language and other personal characteristics (Berthoud, 2003). Similarly, a national study by Blackaby et al (2002) found that, even among the UK-born male population, the chances of employment in the mid-1990s were 10% lower for Indians, 12% for Black people and 24% for Pakistanis compared with White people and earnings were found to be respectively 8%, 5% and 13% lower. Given the ethnic and cultural diversity of London it might be thought that these groups fare better than elsewhere, although Buck et al (2002) concluded that this was not the case. In fact for the Bangladeshi community, they observed that the gap in both the employment rate and earnings differentials was significantly wider in London than elsewhere.

To summarise, the research evidence demonstrates that demand-side factors are contributing to the continued existence of localised concentrations of worklessness. In many local labour markets, and particularly those that are within regions that have suffered most from deindustrialisation, more jobs are needed within acceptable commuting distances of deprived neighbourhoods if more people are to gain access to the labour market. Moreover, these need to be jobs that are sufficiently attractive in terms of pay and conditions to entice people away from a dependence on welfare benefits. These findings are consistent with the perceptions of jobseekers themselves, judging by the results of a survey of 1,200 residents in areas covered by the WNP initiative (Dewson et al, 2007). When jobseekers were asked to identify the various barriers that they experienced, the two most frequently mentioned barriers were that there were no jobs available in the local area (43% of interviewees) and that the jobs available in the local area were poorly paid (also 43%). However, as the examples of localised concentrations of worklessness within areas of substantial employment growth show, the solution is not simply one of providing more 'quality' jobs locally because of the competition from commuters and migrants. Employers' recruitment practices have an important effect in reducing the chances of certain groups obtaining work and various supply-side factors also contribute to an understanding of the causes of high levels of worklessness. We now turn our attention to those characteristics and circumstances of workless individuals and households that constitute obstacles and barriers to the take-up of available job opportunities.

Supply-side considerations

There are a number of interrelated individual and household characteristics that contribute to the reproduction of local concentrations of unemployment and worklessness, sometimes referred to as 'compositional effects'. Figure 3.2, adapted from the work of Gordon (2003), identifies a number of these factors and draws attention to the fact that many of the causal links are two-way, such that local

Figure 3.2: Causal links in the reproduction of concentrated unemployment

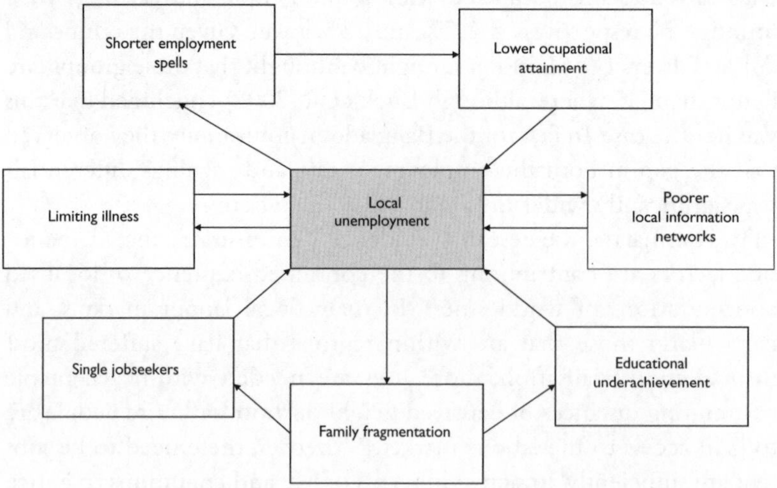

unemployment gives rise to particular social outcomes as well as vice versa.

Educational qualifications and work-related skills

Various studies have highlighted the effects of educational qualifications on employability and particularly the strong association between worklessness and the lack of qualifications. Thus, Berthoud (2003) found that those with no educational qualifications are almost five times as likely to be in a non-earning family as those with degrees, holding other factors constant. A number of studies have demonstrated that low educational attainment among young people becomes translated into poor social and economic opportunities in later life, resulting in a high risk of economic and social exclusion (for example, Bynner and Parsons, 1997; Gregg and Machin, 1997). Largely for this reason, the proportion of young people aged between 16 and 18 who are 'not in education, employment or training' (officially termed 'NEETs') – 11% in England and 13% in Scotland in 2005 – has now become a particular focus of government attention.

Not only is the lack of educational qualifications a barrier to employment but there is evidence to indicate that the experience of not being in work can stand in the way of attaining qualifications and thereby improving the chances of obtaining work. Labour Force Survey (LFS) data show that whereas between 1997 and 2005 the number of households where the reference person had no qualification fell by 44%, the reduction was only 13% in the case of workless households, indicating that people living in workless households have not been sharing in the skills improvement found in the population as a whole (National Audit Office, 2007). Invariably allied to the lack of educational qualifications is the lack of previous employment experience and basic skills such as literacy, numeracy and the kinds of social skills that are crucial to employers. From the perspective of a sample of employers in Newham, some young unemployed people are considered to be so lacking in basic skills and social skills that no amount of vocational training would help their employment prospects (Roberts, 1999).

The concentration of people lacking in qualifications in deprived neighbourhoods is illustrated by the case study areas (see Table 3.5). For example, in Oldham 37.7% of residents aged 16-74 had no qualification according to the 2001 Census, against 28.9% nationally and in four of the most deprived wards the proportion exceeded 50%. Similarly, in Newham 33.6% of the working-age population did not have a qualification in 2001, reaching 43.1% in one of the most deprived

Table 3.5: Highest level of (NVQ) qualification, for those aged 16–74, 2001

Area	Population 16–74	% according to highest NVQ level						
		No qualifi-cations	Level 1	Level 2	Level 3	Level 4/5	Un-known level	Total
Sunderland	206,228	36.9	18.2	18.6	6.8	12.0	7.5	100.0
Hendon NDC	6,177	45.0	15.4	14.8	7.2	11.0	6.6	100.0
Oldham	152,602	37.7	17.5	17.9	6.1	12.9	7.9	100.0
Hathershaw NDC	4,658	51.5	14.8	13.7	6.0	8.4	5.5	100.0
Mansfield	70,510	38.2	19.3	19.1	6.0	10.0	7.5	100.0
Northfield	4,746	45.8	18.5	17.1	5.3	6.5	6.8	100.0
West Titchfield	5,098	42.7	19.6	18.5	5.9	7.5	5.9	100.0
Newham	170,268	33.6	13.9	16.3	8.9	21.3	6.0	100.0
Beckton	4,912	41.4	13.0	15.2	6.9	16.9	6.6	100.0
Green Street	4,621	36.2	13.1	16.3	9.2	20.0	5.3	100.0
Brighton and Hove	185,131	22.1	13.5	17.8	12.5	28.7	5.4	100.0
Saunders Park	5,311	36.5	16.3	15.2	11.7	13.5	6.8	100.0
North Moulsecoomb	6,953	24.0	10.3	12.6	38.4	9.9	4.9	100.0
England	35,532,091	28.9	16.6	19.4	8.3	19.9	6.9	100.0

Source: Census, 2001

wards, compared with 23.7% in London as a whole. Given this evidence, therefore, it seems clear that tackling the problems of concentrated worklessness is closely tied to improvements in the educational attainment of those living in the most deprived neighbourhoods. The lack of English language skills is also a major barrier to accessing both education and employment in those communities comprising large numbers of immigrants, refugees and asylum seekers, as the Newham case study illustrates (see Box 3.2).

Box 3.2: Educational attainment and labour market participation in Newham

A large proportion of Newham residents are disadvantaged in the labour market by their lack of, or low level of, educational qualifications. There is also a negative relationship between education level and the probability of working in Newham, this being most pronounced for women, which becomes reflected in the higher wages of those working outside the borough. Evidence from the Newham Household Panel Survey (London Borough of Newham, 2003) shows that one in three individuals without English as a first language had no qualifications at all, compared with 19% of those with English as a first language. Key informant interviews referred to a high proportion of recent foreign migrants living in Newham and the lack of English language skills associated with them. Where migrants did hold qualifications from their home countries, a lack of recognition of these qualifications combined with limited language proficiency often meant that they were employed in jobs significantly below their skill levels. Respondents also pointed to a worsening mismatch between the demands and expectations of employers, who are increasingly looking for recruits with Level 3 qualifications and above, and the supply of workers available locally, most of whom, if they have had training, have not gained a qualification above Level 2. A consistent view from local interviewees was that the low level of educational attainment lay at the heart of the employment problems experienced by Newham and that much more action was needed in the areas of education and training.

Lone parenthood

There is a lot of research evidence showing a significant association between lone parenthood and non-employment as well as a tendency for single parents to live in the poorest neighbourhoods. Thus, McKay (2003) found a high concentration of lone parents in the most deprived wards, with 49% of all single parents living in the 20% most deprived wards compared with 26% of couples with children. McKay found that, in London, employment rates among lone parents were particularly low, heavily concentrated in deprived wards, and to be associated with being from a minority ethnic background, lacking qualifications and being social tenants. In the case of Newham, 2001 Census data showed that the average number of lone-parent households per 1,000 population was 172 (compared with 127 in Greater London and 105 in England), with more than a fifth of the population comprising lone-parent households in some of the most deprived wards in the former docklands part of the borough. These are among the wards with the highest unemployment and inactivity rates.

Some writers have linked the growth of lone parenthood in deprived areas to economic restructuring and increases in male unemployment. In former coalfield and industrial areas, it has been suggested that the increasing number of female-headed households, particularly lone parents, who are out of work and in many cases living on benefits is a long-term consequence of the collapse of the industrial base and male employment. Thus, Webster (2000) showed a high correlation (0.85) between male unemployment and the proportion of households with children that were headed by female lone parents. Moreover, Rowthorn and Webster (2006) estimated that around 30% of the 1,161,000 increase in lone parents over the 1971-2001 period could be attributed to marital and relationship breakdowns associated with the rise of male unemployment: 'it is not surprising that lone parents have a low rate of employment since they have to contend not only with their competing responsibilities as parents, but also with the fact that they are disproportionately concentrated in areas where it is difficult to get a job' (Webster, 2006, p 111).

The high degree of spatial concentration of lone parents in deprived neighbourhoods has also been seen as helping to explain the low level of educational achievement in these areas (Gordon, 1996). Gordon found that poor levels of educational achievement in deprived neighbourhoods were closely associated with high proportions of non-employed lone parents, much of the effect occurring through unauthorised absenteeism from school. This led Gordon to the conclusion that more attention needs to be given to 'family dynamics' (that is, family structure, attitudes and behaviours) as they operate within deprived urban communities in order to understand educational underachievement and how it contributes to the problems faced by such areas.

Health problems

Worklessness is closely bound up with physical and mental health problems, which may have been the reason for leaving employment in the first place (for example stress-related problems), or may have set in as a result of being out of work (for example depression). In the case of the NDC areas, for example, it has been shown that there is a close association between worklessness and health ($r = 0.506$, significant at the 1% level), with the proportion of the working-age population who are economically inactive decreasing as the health of the population improves (DCLG, 2008b).

More than half of people in workless households are long-term disability and IB claimants (2.7 million, of whom 1.1 million are women) and account for the largest groups of economically inactive working-age people in the UK (National Audit Office, 2007). Moreover, nearly 60% of people receiving IB have been receiving it for over five years. As might be expected, the proportion of the working-age population that is out of work for these reasons is highest in those areas associated with heavy industry in the past. Thus, in Sunderland, for example, at the time of the 2001 Census, 26.3% of those who were economically inactive were classified as permanently sick or disabled compared with 16% in England as a whole, and the proportion of the population claiming IB was almost double the national average.

It has been shown that a large proportion of those who are on incapacity and sickness benefits are interested in and are capable of working, their status having been changed at some stage by the social security system from being unemployed but wanting to work (Beatty et al, 2000). In fact, Beatty et al (2007) have estimated that around 40% of IB claimants could reasonably be expected to be in work in a genuinely fully employed economy. This is therefore an indication of how institutional factors such as the benefit system provide a context that structures and influences individual behaviour and decision making, as will be discussed further below.

Social contacts and networks

A further issue affecting access to jobs relates to the information that workless people have about the jobs that are available within commuting distance. Some studies (for example, Lawless, 1995; Atkinson and Kintrea, 2001) have found that the unemployed tend to have poor knowledge of job opportunities within the local labour market. This may be partly the result of there being inadequate information available at the local neighbourhood scale. Thus, in a study in Newcastle, Speak (2000) found that people were being disadvantaged by the trend towards concentrating employment services in city-centre locations, leaving people in some neighbourhoods without any direct link to up-to-date information about job vacancies.

Recent research has drawn attention to the importance of networks of families, friends and social contacts not only in obtaining information about jobs, but also in being successful in competing for them (for example, Meadows, 2001; Shuttleworth et al, 2003). This focuses the attention on the social relationships and resources (that is, social capital) found in deprived neighbourhoods, rather than on the characteristics of unemployed individuals themselves, and particularly on the ways in which employment prospects are affected by the mix of 'bonding' and 'bridging' social capital (see Chapter Two, p 51). The resources provided through social networks are particularly significant given the importance of informal recruitment processes. As Watt (2003) showed in his study of the work histories of local authority tenants in Camden, 'reputation' needs to be transmitted by word of mouth to employers so that being enmeshed in the appropriate social networks proves crucial in providing the routes by which information about jobs and workers' reputations can be circulated. In fact, Watt concluded that having the right reputation and social contacts are probably as important as the possession of training certificates.

The disadvantaged, therefore, are likely to be more dependent on family and friends as they have fewer ties to paid work and less access to job information. Yet, if members of their family and friends are also out of work, this is going to separate them further from the kind of information that they need and make it more difficult for them to obtain employment. Dickens (1999) suggested that this kind of 'network failure' is an important factor underlying the problems in deprived neighbourhoods, reinforcing other processes that create inequalities in labour market outcomes and thereby 'tipping' deprived neighbourhoods further into a vicious cycle of decline.

Institutional barriers

The housing market

As discussed in Chapter Two, the housing market and residential sorting mechanisms in particular, play a key role in segregating poorer and more disadvantaged groups, which then become translated into labour market outcomes. Housing status is the principal factor influencing where workless people live (Cheshire et al, 2003).Various studies have shown that people who live in social housing are more likely to be unemployed, becoming trapped into neighbourhoods where there appears to be little hope of economic improvement (Green, 1997, p 507).According to government figures, 54% of the 2.6 million people of working age living in social housing in the UK in 2007 were not working, rising to nearly three quarters in the case of those under the age of 25. Public housing allocation policies have tended to concentrate the most disadvantaged onto particular estates, which then perpetuates problems of acute localised deprivation in which non-participation in the labour market becomes the norm (Brennan et al, 2000, p 142). Moreover, the process of residualisation that has occurred within the social housing sector from the sale of better-quality council housing in more desirable neighbourhoods has accentuated the tendency for the most vulnerable people, a high proportion of whom are workless, to be concentrated in particular areas, leading to increased polarisation across cities (Gordon and Turok, 2005).

However, various authors consider that it is difficult to disentangle the direction of causal effects in the relationship between the housing and labour markets (Coulson and Fisher, 2002). Fieldhouse (1999) has suggested that housing tenure might be both an influence on the propensity to unemployment and a consequence of unemployment. Thus, people may find themselves allocated to particular housing estates because they are unemployed, but then their chances of obtaining employment become adversely affected by the various barriers that stem from where they live – such as constraints on their ability to access jobs, their ability to move to somewhere closer to employment, or employers' discrimination because of where they live. As Fieldhouse's analysis of minority ethnic unemployment in London based on 1991 Census data showed, there was a clear residential segregation of unemployed people, with the geographical pattern of minority ethnic unemployment being similar to that of white unemployment, demonstrating that 'unemployment is a problem of specific areas, regardless of ethnicity' (Fieldhouse, 1999, p 1592).

One of the effects of such concentrations is the creation of a way of life characterised by a loose attachment to the mainstream labour market. In his study of the work histories of local authority tenants in the London Borough of Camden, Watt (2003) found that joblessness, homelessness and entry into local authority housing often went together. His study provided examples of how local authority tenants were struggling to survive in an increasingly precarious metropolitan labour market, with a reliance on casual and temporary jobs, and with a process of 'bumping down' to lower-tier jobs following periods of unemployment or childrearing being common. However, the extent to which the concentration of workless people in the same neighbourhood encourages a 'culture of worklessness', that is, negative attitudes towards employment, low aspirations for work and study and narrow travel horizons, continues to be a matter for debate (see Chapter Two). On the one hand, the government's Housing Minister has recently suggested that living in social housing acts as a deterrent to people seeking work due to the peer group pressure of 'no one works around here' and has controversially suggested that agreeing to look for work should be part of the tenancy agreement for new social housing tenants (*The Guardian*, 5 February, 2008). On the other hand, two recent studies found no consistent evidence to indicate that people in deprived areas had different attitudes and aspirations relating to work than the rest of the population (SEU, 2004; Gore et al, 2007).

From the perspective of renewing neighbourhoods, one of the adverse effects of these concentrations of jobless people is the out-migration of those who do obtain employment, with jobseeking individuals wanting to 'get on and get out', only to be replaced by those in a weaker labour market position, leaving the overall level of unemployment and worklessness in the neighbourhood unchanged. For example, drawing on evidence from the British Household Panel Survey, 40% of people in paid employment were found to have moved away from inner East London over the 1991-99 period (see Buck et al, 2002, p 219). Similarly, research on several areas that received Single Regeneration Budget (SRB) funding estimated that half of the base population of an area is likely to change within a 10-year period (Rhodes et al, 2007). In the case of NDC areas, it also was found that those moving out tended to be less disadvantaged than the NDC population as a whole and in particular were more likely to be in employment than either those moving into or those staying in the area (CRESR, 2005, p 254).

This is clearly a problematic issue from the standpoint of area regeneration, as one of the effects of supply-side labour market initiatives is to improve the prospects of certain individuals successfully accessing employment while at the same time, albeit inadvertently, leading to the reproduction of deprived areas as others experiencing various forms of social exclusion move in. This situation is neatly summarised by a quote from an interviewed community worker in the Hendon area of Sunderland: 'we have been doing this work for 25 years and we have changed individuals but we ain't changed communities'.

Lack of affordable transport

Not surprisingly, the lack of private transport coupled with inadequate or costly public transport services prove to be significant constraints on the ability of those who are out of work to secure employment, given that much employment is unlikely to be within walking distance of deprived neighbourhoods. In fact, in the last few decades there has been a spatial reconfiguration of employment opportunities as employers have moved away from areas close to town and city centres to retail and business parks, which are invariably on the edge of urban areas. This has led to an increasing separation between residential and employment areas and made it more difficult for those without transport to access jobs. Levels of vehicle ownership are low in deprived neighbourhoods. For example, in the Hendon ward in Sunderland, at the time of the 2001 Census 46.6% of households did not have their own vehicle compared with 26.8% nationally, and similarly in Newham, more than half of households in some of the most deprived wards had no car. There is a wide range of evidence showing how the probability of obtaining work is increased for those with access to private transport. For example, a quarter of surveyed participants on the New Deal for Young People (NDYP) cited lack of their own transport as a barrier to obtaining employment (Bonjour et al, 2001), and research by Stafford et al (1999) on young people found that having a driving licence increased the likelihood of leaving unemployment by a factor of 1.98 for young men and 2.2 for young women.

The lower incidence of private transport among poorer households highlights the importance of having good, reliable and affordable public transport serving the more deprived neighbourhoods, yet several studies indicate that these areas often suffer from inadequate public transport (for example, DETR, 2000a; SEU, 2003). Women and young people are the most dependent on public transport for accessing employment and training, yet bus routes do not always link residential and employment areas and many new jobs in the service sector involve working in the evenings and at weekends when bus services are more limited. Many women also face particular problems because of combining journeys to work, school, childcare and shopping, made worse in areas where there are fears about safety as well. While there are examples where initiatives have been taken to provide solutions to transport problems at the individual level (for example the use of discretionary funding as part of the Action Teams for Jobs (ATJ) initiative to pay for travel cards, driving lessons or mopeds), action at a strategic level is seen as being crucial to addressing transport as an institutional barrier to improving the employment prospects of those living in deprived neighbourhoods (Sanderson, 2006).

Operation of the benefits system

The operation of the benefits system acts to condition the perceptions and attitudes of workless people towards available jobs, especially when these are predominately low-wage jobs that are perceived as being insecure. For example, research among poor households in South London found that the potential loss of Housing Benefit was a key factor influencing people's attitudes towards low-paid jobs (Smith, 2000) and the House of Commons Education and Employment Committee in their report on employability and jobs (House of Commons, 2000, para 53) concluded that 'for many, the financial risks of leaving benefits for work are a very real barrier to employment', such as concern over whether it would be possible to re-establish the same level of benefits if a job was not to last. This fear of loss of benefits combined with the inflexibility of the benefits system when people earn small sums of money can encourage those on low incomes into irregular working as a means of developing supplementary income (Katungi et al, 2006).

While it is sometimes alleged that the benefits system can engender a culture of dependence that discourages the unemployed, especially the long-term unemployed, from active job search, others argue that those who prefer to remain on benefits are making a rational choice when confronted with the poor quality of the jobs available to them, fearing 'in-work' poverty. There is a range of research evidence that supports this argument. Hogarth and Wilson's (2003) research with employers experiencing hard-to-fill vacancies found that many employers detected a reluctance of people to come off benefits for jobs that were perceived as offering low pay and a lack of security. Furthermore, the survey of 1,200 residents as part of the evaluation of the government's WNPs (Dewson et al, 2007) found that 25% of those who were looking for work had concerns about coming off benefits or switching to tax credits, with many saying that benefits offered some 'financial security', particularly for those eligible for more than one benefit. Some recent survey evidence of those on IB suggests that wages well above the National Minimum Wage need to be on offer in order to entice people off benefits (Beatty et al, 2007); this is likely to be particularly the case in London where high housing and childcare costs make it particularly difficult for the disadvantaged to find work that pays.

There have been a number of initiatives taken by the government to reduce the number of 'benefit traps' and to 'make work pay' (for example, the National Minimum Wage introduced in 1999 and the Child Tax Credit and Working Tax Credit reforms in 2003), but it would seem that they have not been sufficient to make entering the labour market sufficiently attractive for many people. It is interesting to note here a recent local initiative taken in Newham to try to overcome continuing fears about the loss of benefits and the fact that wages of entry-level employment do not always cover the loss of Housing Benefit. In 2007 the Mayor of Newham introduced a three-year pilot project to test whether providing Housing Benefit protection on entering employment would increase the likelihood of an unemployed or economically inactive person moving into sustainable employment. As part of a wider package of personalised support to unemployed and jobless residents, the intention was to provide extended Housing Benefit protection for up to a year to qualifying individuals. As the Mayor stated, 'we believe it is far better to provide a rent subsidy until people earn enough to pay their way, rather than settle for less than the best opportunity for all' (quoted in *The Guardian*, 6 February 2008, p 31).

Lack of affordable childcare

The lack of affordable childcare is a significant barrier to employment for parents with young children, and especially for lone parents. As the House of Commons Work and Pensions Committee concluded (House of Commons, 2002a, para 47): 'It is our belief ... that affordable and available childcare is crucial to raising employment levels and lifting individuals, particularly lone parents, out of poverty'. In their evaluation of the New Deal for Lone Parents (NDLP), Evans et al (2003) reported that more than half of lone parents on Income Support identified lack of suitable childcare in their area to be a barrier to work. A study by Woodland et al (2002) also found that 23% of all non-working mothers and 30% of lone parents gave the lack of free or cheap childcare as a reason for not working. Moreover, lone-parent families living in deprived neighbourhoods were the least likely to have used paid childcare. The main reason for this was that they could not afford it, despite the expanded provision given to deprived neighbourhoods in the government's National Childcare Strategy and the Sure Start programme (Kasparova et al, 2003). The low provision of childcare in deprived wards is also a factor – the level of childcare provision in the 20% most deprived wards in England being half the national average of 12 to 14 places per 1,000 children. Childcare providers have been found to face particular difficulties in achieving financial viability in deprived areas because of problems in obtaining access to capital to buy premises, in covering losses in the first year of operation due to the need to keep fees low, and in ensuring ongoing sustainability (Strategy Unit, 2002).

The extent to which the availability and affordability of childcare is a major barrier to work is likely to be greatest in those deprived areas where there is a high proportion of households with dependent children. At the time of the 2001 Census, Newham, for example, had 59.9% of family households with at least one dependent child compared with 47.9% in Greater London as a whole, and the proportion of households that had lone parents with dependent children was the highest in England and Wales (11.9% of households in 2001 compared with 7.6% in London).

Policy responses

The review of research evidence presented so far in this chapter has identified a wide range of factors relating to labour market conditions that structure labour demand, individual and household characteristics, and characteristics of the local institutional context, which together contribute to an understanding of unemployment and worklessness in deprived neighbourhoods. Clearly, it is not possible to derive an overall assessment of the relative importance of these factors since the interplay between them is invariably complex and will vary according to specific local circumstances, reflecting differences in regional economic contexts, employment histories and population compositions, as well as institutional contexts. Thus, the balance between demand- and supply-side factors will not be the same everywhere and the extent to which both formal and informal institutions and practices contribute to the problem will also vary.

It is against the background of this analysis that we now turn to discuss a number of government policy interventions that over the last decade have sought to tackle the problems of unemployment and worklessness, starting with national-level welfare-to-work programmes before considering various area-based interventions targeting localised concentrations of employment deprivation. All these policy responses are based on moving workless people into formal paid employment. Although non-formal work plays an important role in helping people living in deprived neighbourhoods to get by on low incomes (Williams, 2001; Evans et al, 2006; Katungi et al, 2006), within this policy discourse there is no consideration of work that takes place outside of the formal sector. Whereas paid informal work is viewed as something to be deterred (Grabiner, 2000), the role of mutual aid and self-provisioning is largely ignored.

The key features of the government programmes analysed are summarised in Table 3.6. This section also looks at some local initiatives that have been funded under broader regeneration programmes before briefly considering the latest developments in policy thinking as exhibited in the Department for Work and Pensions' (DWP's) City Strategy Pathfinders initiative.

Welfare to Work and the New Deal for the Unemployed

Over the last 10 years there have been a number of mainstream policy interventions aimed at reducing levels of unemployment and inactivity and helping individuals to overcome the various barriers to entering the labour market. As previously outlined, a defining feature of New Labour's approach to reducing social and economic exclusion has been to increase labour market participation among the working-age population, this being in line with the ideological shift towards a work-focused welfare state that started under previous Conservative governments (Evans, 2001a). Building on the thinking behind the JSA introduced in 1995 by the previous government, the first New Labour government introduced a range of measures concerned with linking the receipt of welfare benefits to undertaking training, actively looking for a job and taking on low-paid work. Sometimes referred to as a message of 'tough love', the aim was to reduce the number of people who were living off benefits and to incentivise those out of work to acquire skills and to seek employment. The approach has essentially been a supply-side one, focusing on changing the attitudes and behaviour of workless individuals and households, rather than one that has sought to influence the decisions and recruitment practices of employers.

The centrepiece of this approach has been the NDU, introduced in 1997, and comprising a family of schemes targeting different marginalised groups (that is, the young unemployed, the long-term unemployed aged 25 and over, those aged 50 and over, lone parents and disabled people). The New Deal focused on disadvantaged groups rather than deprived areas, therefore making links with deprived neighbourhoods only indirectly because of where a large proportion of the targeted groups lived. Although there is some justification in the government's claim that the New Deal has made a major contribution to falling unemployment over the last 10 years, evaluations of the various variants of the New Deal paint a more differentiated picture.

Table 3.6: Government programmes for tackling unemployment and worklessness

Programme	Period	Target groups	Key elements	Cost per job in 2005–06*	Availability in case study areas
New Deal for Young People	1998–	18–24 year olds unemployed for 6 months	• gateway period of intensive advice and guidance • options of (i) subsidised employment; (ii) full-time education and training; (iii) work placements	£2,620	available across the UK
New Deal 25 plus	1998–	Over-25s unemployed for 18 months	• weekly meetings with a personal advisor • basic skills screening • development of job search skills	£3,530	available across the UK
New Deal for Lone Parents	1998–	Lone parents	• support from a personal advisor • payment of training premium • help with cost of childcare while training/searching for work	£840	available across the UK
New Deal for Disabled People	2001–	Unemployed people with a disability	• support from a job broker to match skills and abilities to employer needs • advice on suitable vacancies locally	£2,370	available across the UK
Employment Zones	2000–	Long-term unemployed people who live in a zone	• introduced in 15 areas of high and persistent long-term unemployment • develop innovative ways of helping long-term unemployed to secure and keep work • assistance customised to needs of individuals in form of 'personal job accounts' • delivered by private sector providers	£4,770	Newham (merged with Tower Hamlets for 2nd round) Brighton and Hove

Table 3.6: Government programmes for tackling unemployment and worklessness (continued)

Programme	Period	Target groups	Key elements	Cost per job in 2005–06*	Availability in case study areas
Action Team for Jobs	2000–06	Long-term unemployed residents in disadvantaged groups	• set up in the 65 deprived local authority areas with lowest employment rates • each Action Team developed initiatives that reflected the needs of the area • use of community-based outreach methods to reach clients • provision of specialist advice and financial assistance with costs of finding work • from 2004 targeted people on IB or with significant barriers to work	unavailable	Brighton and Hove Newham Sunderland
Working Neighbourhood Pilots	2004–06	Unemployed and workless residents of pilot areas	• 12 pilot areas defined at the neighbourhood scale • aim to test new approach to offering intensive support in areas suffering from a 'culture of worklessness' • provision of range of support to help people find work, including offering work-focused contacts • provision of in-work support and incentives including retention payments	unavailable	None
Pathways to Work	2003–	Incapacity benefit claimants	• package of measures piloted in seven areas • ongoing support from personal advisor through series of work-focused interviews • work-focused rehabilitation support offered by JCP and NHS • financial incentives to return to work • programme to roll out nationally from April 2008	£2,970	Sunderland (as part of the South Tyne and Wear Valley Jobcentre Plus District)

Note: * Cost per job is the total cost of the programme, divided by the total number of job outcomes

Source: Adapted from NAO, 2007 (Table 1, p 7 and Appendix 3, pp 52–9).

Various evaluations of the NDYP found, perhaps unsurprisingly, that it was more likely to lead to successful job outcomes in the buoyant labour markets of southern Britain than in the slack ones found in the former industrial and coalfield areas of northern Britain (for example Martin et al, 2003). Research on the NDYP in Scotland showed that the New Deal was best able to help those facing more conventional labour market problems (that is, a lack of work experience and qualifications) but less able to help those with problems of a more personal or social nature (that is, problems of drug or alcohol abuse, a prison record or homelessness) (Bonjour et al, 2001). Similarly, a number of assessments showed that the NDYP has been relatively successful among those on the margins of entering the labour market but in need of help with the process of finding and securing employment, but less successful among those experiencing multiple barriers to entering the labour market and requiring a more holistic approach (for example House of Commons, 2002b). The evaluation of the New Deal 25 plus reached similar conclusions (Hasluck, 2002; Wilkinson, 2003). Other research showed that people from minority ethnic groups have been underrepresented on the employment option of the New Deal (Fieldhouse et al, 2002) while the evaluation of the NDLP (a voluntary programme) found that it had not been very effective in addressing the needs of minority ethnic (especially Pakistani, Bangladeshi and African-Caribbean) groups and those living in deprived urban areas (Evans et al, 2003).

Area-based programmes for tackling worklessness

It soon became clear that the NDU was not designed to deal with the problems associated with those furthest from entering the labour market, nor the tendency for persistent worklessness to be concentrated in small geographical areas. This resulted in the government introducing a series of policy initiatives targeted at those disadvantaged groups and areas that have the highest levels of worklessness and experience the most serious barriers to work. This move represented an extension of the welfare-to-work agenda beyond those who are unemployed but seeking work to embrace those economically inactive for various reasons, including sickness and incapacity, or the lack of a desire to enter the labour market.

There have been four main area-based programmes over the 10 years, the key features of which are shown in Table 3.6. As the table also shows, three of the case study areas (Brighton and Hove, Newham and Sunderland) were selected for the implementation of more than one of these programmes whereas the other two (Mansfield and Oldham) were not selected for any of them. Although there are a number of similarities between the four programmes, they do indicate something of a learning process about the difficulties of reaching those furthest from entering the labour market, the kind of difficulties they face and the nature of the support required, and also the best spatial scale at which to engage with them.

The first area-based initiative (ABI) was *Employment Zones*, introduced in selected local authority areas experiencing a high level of long-term unemployment (defined as more than 18 months out of work) among the over 25s, initially in five locations in 1998 and then extended two years later to a further 10. The aim was to encourage a more client-focused approach to overcoming barriers to work than that provided by Jobcentre Plus, with personal advisors providing assistance customised to the needs of the individual in the form of 'personal job accounts'. The idea was to make more flexible and innovative use of the resources available to overcome individual barriers to work and to tailor these to individual circumstances. A radical feature of Employment Zones when they were first introduced was the contracting out of the delivery of services to private providers rather than relying totally on the government's own Employment Service (that is, Jobcentre Plus).

Running in parallel with Employment Zones was the *Action Team for Jobs* (ATJ) initiative, which ran from 2000 until 2006 and led to the setting up of 65 Action Teams in local authority areas with low employment rates and high unemployment claimant counts. It shares many features with the Employment Zone initiative and in fact all 15 Employment Zone areas were included in the first-phase Action Team areas. The overall aim of the ATJ programme has been to increase employment rates among disadvantaged groups in deprived areas, using discretionary funding and partnership working between private and voluntary sector organisations and employers. The ATJ programme involved more outreach work than Employment Zones and the involvement of community and voluntary organisations was seen as crucial to building trust and credibility within deprived communities. Since 2004 there has been a particular focus on helping IB claimants and those facing significant barriers into work, the providers of ATJ services being required to ensure that 70% of those entering work would be from those who were not already receiving JSA.

A growing concern over the emergence of communities in which worklessness appeared to be the norm together with evidence showing the highly localised geography of worklessness (that is, a few streets or a housing block) resulted in the announcement of yet another government pilot initiative in 2002, the *WNP*. This aimed to test out a new approach to helping people access employment. Twelve pilot areas were chosen, each being at the neighbourhood or sub-ward scale with populations of between 4,000 and 5,000 people of whom between 35% and 50% of those of working age were considered 'workless'. Some of the pilots had previously been covered by Action Teams, while others had been part of Employment Zones. The underlying premise of the WNP, which ran for just two years from April 2004, was that existing policies were insufficient to deal with the problems in those deprived neighbourhoods where a 'culture of worklessness' appeared to be taking root.

A further incarnation of the area-based approach targeting workless people has been the *Pathways to Work* (PtW) programme, originally launched in seven Jobcentre Plus districts during 2003 and 2004 and then extended to a further 13 districts. Focusing specifically on IB claimants, PtW aims to move people into work through a combination of work-focused interviews, help from specialist advisors, comprehensive provision of support, and a return-to-work credit. Distinctive features of PtW include the involvement of the National Health Service (NHS) (via the Primary Care Trusts) to help participants manage their health in a working environment and also the payment of a return-to-work credit for up to six months to encourage people to stay in work.

A number of key lessons can be drawn from the research and evaluations that have been undertaken on these four area-based programmes for tackling worklessness. First, in terms of getting people into work, the research evidence shows the benefits of a more intensive, client-focused approach administered by personal advisors who are able to tailor flexible and innovative forms of provision to meet individuals' needs and circumstances. Evaluations of the Employment Zones have shown a positive effect with the client-centred approach leading to more Employment Zone participants than New Deal participants finding employment (34% compared with 24%) (Hales et al, 2003), although the numbers leaving unemployment have dropped off over time (Hasluck et al, 2003). The government's own evaluation of the WNP (Dewson et al, 2007) also concluded that it improved job entry rates of those who participated (up from an estimated 30% to 43%).

A key element in the ATJ initiative was the client-centred approach and the use of community-based outreach methods to reach clients, often based in the target communities. Through regular contact with their clients, advisors built up a good understanding of clients' situations and the barriers to work they faced and were able to provide a range of tailor-made services. These included job search and guidance, support to overcoming financial barriers to taking up work such as childcare costs, various types of training, some of which were certified, and help with travelling to work. The government's evaluation of the ATJ programme found that it had had most success in helping lone parents into work, with 36% of them obtaining employment, whereas only 22% of clients where English was their second language and 23% of those with drug and alcohol problems obtained employment through the scheme (Casebourne et al, 2006).

Second, as the experience of ATJ and other 'work first' initiatives indicates, the greatest success has been with those nearest to entering the labour market. Forty per cent of all the clients accessing the ATJ services in the first phase of the initiative secured work, and this was highest for those who had been claiming JSA (44%) and lowest for Income Support and IB claimants (32%) (Cox et al, 2002). Similarly, it was found that participants in the WNP who were on Income Support or IB were less likely to move into work (only a fifth of them) than those who had been receiving JSA (over two fifths), indicating not only that it was those furthest from the labour market who encountered the most barriers, but also that it proved most difficult for WNP advisors to engage with this group (Dewson et al, 2007).

Third, the better success rate among those who are closest to obtaining employment was compounded by the pressure on service providers to reach their targets, particularly in the earlier programmes. For example, Employment Zones have been described as a 'work first' policy as the financial rewards to the providers were tied to achieving 13-week job outcomes rather than training or other personal development outcomes. This output-related payment structure has been criticised for inevitably leading to a 'creaming off' of the most employable and 'job-ready' clients and a reluctance to spend time and resources on the more difficult clients (Bruttel, 2005). This led one commentator (Hirst et al, 2002, p vii) to conclude that: 'they [Employment Zones] do struggle to deal with the very hardest to help and are therefore not a panacea for the problems of long-term unemployed people'.

Fourth, a key issue has been the sustainability of the jobs that people have moved into. The 13-week job outcome used in the Employment Zone programme (based on the standard Jobcentre Plus outcome measure) is hardly an indication of sustainable employment. The evaluation of the ATJ also identified problems with job sustainability, reflecting in some cases a lack of job-readiness and in others a lack of post-employment support (Casebourne et al, 2006). In order to try to address this issue, the WNP included 'retention payments' to incentivise participants to stay in a job. Of those who started employment, just over half (55%) stayed in work for at least 13 weeks and qualified for their first retention payment, while over a third (37%) stayed in the job for 26 weeks or more and received the full back-to-work bonus of £1,250 (Dewson et al, 2007). However, nothing is known about the job retention of WNP participants beyond this six-month period.

Fifth, an important conclusion of the evaluation of the ATJ programme was the need for an understanding of 'the extremely localised geography of worklessness within a variety of different labour market contexts' (Casebourne et al, 2006, p 95). Although the WNP initiative was designed to address this and has undoubtedly improved the chances of particular individuals gaining employment, the extent to which it has brought about improvements at the neighbourhood level (that is, place-based improvements) is more questionable. Clearly, a much longer time period than just two years is necessary in order to make serious inroads into the high levels of worklessness in deprived neighbourhoods, not to mention bringing about the cultural changes that the WNPs were supposed to be addressing.

Sixth, the more recent programmes such as WNP and PtW have demonstrated the importance of working with a range of partner organisations in order to provide the comprehensive support that people with multiple barriers face if they are going to enter paid employment. This invariably involves new ways of working between organisations in order to provide the integrated support provision that is needed and overcoming the silo mentality that so often obstructs effective joint working. Also, a noticeable weakness in all of these programmes has been the difficulty of involving employers themselves more fully in the implementation of the programme rather than just informing service providers of their current job vacancies.

And finally, the shift towards developing a series of area-based programmes for tackling worklessness indicates some recognition that these are more effective than mainstream programmes in getting people into work. Interestingly, a review of various evaluations of government employment programmes comparing the effectiveness of person-targeted initiatives with place-targeted ones concluded that while both have a role to play in getting people into work, a straight comparison between person-based and place-based policies targeted at similar groups showed the latter to be noticeably better in terms of the outcomes achieved (Griggs et al, 2008). This provides some evidence to support place-targeted programmes, particularly in terms of their ability to provide the outreach and more intensive levels of support required by those people facing the most severe and multiple barriers to employment.

Local initiatives to address worklessness

All the interventions discussed so far have been part of New Labour's welfare-to-work programme and as such have a consistent rationale – a strong belief that the main obstacles to further improvements in employment participation rates are to be found on the supply side, and particularly in relation to the individual and household characteristics of those who are out of work. However, at the same time that these mainstream programmes have been pursued, there has been a diverse range of *local-level labour market initiatives*, which have been less constrained in their approach. Many of them have been funded through major regeneration programmes such as the SRB and NDC and others from European Social Fund (ESF) monies (see Box 3.3).

Box 3.3: Example of Sunderland's Job Linkage programme

Starting in 1996, Sunderland City Council in partnership with the Careers Service and the Learning and Skills Council (LSC) developed its own 'Jobs Linkage' service, which aimed to 'link local people to local jobs'. On the supply side, the aim was to provide a personalised counselling and job support service that is tailored to the needs of the individual client and divorced from the provision of welfare benefits that can constrain the mainstream programmes administered by Jobcentre Plus. As one Jobs Linkage advisor explained: 'we spend time with people and make them feel comfortable in order that we can help them find the training or jobs that are right for them'. On the demand side, Jobs Linkage aims to respond to the human resource needs of existing employers and inward investors by offering recruitment and training grants to offset the initial costs of employing local residents and developing customised training and employment support for local people. The services, which are free to employers, include recruitment advice, links to applicants who are committed to looking for work, specific training for applicants if it is linked to a guarantee to interview them for the vacant position, and an after-care service to try to ensure that the client remains in the job. Funding for the programme has come from a range of sources, including One NorthEast (the Regional Development Agency), the Neighbourhood Renewal Fund and the ESF. Jobs Linkage has also received funding from the NDC programme in the East End and Hendon part of the city, resulting in 221 local people from this deprived neighbourhood being helped into employment between April 2006 and March 2007.

Based on detailed research in six different SRB areas, the evaluation of the SRB commissioned by the government provides important evidence on the effectiveness of local actions to address worklessness at the neighbourhood level (Rhodes et al, 2007). It found that some 15% of total SRB expenditure in seven case study areas was allocated to training and employment schemes. The evaluation concluded that there had been significant outcomes from training and employment schemes, after allowing for deadweight and displacement effects, in terms of qualifications gained from training and residents accessing jobs through training or advice. However, a notable finding was significant 'leakage' of benefits from the local area, as 29% of the net jobs created and 23% of those accessed through training or advice were taken either by people who moved out of the area once they had obtained employment or by in-commuters (Rhodes et al, 2007, p 224).

This evaluation also found that the proportion of people unemployed or economically inactive in SRB areas declined at a faster rate than the national average, although much of the movement was into retirement rather than into work, the latter being mainly among younger age groups (Rhodes et al, 2002). Moreover, there continued to be a considerable gap in full-time employment levels between the seven SRB areas (36%) and England as a whole (54%) by 2001 (Rhodes et al, 2007, p 225). Other evidence of SRB-funded local schemes comes from a study by Sanderson et al (1999), which shows that although the seven schemes that were examined had some success in helping participants into work, they were less effective for more disadvantaged groups, particularly men with poorer skills and qualifications and those with less previous work experience. The study also highlighted the value of integrated and holistic packages of support to address the full range of clients' needs, underpinned by the need for outreach work and good partnership working with all relevant agencies who can provide the support needed.

The need to tackle unemployment and economic inactivity in turning around the poorest neighbourhoods has also been a critical element of the government's NDC, launched in 1998 as a 10-year £2 billion programme focused on 39 designated areas. The severity of the worklessness problem found in the NDC areas is indicated by the fact that in 2002 just 42% of those aged 16 and over were in paid work (18 percentage points lower than the national average) and 47% were economically inactive (11 percentage points higher than the national average) (CRESR, 2005). In 1999 there were an estimated 50,710 workless people (defined as being involuntarily excluded from the labour market and claiming out-of-work benefits) in NDC areas, representing 23% of the total working-age population. Almost £50 million, representing 11% of total NDC expenditure, was allocated to tackling worklessness over the four-year period from 2000/01 to 2003/04 (CRESR, 2005), resulting in a diverse range of labour market interventions with individual NDCs invariably working in partnership with other organisations, such as Jobcentre Plus, LSCs, local authorities and the voluntary sector. Projects typically had supply-side objectives such as increasing the employability of local residents, removing barriers to labour market participation especially for the most disadvantaged, and promoting skills development and the attainment of qualifications. However, job brokerage projects were often favoured as a way of involving local employers with a view to increasing their confidence in employing residents of NDC areas. Core elements of these projects normally involved personalised and customised advice, a pathway of training, job search and job matching, job interview preparation and support, and ongoing mentoring for those obtaining work (see Boxes 3.3 and 3.4).

Box 3.4: Example of NDC employment initiatives in Newham

The West Ham and Plaistow NDC programme started in 2000 with a budget of £54 million over 10 years. The area covers a population of 10,000 people, or 4,000 households, 51% of whom are White British, the rest being mainly Black African or Caribbean. The NDC is divided into five neighbourhoods, each of which tends to differ in terms of housing and population characteristics. The 'economy theme' of the NDC focuses on reducing unemployment and increasing the employability of the resident population. The emphasis of the local employment strategy has been on tackling person-related barriers such as language skills among the minority ethnic community that prevent them taking advantage of the employment opportunities in this part of East London. Many projects are training related, such as those concerned with childcare/childminding training, training for the construction sector and language training. One key project is 'Elite', a job brokerage project started in 2000 that targets the hardest to help, including those on IB. Although it was initially delivered by Reed Partnership, the Elite project is now run 'in house' by the NDC to ensure a close integration with other projects. Another initiative associated with the Elite project is the Construction Labour Initiative, which aims to encourage local construction companies to source local labour, including those companies undertaking the housing redevelopment projects within the NDC area itself. More generally, the NDC economic theme manager works alongside intermediary agencies such as

Jobcentre Plus on other sector projects (such as Excel in the Royal Docks and the Gallions Reach retail development in Beckton) to help make residents of the NDC area aware of these job opportunities.

Evidence from the national evaluation of the NDC programme, based on longitudinal analysis of the movement of individuals into and out of worklessness in NDC areas and a number of non-NDC deprived areas, found that unemployed people living in NDC areas were 1.1 times more likely to exit unemployment benefits than claimants in other areas and that sick and disabled people living in NDC areas were 1.6 times more likely to exit sickness/disability benefits than claimants from other areas. In fact, over the 2002-04 period, it is estimated that there was an 'NDC effect' of an additional 7,400 people of working age in NDC areas entering employment compared with comparator deprived areas. This suggests that job brokerage projects are contributing to increased transitions out of unemployment and worklessness in NDC areas – 'there is a feeling that job brokerage projects are "working"' (CRESR, 2005, p 262).

Intermediate labour markets

Given the difficulties of bridging the gap between the world of work and those who have spent long periods out of work, or even have never worked, increasing attention has been given to the potential of *intermediate labour markets* (ILMs) as a means of making the transition into employment while also promoting community-based regeneration. The ILM model originated in Scotland in the 1990s where the Wise Group recruited and trained a workforce drawn from local long-term unemployed people to carry out housing improvement and physical regeneration activities in deprived neighbourhoods of Glasgow (McGregor et al, 1997). As well as providing jobseekers with training and personal development to provide skills and work discipline in a supportive real-work environment, ILMs provide waged work and therefore avoid the stigma attached to many government 'make work pay' schemes by the unemployed and some employers. They also have the benefit of providing employers with evidence of work experience and commitment. A review that identified 73 organisations across Britain that were running ILMs concluded that they made a useful if modest contribution to tackling long-term unemployment, especially in high unemployment areas (Finn and Simmonds, 2003). Intermediate labour markets have tended to be most effective among young unemployed people and more evidence is needed with regards to their effectiveness with more disadvantaged groups.

City Strategy Pathfinders

In 2006, as part of its aspiration to achieve an 80% employment rate – by reducing the number of people on IB by one million and moving one million older workers and 300,000 more lone parents into work – the government announced a more devolved and flexible approach to tackling high levels of economic inactivity in major cities throughout the UK. The DWP's City Strategy initiative marked a departure from the centrally determined approach of previous welfare-to-work programmes and also a recognition that local stakeholders are in the best position to produce policy interventions that are tailored to specific local circumstances – 'the City Strategy will test whether locally determined solutions can add significant value to driving up employment outcomes' (DWP, 2007b, p 64). City Strategies were also seen as a way of pooling resources and funding streams as well as integrating a range of employment, training and health provision targeted at disadvantaged groups and neighbourhoods.

Fifteen cities and city-regions[2] with employment rates below the national average were awarded City Strategy Pathfinder status in 2006, each receiving seedcorn money to establish consortia made up of government agency providers (namely Jobcentre Plus, LSCs, Regional Development Agencies, and Primary Care Trusts), local government and Local Strategic Partnerships (LSPs), the private sector (chambers of commerce and key employers), the voluntary sector and the Trades Union Congress (TUC). Each city consortia was given just two years, until April 2009, to achieve the centrally determined target of a 3% reduction in benefit numbers and an equivalent increase in the employment rate through developing innovative ways of tackling worklessness that are appropriate to the circumstances found within specific cities and city-regions. A £65 million Deprived Areas Fund (drawn from monies saved from the closure of Action Teams, Ethnic Minority Outreach and the WNPs) was created to assist city consortia in the implementation of their local strategies with the promise of at least £5 million reward funding. Although a recognition of the need to develop strategies that are appropriate to local circumstances is a positive move, it remains to be seen what can be achieved by this model of partnership working within an extremely short timescale and the extent to which the consortia are able to get to grips with the complex interplay of factors that prevent many people living in deprived neighbourhoods from entering the labour market.

Conclusions

The discussion presented in this chapter has demonstrated the multiple causes of high levels of unemployment and economic inactivity associated with deprived neighbourhoods. The precise interplay between demand-side, supply-side and institutional factors is spatially constituted within particular local labour markets. As the relative importance of these factors varies spatially, it follows that strategies to tackle concentrated worklessness need also to be spatially differentiated and interventions based on a sound understanding of the dynamic interplay of causal factors that lie behind the problems of a given area.

What is readily apparent from the review of the policy agenda developed under New Labour is a fundamental and restated commitment to the basic rationale that formal employment represents the best route out of poverty combined with an acceptance that the primary factors limiting labour market integration of disadvantaged groups and those living in disadvantaged areas relate to the supply side of the labour market. In consequence, the vast majority of policy activity targeted at worklessness has had a narrow supply-side focus. Acceptance that individual and household characteristics form a large part of the explanation has meant a strong emphasis on measures to address key person-related factors that have been shown to be strongly associated with worklessness. In contrast, interventions related to demand-side factors have been minimal while those related to institutional factors have been variable and often poorly integrated. Furthermore, the focus exclusively on formal employment has meant that little attention has been paid to work outside employment despite its considerable importance within deprived areas, whether in terms of cash-in-hand activity or work undertaken for mutual benefit or associated with self-provisioning.

A notable characteristic of policy development has been the introduction of a series of area-based interventions to augment mainstream provision in an attempt to better reach more marginalised individuals and groups living within deprived areas. This marks ongoing recognition of the relative failure of mainstream policies to reach effectively the most disadvantaged living in poor neighbourhoods and the limitations of a highly centralised policy agenda focused primarily on national-level analysis of aggregate supply and demand.

The approach of the government department primarily responsible for this policy agenda – the DWP – has a traditional focus on the development and delivery of geographically undifferentiated national policies. Recent years have seen a grudging acceptance that standardised 'one-size-fits-all' solutions are ineffective in tackling concentrated deprivation and that strategies to tackle worklessness need to be tailored to local circumstances, most notably through the introduction of the City Strategy Pathfinders. However, there still remains strong resistance within the DWP to the development and delivery of policies that are more devolved locally.

Localised employment policies variously developed under an array of area-based interventions have demonstrated an ability to respond to the particular problems of those living within areas of concentrated worklessness – whether this relates to the issues of the lack of English as a first language in Newham or training targeted at young single mothers in Mansfield. In the development of these localised, largely supply-side-oriented interventions, there is an emerging consensus at an operational level about what kind of actions are most likely to work best and the key elements of 'good practice' (Sanderson, 2006; North et al, 2007; Policy Research Institute, 2007). These include:

- *Outreach activities* – engaging with the most disadvantaged groups who are furthest from entering the labour market requires a proactive approach based on voluntary rather than compulsory involvement. Experience has found that this is best facilitated by involving local voluntary and community organisations in the development and delivery of local initiatives, in order to build the trust and confidence of the local community and overcome the reluctance to deal directly with government officials. When targeting particular minority ethnic communities, the involvement of outreach workers and groups from those communities is likely to be crucial. The location of outreach services in familiar and accessible community-based locations is also important in order to facilitate initial engagement.
- *Personalised and holistic approach* – this is needed in view of diverse and multiple barriers to employment that individuals face, which often require specialist help with issues of health, drug or alcohol abuse, debt, housing and family breakdown before more employment-related issues such as skills, language difficulties, job search and making applications can be addressed. The experience of a number of policy initiatives highlights the important role played by a trusted and motivated personal advisor who can operate flexibly in relation to an individual's needs, providing continuity of support and guidance

to appropriate sources of specialist help at the right times. Provision needs to include support throughout a long-term process of labour market engagement that starts with pre-employment training and confidence building, and continues through to support for job search and interview preparation and ongoing training both in and out of employment.

• *Involvement of employers* – evidence from a number of initiatives highlights the importance of developing good relations with employers and addressing employers' needs since it is employers who control access to job opportunities. This involves finding out about job vacancies and what employers are looking for in order to help workless people become job ready and in a position to compete for the jobs on offer. Being able to influence employers' recruitment practices in favour of disadvantaged groups is likely to depend on building a trusted relationship with them over time, sometimes helped by having someone dedicated to employer engagement. A more targeted, sectoral approach to involving employers has tended to prove more effective than a more scattergun approach. The government's initiative to involve major private and public sector employers in the creation of Local Employment Partnerships that are focused on employing marginal groups demonstrates a degree of recognition of the vital, yet still underdeveloped, role that employers play in reducing worklessness at the local level (DWP, 2007b).

• *Job retention and progression* – a major limitation of several of the national employment programmes is that they are concerned with getting unemployed and workless people back to work rather than into sustained employment. Little is achieved if someone returns to being out of work after a period of just 13 weeks in a job – the period that was defined as a successful job outcome in a number of government schemes. This points to the need for continuing support for people once they have obtained work, particularly for those who have no previous work experience or those likely to be most vulnerable to losing their job, such as lone parents and disaffected young people. Encouraging people to move up the job escalator is also important not only to avoid them becoming stuck in 'entry-level' jobs, but also to free up these jobs for others, thereby avoiding congestion at the bottom end of the labour market. This does depend of course on there being opportunities for job advancement in the local labour market and sufficient incentives for taking on a higher-skilled and more demanding job.

Given that unemployment and economic inactivity have remained stubbornly high for certain groups and areas over many years, it is perhaps understandable that government has tended to pursue a 'work-first' approach to tackling the worklessness problem in order to be able to show results in the short term. However, to tackle worklessness more effectively, broader long-term strategies and coordinated actions are required that address the various barriers that prevent people from deprived neighbourhoods and disadvantaged groups more generally obtaining sustainable employment and better life chances. Where various aspects of labour demand contribute a large part of the explanation, stronger efforts are needed to generate and attract particular kinds of employment and to work more closely with local employers to try to influence their recruitment practices. Particularly in those areas still suffering from the legacy of industrial decline, there continues to be a case for demand-side policies aimed at producing the kinds of jobs that are likely to be accessible, in terms of skills and location, to the residents of the most deprived neighbourhoods. To date, national and regional economic strategies have largely ignored this issue. Nor should the potential contribution of employment creation in the public and voluntary sectors be overlooked given the wider need for regeneration and improved public services in these areas.

Where barriers to work relate to the institutional context, the policy focus needs to be on addressing the various institutional factors that will make it easier for people entering at the bottom end of the labour market to access decent-quality employment that provides a stable, living wage. Policies here need to be pursued at different spatial levels. Much important regulatory activity in relation to the labour market is nationally based, and other key areas of related provision, such as childcare, transport and housing, are also strongly structured by central government regulation and policy. Although there have been various attempts to reform the benefits system to 'make work pay', for many disadvantaged groups coming off benefits to take up low-grade insecure employment still remains unattractive, given the real possibility that it will lead to a worsening of their material circumstances.

Interestingly, with regard to pay and working conditions for low-income workers, aside from the early introduction of the minimum wage and the working time directive, it has been notable that the overwhelming desire to retain and promote labour market flexibility has resulted in a marked reluctance by government to intervene further. The commitment to open, flexible and lightly regulated labour markets has been similarly evident with regard to issues of inward labour migration and irregular working. Only more recently when the scale of labour inflows raised public concern has regulation been tightened with regard to the recruitment of migrant workers (through the introduction of a 'points-based system' for entry into the UK in 2008) and a more active pursuit of employers who employ undocumented workers. However, the issue of the inability of marginalised residents in deprived neighbourhoods to compete successfully against migrant workers for available low-wage jobs remains largely unacknowledged.

There is also considerable scope to address institutional factors at the level of city/subregions and the locality, given that the importance and interplay of institutional factors varies between local labour markets. Some of these may be easier to tackle than others, as for example providing a subsidised bus service linking deprived neighbourhoods with employment areas compared with making changes to the allocation of social housing or the mix of housing tenure in an area. It is notable that London, with its greater devolved power, has been more proactive in seeking to address the particular employment problems affecting those living in a high-cost city, with key policies aimed at the lack of affordable childcare, housing and public transport, and attempts to better integrate employment and training provision (Syrett, 2006). Yet in practice, local and city-based institutions generally lack the resources and power to advance and implement more ambitious strategies to reform the institutional setting, although there remains a highly important role at this level in terms of tailoring existing provision to local labour market conditions and improving its coordination and delivery.

Notes

[1] The ILO measure generally gives a higher unemployment rate than the claimant count measure as it includes those who want to work but are not on Jobseeker's Allowance (JSA). However, it is an estimated figure based on sample data from the government's annual Labour Force Survey (LFS) and can prove less reliable at the local authority scale than at higher spatial scales.

[2] The cities and city-regions funded as City Strategy Pathfinders were: Birmingham, Blackburn, Dundee, East London, Edinburgh, Glasgow, Heads of the Valleys, Leicester, Liverpool, Greater Manchester, Nottingham, Rhyl, South Yorkshire, Tyne and Wear and West London.

FOUR

Enterprise and entrepreneurship

Introduction

This chapter considers the role that enterprise and entrepreneurship can play in renewing neighbourhoods as well as reviewing the various kinds of policy intervention that have sought to stimulate enterprise in deprived neighbourhoods. Of the three different rationales that were put forward in Chapter Two for policy intervention in deprived areas, both strengthening economic competitiveness and the pursuit of social inclusion currently feature prominently in the discourse concerning the importance of enterprise and entrepreneurship in tackling the problems of deprived localities. A central question underlying this chapter is the extent to which these two rationales are in conflict with each other and whether this is reflected in a degree of confusion and tension between policies relating to enterprise in deprived areas.

From a national and regional economic perspective there is a concern that the low levels of enterprise activity associated with many deprived neighbourhoods impede the pursuit of improvements to economic performance at various spatial scales. This is based on econometric evidence supporting the Schumpeterian thesis that entrepreneurship is a vital determinant of economic growth. For example, Audretsch et al (2002, p 2) claim that 'the positive and statistically robust link between entrepreneurship and economic growth has been indisputably verified across a wide range of units of observation, spanning the establishment, the enterprise, the industry, the region and the country'. Creating enterprises that survive and grow in deprived areas is therefore seen as helping achieve national and regional objectives of increasing economic growth, improving productivity and enhancing competitiveness. According to the government's own estimates, there would be an additional 155,000 businesses in the UK if the levels of business activity in deprived areas matched those in the least deprived areas (HM Treasury, 2005a, p 29). Thus, developing the entrepreneurial potential of those deprived areas suffering from low rates of new business formation and below-average levels of enterprise activity has become a key objective of most strategies concerned with improving regional economic performance.

Policy interventions to stimulate enterprise in deprived neighbourhoods have also been argued for on social justice grounds, focusing on the contribution that enterprise formation and growth can make from the perspective of reducing unemployment and worklessness. The creation of new businesses and the growth of existing businesses are seen as important sources of much-needed jobs and skills for the local working-age population, especially where there is little prospect of attracting large employers to an area. Going into self-employment and starting a new business are considered to be valid options for unemployed residents of deprived neighbourhoods not only as sources of income, but also because of the opportunities they create for acquiring a range of skills and developing confidence and self-esteem. Enterprise formation has therefore been linked to combating social and economic exclusion and been a central plank of New Labour policy. As a Policy Action Team report in 1999 stated: 'promoting enterprise to expand employment opportunities can build confidence and capacity and offer a route out of exclusion through economic opportunity – enterprise development should therefore be an important indicator of the success or failure of neighbourhood renewal' (HM Treasury, 1999, p 6).

As well as distinguishing between different rationales for stimulating enterprise in deprived areas, it is also important to clarify and define a number of concepts that all too frequently are lumped together or left undefined. 'Entrepreneurship' tends to be used as an all-embracing term, being defined by the Global Entrepreneurship Monitor (GEM) as 'any attempt at new business or new venture creation, such as self employment, or the expansion of an existing business by an individual, a team of individuals or by established businesses' (Zacharakis et al, 2000, p 5). Much of the policy discussion about encouraging entrepreneurship and enterprise in deprived neighbourhoods would seem to implicitly adopt this broad definition.

Other definitions relate to a number of specific qualities of those running the enterprise, with entrepreneurship defined as 'the mindset and process to create and develop economic activity by blending risk-taking, creativity and/or innovation with sound management, within a new or existing organisation' (EC, 2003, para 7). Under this narrower definition, entrepreneurs are people who have a high degree of self-motivation and self-belief, a willingness to accept risk and uncertainty, an ability to recognise new opportunities, a vision and an aptitude for innovation and creativity, and above all, an instinct for growth. These form a set of natural attributes that go beyond the technical skills needed to set up a new business venture and, it might be suggested, are not immediately apparent among the majority of people who go into self-employment or run their own business; 'it is this sense of entrepreneurship that distinguishes the entrepreneur from the owner-manager or life-style business founder' (Chell, 2007, p 8). Most small business owner-managers and the self-employed are not entrepreneurial in the above sense as they are essentially concerned with managing various assets for trading purposes and to earn an income (Scase, 1997; Burns, 2007, p 12). The terms 'entrepreneur', 'entrepreneurship' and 'entrepreneurial behaviour' are often applied very loosely in the context of the economic regeneration of deprived neighbourhoods, yet it is questionable as to how much of the business activity that takes place is 'entrepreneurial' in the narrower sense of the term.

In the first part of this chapter, research evidence relating to various kinds of enterprise activity will be discussed within the context of regenerating deprived local economies and communities, distinguishing between exogenous (that is, external to the local economy) and endogenous (that is, internal to the local economy) sources of enterprise investment. Following a brief review of evidence relating to inward investment, the enterprise demographics of deprived neighbourhoods will be discussed, including the roles played by black and minority ethnic businesses (BMEBs), social enterprises and informal economic activities. The second part of the chapter examines how the issue of stimulating enterprise has been treated under different policy approaches to tackling the problems of deprived areas over the last three decades, drawing on research evidence that helps identify the limitations as well as the achievements of policy interventions in this field. Under the New Labour governments, there have been numerous policy initiatives aimed at stimulating new and existing enterprises in deprived areas and encouraging people from various marginalised groups to consider self-employment or starting a new business, justified on the grounds of both economic competitiveness and social inclusion. This contrasts sharply with the approach of the 'New Right' Conservative government of the 1980s where the focus was more single-mindedly on the economic growth and competitiveness rationale for stimulating enterprise in deprived areas, particularly the inner cities. The differences between these approaches are discussed further in the second half of this chapter.

Exogenous versus endogenous investment

Historically, prioritising exogenous sources of investment has been the preferred way of generating new investment and employment within lagging regional and local economies, especially in situations where the prospects for endogenous investment in the form of new and small enterprises are limited. Attracting inward investment has been favoured as a way of kickstarting the economic regeneration of an area, principally because it is capable of providing significant numbers of jobs 'at a stroke' and thought to boost local economies via supply chain benefits and increased spending. There are a number of examples of substantial foreign direct investment projects being attracted to the case study areas, particularly during the 1980s when the Thatcher government courted a number of multinational enterprises, especially from the Far East, with generous financial incentives to invest in the old industrial regions that had suffered most from her government's policy of privatising and running down the nationally owned industries. For example, the decision by Nissan, the Japanese car manufacturer, to locate its first European integrated car manufacturing facility in Sunderland was heralded in the early 1980s as one of the major achievements of the government's inward investment policy. The combination of the low cost of land and labour, high levels of unemployment, the chance to recruit labour in a region unaffected by previous labour disputes in the British car industry and a high level of public subsidy amounting to a third of the cost of the original investment were all crucial factors in the location decision (Garrahan and Stewart, 1992).

From the perspective of the regional economy, it is generally accepted that the Nissan investment has been a major benefit to the North East as a whole, with the total invested in the Sunderland car production plant over the last 20 years exceeding £2 billion, 4,000 jobs being provided directly and an estimated 5,000 indirectly in the regional supplier base, providing anything from local services to hi-tech automotive components (Sunderland Partnership, 2006). However, it is not clear to what extent the company's rhetoric at the time of opening the plant to be joining hands with the local authority to 'create jobs for local people' has been met and what proportion of the thousands of jobs generated in Nissan and its suppliers have benefited people from the most disadvantaged groups and neighbourhoods within the city. There are grounds for expecting this to be small, given the difficulties of accessing a plant located on the outskirts of the city, several miles from the deprived inner-city neighbourhoods, and more particularly, as the company has operated highly selective recruitment practices, drawing workers from a catchment area extending well beyond the Sunderland Travel to Work Area (TTWA).

Although much of the research that has been conducted on inward investment has concentrated on foreign direct investment and relates to the national and regional scales, some useful insights on the nature and impact of inward investment on deprived localities of the UK emerge from a study of the Enterprise Zone policy of the 1980s and 1990s (Potter and Moore, 2000).This was essentially an incentive-driven approach (most notably via exemption from local business rates and tax allowances for property development) to regenerating run-down local economies in a range of different regional and subregional contexts (as discussed later in this chapter, at pp 166-9). Significantly, as it turned out, 'inward investor' was defined broadly in the study to include firms relocating into an Enterprise Zone from elsewhere in the region (where over 10 miles from the zone) as well as firms from other regions and abroad. Based on a survey of 185 inward investor establishments in 22 Enterprise Zones, it was found that 69% of 'inward investors' took the form of business relocations within the region, with only 2% originating from abroad. This is a striking finding that has wider implications as it indicates that the main source of inward investment into deprived areas is likely to be businesses that already exist in other parts of the same region. While the authors concluded that the skills profile of inward investors was a good match with that of the local unemployed population, they also found that inward investors in inner-city zones were more likely to recruit people who were already employed than provide jobs for the unemployed. In terms of other forms of local economic impact, Potter and Moore found that the inward investors were less likely to purchase locally than other firms (13.3% of purchases being from local suppliers compared with 24.8% in the case of other firms) and that they were unlikely to have a major role in building or strengthening local clusters. In other words, inward investors were found to have a relatively low level of local embeddedness, which is consistent with the findings of other research on the local impact of inward investment (for example Turok, 1993, 1995).

In recent years, a common form of inward investment project has been the establishment of 'call centres' (or 'contact centres'), largely because their intensive use of 'distance shrinking' technologies gives them considerable locational flexibility and makes them especially sensitive to labour cost differentials given operational labour costs typically comprise 58% of total costs (Bristow et al, 2000). Within the UK this has drawn call centres to locations close to the centres of provincial cities, notably Edinburgh, Glasgow, Leeds and Newcastle (Richardson and Marshall, 1999, p 109). Sunderland has been particularly successful in attracting a number of call centres, including Barclaycall, London Electricity and the Post Office Customer Management Centre, which together brought over 7,000 jobs to the city. The ready supply of 'willing', 'reliable' and 'cheap' labour has been extolled by the City

Council to attract call centres to Sunderland. Although none of the research on call centres addressed the question of employment provision for people from deprived communities, the location of many call centres close to urban centres makes these jobs reasonably physically accessible to people living in more deprived inner-urban areas. Yet there remain concerns about the low quality of most of these jobs, the lack of career progression and the coercive employment relations in many call centres. A lack of employee autonomy, combined with the intense, repetitive and stressful nature of the work, can lead to staff 'burn-out' and high rates of staff turnover (Richardson and Marshall, 1999, p 98). Moreover, the risk of losing the jobs to other parts of the world offering much cheaper labour and other advantages has become ever greater with the increasing intensity of global competition for inward investment.

The research evidence therefore presents a number of sound reasons against placing a heavy reliance on exogenous sources of enterprise investment for regenerating disadvantaged local economies and generating job opportunities for those living in deprived neighbourhoods. These doubts have contributed to a shift of emphasis on the part of economic development policy makers towards stimulating more endogenous forms of investment and enterprise development, including unleashing latent 'entrepreneurial' talents within deprived communities, encouraging business start-ups and overcoming the barriers to small business growth.

The enterprise demographics of deprived neighbourhoods

The enterprise deficit

At the core of the rationale for stimulating enterprise in deprived neighbourhoods is an economic case for the need to address the low level of enterprise activity in these areas by bringing them closer to the overall national level of enterprise formation. The 'enterprise deficit' is seen to contribute to the relative poor economic performance of certain regions and thereby acts as a constraint on improving national economic growth. Increasing levels of enterprise formation in deprived areas is central to New Labour's objective of achieving sustainable improvements in the economic performance of all English regions and reducing the persistent gap in growth rates between the English regions (HM Treasury, 2001).

Various indicators of enterprise activity have been used to show the extent to which the most deprived areas suffer from the existence of an enterprise deficit when compared with less deprived areas. As Figure 4.1 shows, there is an inverse relationship between the level of deprivation (based on the Index of Multiple Deprivation; IMD) and the rate of new business formation (as measured by Value Added Tax – VAT – registration data[1]). In 2000, the 20% most deprived Super Output Areas (SOAs) in England had 25 businesses registering for VAT per 10,000 resident adults compared with 43 in the 20% least deprived SOAs. While there was a slight narrowing of the gap by 2005 (the equivalent figures being 27 and 42 respectively), there continued to be a marked disparity between the most deprived and least deprived SOAs. Although the enterprise deficit is evident in the most deprived areas in all English regions, this is superimposed on significant regional differences in enterprise formation rates, as shown in Table 4.1. The lowest levels of business formation are to be found in the most deprived SOAs within the North East, which had 17 VAT registrations per 10,000 residents in 2005 compared with 24 in the least deprived SOAs. At the other extreme, the most deprived SOAs in London had a much higher level of enterprise formation, with 36

Figure 4.1: Business start-ups and deprivation in English local authority areas (excluding London boroughs)

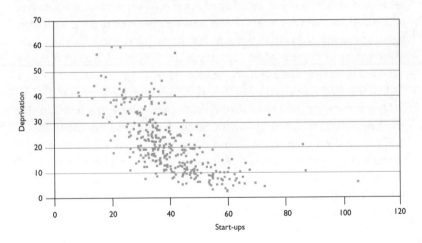

Source: HM Treasury (2005a)

Note: Start-ups = number of VAT registrations per 10,000 adult population during 2001. Deprivation = average number of ward scores on IMD 2000.

Table 4.1: Business start-ups by region and level of deprivation, 2000–05

Average annual number of VAT registrations per 10,000 resident adults, 2000–05

	20% most deprived SOAs	20% least deprived SOAs	% gap in rates of most and least deprived SOAs
England	26.5	42.8	38.1
North East	16.8	22.5	25.3
North West	24.2	36.2	33.1
Yorkshire, The Humber	22.0	32.6	32.5
East Midlands	27.3	38.2	28.5
West Midlands	24.8	35.8	30.7
East of England	28.8	45.7	37.0
London	35.7	46.8	23.7
South East	28.5	49.7	42.7
South West	31.5	37.0	14.9

Source: ONS Inter-Departmental Business Register (IDBR), Enterprise Directorate, DBERR

VAT registrations per 10,000 residents, but this was still below that of the least deprived SOAs in London (47).

Not only are there fewer enterprises being set up in the most deprived areas, but those that are established have a lower chance of survival according to the VAT registration and deregistration data, although again there are signs that the gap has been narrowing (Figure 4.2). Whereas in 1995, 58% of enterprises in the 20% most deprived SOAs survived their first three years compared with 70% in the least deprived SOAs, this had narrowed to 66% and 73% respectively by 2002.

Data on self-employment also indicate particularly low levels in the most deprived areas. A study by the Social Exclusion Unit (SEU, 2004, p 97) using 2001 Census data showed that the level of self-employment in the most deprived wards is disproportionately low, being 1 in 20 of the working-age population compared with 1 in 12 in England as a whole. The study estimates that an extra 130,000 people would need to become self-employed if rates of self-employment in the most deprived areas were increased to the national average.

The enterprise deficit is clearly evident in several of the case study local economies, although there are differences between them in the form that this takes (Table 4.2). The first point to note is the sharp north–south difference with respect to the growth in the numbers of businesses over the 1994–2006 period, with the business stock in both Sunderland and Oldham growing much more slowly than in England

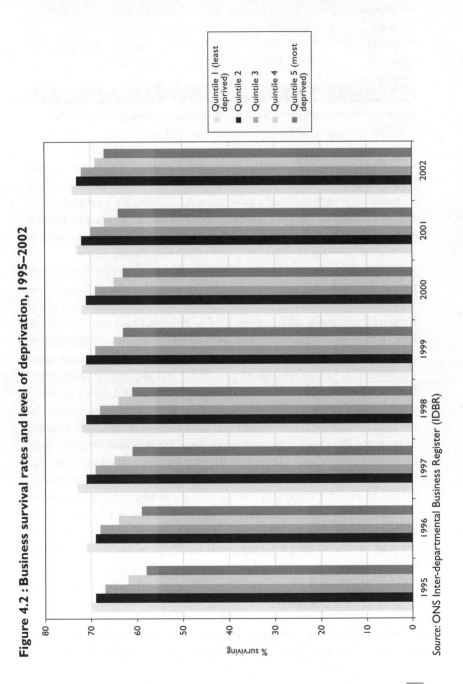

Figure 4.2 : Business survival rates and level of deprivation, 1995–2002

% surviving

Quintile 1 (least deprived)
Quintile 2
Quintile 3
Quintile 4
Quintile 5 (most deprived)

Source: ONS Inter-departmental Business Register (IDBR)

Table 4.2: Business formation rates in the case study areas

	Net change in business stock 1994–2006 (%)	Average annual number of new VAT registrations per 10,000 adult population (aged 16–74), 1994–2006
Sunderland	13.5	18.8
Oldham	9.2	28.1
Mansfield	26.5	26.2
Newham	31.9	31.5
Brighton and Hove	35.2	47.9
England	19.6	39.4

Source: ONS Inter-Departmental Business Register (IDBR), Enterprise Directorate, DBERR

as a whole, compared with Brighton and Newham where the growth in the business stock has been almost double the national rate. In these respects, the trends within the case study areas are largely consistent with regional differences in the growth of the business stock over this period. However, in terms of their business formation rates, as measured by the number of new registrations per 10,000 adult population, four of the case study areas fall below the national average rate of 39.4 for the 1994–2006 period. The very low business formation rates in Mansfield, Oldham and particularly Sunderland, all places located in former coalfields and older industrial regions, is often interpreted as being an indication of a lack of an enterprise and self-employment culture in regions where there is a legacy of previous dependence on a small number of large employers (for example, in coalmining, shipbuilding and the textile industries). Surprisingly, Newham's business formation rate is also low, especially considering that it is within London, which has the highest rate nationally (57 registrations per 10,000 people in 2006). While there is still a legacy of previous dockyard employment in some parts of the borough, it is likely that other factors linked to deprivation are contributing to the low level of business formation in this part of East London. Brighton, on the other hand, has enjoyed a rate of business formation that is above the national average, this being an indication of the dynamism of this coastal city economy with its strong entrepreneurial culture, 20% of working residents being self-employed in 2005 compared with a national average of 13%.

Quality of new businesses

At the heart of the debate about increasing the level of enterprise formation in deprived areas is a concern about the quality and economic viability of new enterprises formed in the most deprived areas, as indicated in Figure 4.2 in relation to their lower survival rates. Research evidence shows that a high proportion will be 'imitative' rather than 'innovative' in that they are most likely to be in low value-added sectors where competition is intense and the chances of survival low. For example, a study of young self-employed people during the 1990s in an area of high unemployment and economic deprivation showed that most set up very small firms in the service sector 'where the market was saturated with similar businesses run by similar people with similar motivations in similar ways. The local economy simply could not support another freelance photographer, another mobile hairdresser, another graphic designer' (Macdonald, 1996, p 444). Moreover, self-employment has been shown to be a difficult way out of unemployment, with higher rates of involuntary exit compared to those who have entered self-employment from being in employment, with those experiencing long-term unemployment being the least likely to survive in self-employment (Taylor, 1999; Cowling and Hayward, 2000).

A series of studies focused on the depressed area of Teesside in the North East region have found a heavy concentration of self-employed people and business start-ups in low value-added sectors; for example, a survey in 2001 found that 23% of new firms in Teesside were in hairdressing, beauty therapy and motor repairs compared with only 4% in Buckinghamshire and 9% in Shropshire (Mole et al, 2002). The issue of whether 'more means worse' was addressed through looking at new business start-ups in Teesside over three decades – the 1970s, 1980s and 1990s (Greene et al, 2004, 2007). This showed that while the rate of small business start-up was higher in the 1980s than previously or subsequently, failure rates were also higher. The quality of the new businesses founded in the 1980s was found to be poorer in terms of growth in employment, the human capital of their founders and their choice of legal form. This led to the authors questioning the ethics of stimulating enterprise in disadvantaged areas: 'seeking to raise new firm formation rates in an area where one in four new business starts are in motors, hairdressing or beauty seems unlikely to enhance substantively employment, productivity or the welfare of that area' (Greene et al, 2004, p 1223). Thus, it is being argued on the basis of this evidence that attempts by policy makers to increase the rate of new business formation in deprived areas will be offset by more business failures, primarily because of the limited human capital (that is, educational attainment, qualifications, skills and relevant work experience) in these areas (van Stel and Storey, 2004).

Without sufficient attention being paid to the quality of start-up enterprises, increasing the rate of new enterprise formation in disadvantaged local economies can all too easily result in high rates of displacement as low value-added businesses compete with each other in overcrowded local markets. Although it might be argued from an economic standpoint that a high level of churn in the local business population may not be a bad thing if more efficient and productive businesses replace less efficient and productive ones (HM Treasury, 2002, 2005a), this is unlikely to help the achievement of employment objectives if one person moves from being unemployed into self-employment at the expense of another. Nor will this kind of enterprise development help attain greater social inclusion if it results in 'self-exploitation', 'in-work poverty', and further disillusionment if the new business venture proves to be shortlived. Thus, any economic gains in terms of improved competitiveness and productivity may be at the cost of further deepening social and economic exclusion experienced by disadvantaged groups. To try to avoid this, any attempt to raise the rate of enterprise formation in deprived neighbourhoods needs to address the factors that influence the type and quality of the enterprises created, especially the attitudes and skills of those setting up in business. This is where successful enterprise development in deprived areas cannot be divorced from the wider aspects of neighbourhood renewal, not least those concerned with improving educational attainment and skills development.

Business growth

In terms of reviving the local economies of deprived areas, much of the interest in small enterprises relates to their potential contribution to creating new employment opportunities, particularly in those local contexts where larger firms have been shedding employment. In fact at a national level, job generation has been one of the main rationales for policy interventions to support new and existing small firms ever since the influential but also much criticised paper by Birch (1979) arguing that two thirds of new jobs in the US during the early 1970s were in firms with less than 20 employees. Although the data and methodology used by Birch have been shown to have inflated the contribution of small firms, further analysis based on more reliable data still shows that small firms provide a disproportionate share of new jobs within the US (Storey, 1994). This has been backed up by evidence from the UK showing that new and small firms accounted for 70% of the net increase of 800,000 jobs over the 1995-99 period (Dale and Morgan, 2001; Small Business Service, 2004).

However, this aggregate picture needs to be interpreted carefully as it would be wrong to conclude that most new and small enterprises are generating significant numbers of jobs. More detailed research evidence, based on monitoring sample panels of small enterprises over a period of time, shows that very few small enterprises grow to any significant size. A much-quoted statistic is that over a decade, only 4% of the businesses that are started would be expected to create 50% of the employment generated (Storey, 1994, p 115). Because of the need to make productivity improvements to remain competitive, significant employment growth is only likely to be found in those small enterprises achieving rapid output growth. This was demonstrated by a longitudinal study of manufacturing firms during the 1980s, which found that 83% of the additional jobs created in those firms that survived the decade were in the firms that at least doubled their sales turnover in real terms (North et al, 1994). The majority of small firms that are established therefore stay small, in many instances because their owners are not seeking to grow the business and have no desire to become 'entrepreneurial' in the sense of starting a number of businesses (that is, becoming 'portfolio entrepreneurs'). It also has been found that 75% of the self-employed do not employ others and only 5% employ more than 20 people (Gray, 1998). Although this evidence relating to employment growth in new and small enterprises relates to a national or regional scale, there is no reason for expecting job generation among the self-employed and small businesses to be greater in deprived areas than elsewhere. If anything, their job generation potential is likely to be less, given the concerns over the inferior quality of businesses in deprived areas.

Given the rarity with which fast-growing new and small enterprises are found, a key challenge facing investors and policy makers is to identify ex ante those businesses that do have high growth potential and to identify the characteristics of growth businesses and their entrepreneurs (Deakins and Freel, 2006). Storey (1994) suggests that there are three sets of interdependent influences: the characteristics of the entrepreneur, the characteristics of the firm and the characteristics of the corporate strategy, each of which need to combine appropriately for a business to achieve rapid growth. Drawing on a wide range of research evidence, Storey isolates those characteristics within each of the three components that are most associated with rapidly growing businesses.

With respect to the characteristics of the entrepreneur, the motivation to start a business has been found to be particularly important, with those being pushed into starting a business (for example, because of redundancy or the lack of alternative employment) being less likely to grow their business than those individuals with more positive motivations (for example, identifying a market opportunity). It has also been found that there is a broad relationship between firm growth and the educational background of the entrepreneur, indicating that education is a key element of the human capital needed for business success. The available evidence also indicates that having previous managerial experience is positively associated with new firm growth, as are businesses that are started by more than one individual. These findings are clearly important when considering the entrepreneurial potential of deprived neighbourhoods since it is in these areas that people are more likely to be 'pushed' into starting a business because of the lack of alternative employment, and to have lower levels of educational attainment, and are less likely to have had previous managerial experience. Compared with more prosperous areas, there are grounds for expecting a higher proportion of those deprived neighbourhood residents who start their own business to be chiefly concerned with providing a reasonable source of income for themselves and their families rather than pursuing business growth objectives. The majority of these people are better described therefore as self-employed individuals, small business owner–managers and lifestyle business founders, rather than 'entrepreneurs' in the narrower sense of the term. The evidence relating to the characteristics of successful entrepreneurs also provides further support for the argument that initiatives aimed at realising the entrepreneurial potential of deprived neighbourhoods need to be closely tied to developing the human capital within these communities, including the provision of entrepreneurial education and training.

In terms of the characteristics of corporate strategy associated with high-growth enterprises, the elements that stand out as being particularly important include making a conscious decision about market positioning through focusing on niche markets and differentiating their products and services from those of their competitors (Storey, 1994). Again, in view of the earlier discussion concerning the quality of enterprises, it would seem that enterprises located in deprived areas are less likely to have these characteristics than those located in more affluent areas.

It was largely in an attempt to rebut these arguments and to challenge the commonly held perception that growing and successful businesses were not to be found in deprived areas that the New Labour government launched its Inner City 100 programme concerned with identifying and promoting the most rapidly growing enterprises in inner-city locations (NEF, 2004). Over four years, from 2001 to 2004, the programme produced an annual index of the fastest-growing 100 inner-city firms, as measured by their growth in sales turnover. Eligible firms had to be located within postcode areas that were within the 20% most deprived wards on the IMD, to be independently owned, and to be employing at least five people in 2001. The Inner City 100 companies were found to perform favourably in terms of growth and profitability against various national business performance benchmarks, with many of them being innovative fast-growing firms across a wide range of sectors. It was concluded that over half of the companies were making significantly positive impacts on the inner-city economies, with an estimated 11% of their combined sales turnover going into these areas in the form of wages, local purchasing and community giving. This rose to 19% in the case of the micro firms (that is, those employing fewer than 10 people), compared with just 8% for the large firms (that is, those employing more than 250 people). This indicates that as firms grow the proportion of their income that finds its way back into the local economy decreases. As to the local employment being generated, it was found that, on average, 15% of the workforce of these firms lived locally (defined as being within one mile of the workplace). While the Inner City 100 report authors describe this as contributing 'significant' numbers of local jobs, it might be more accurate to say that six out of every seven jobs are in effect 'leaking' out of these inner-city locations as a result of commuting, although of course some of these jobs may be filled by people from other deprived inner-city neighbourhoods.

Another problem that the Inner City 100 study draws attention to is the difficulties of retaining growing businesses within the inner cities. Rapidly increasing commercial property prices and rental costs in inner-city locations were making it impossible for many of the surveyed businesses to expand into new premises or remain at their current locations. Moreover, the conversion of business properties to residential uses has exacerbated the situation in many inner-city areas. This, of course, is not a new problem, as the lack of affordable space for expanding businesses in urban areas has been an important factor leading to their outward movement to cheaper locations over several decades. In the case of Inner London, for example, it has been shown that there is a mismatch between the demand and supply of business space in the City Fringe area, with a particular shortage of mid-sized premises making it difficult to retain growing small businesses (Renaisi Ltd and Ancer Spa, 2003). Thus, even when deprived areas do spawn new firms capable of growth, the operation of the urban land and property market can either constrain their growth or result in their movement away to other areas. In this respect the relocation of successful, growth-oriented businesses from deprived localities has certain parallels with the out-movement of those residents of deprived neighbourhoods who succeed in entering the labour market and bettering themselves (as discussed in Chapter Three). This raises the question of whether or not interventions aimed at stimulating enterprise activity in deprived neighbourhoods are more likely to benefit individual businesses rather than setting in motion processes leading to the wider economic regeneration of these localities. Furthermore, it has been argued that policy initiatives aimed at encouraging enterprise in deprived areas are most likely to influence individuals who are on the cusp of social marginality rather than the most seriously disadvantaged (Blackburn and Ram, 2006, p 86). This again echoes the findings previously discussed with regard to labour market intervention where there is a consistent failure to reach the most marginalised individuals.

Black and minority ethnic business

There are a number of reasons why BMEBs[2] might be expected to make an important contribution to the regeneration of deprived neighbourhoods and therefore warrant further separate discussion here. First, as noted in Chapter Two, there is a concentration of the black and minority ethnic (BME) population in the most deprived neighbourhoods, particularly within inner areas of certain cities (such as Birmingham, Leicester and London). It follows therefore that there is likely to be a higher concentration of BMEBs in these areas, both because this is where the owners live and to supply the local ethnic markets. Second, there is an above-average propensity for some BME people to be involved in self-employment and business ownership; for example, 21.8% of people of Pakistani origin who are in employment are self-employed as are 19.1% of Chinese people, compared with just 6.6% of Black Africans (Office for National Statistics, 2005).

The 'Enterprise People, Enterprising Places' study of minority ethnic employment and business growth draws attention to the increasing importance of BMEBs. Using data from a specially commissioned GEM survey, it shows that entrepreneurial activity[3] among minority ethnic groups is higher than among the white population (7.4% and 4.7% respectively) and that this difference is particularly marked for the 18-34 age group (National Employment Panel, 2005). Although some minority ethnic people may have positive motivations for starting a business, for many self-employment and business ownership has been a response to economic and social exclusion in mainstream society and the only alternative to being unemployed (Blackburn and Ram, 2006). Moreover, Deakins and Freel (2006) present evidence from surveys of a sample of entrepreneurs of African, Caribbean and Asian origins showing that over 40% thought that discrimination in the labour market and frustrated career ambitions had been significant push factors. Evidence from London also shows that the lack of job opportunities and overt discrimination in mainstream labour markets are the main reasons why immigrants from new and emerging minority ethnic groups are being pushed into self-employment and enterprise activity (Sepulveda et al, 2006).

From a policy perspective, the social inclusion and cohesion rationale for encouraging people from BME groups to set up enterprises has been highlighted in a number of influential reports, including that of Lord Scarman[4] following the riots in Brixton in the early 1980s as well as more recent government reports (HM Treasury, 1999). One of the factors influencing the potential contribution of BMEBs to the regeneration of deprived areas is the extent of their local embeddedness and their ability to generate social capital (Smith and Wistrich, 2001). Thus, BMEBs have been encouraged not only as a key factor in the economic regeneration of those deprived neighbourhoods with a large minority ethnic population, but also because of the role they can play in developing community capacity, social cohesion and economic inclusion. In this respect, 'current policy interest in promoting "social inclusion" resonates strongly with the *raison d'être* for enterprise support articulated by Lord Scarman nearly two decades ago' (Ram and Smallbone, 2003, p 151).

Various studies have also highlighted the importance of ethnic networks to the development of BMEBs, providing them with financial backing, low-cost labour, trade and information exchange and a means of building trust within the local community (Song, 1999; Ram et al, 2000). While a reliance on co-ethnic labour can help to ensure that the benefits of the growth of the business stay within the local community, these benefits may be limited by a dependence on family and low-wage labour. Also, an excessive reliance on ethnic networks could prove to be inward looking and impede subsequent enterprise development, making it more difficult for BMEBs to 'break out' into mainstream markets and to diversify their activities (Ram and Smallbone, 2001).

There are other features of BMEBs that can limit their economic regeneration potential. As Blackburn and Ram (2006, p 83) point out, 'many Asian small business owners are stuck in highly competitive and precarious market niches (notably, lower-order retailing); are under capitalised; work long hours, intensively utilising familial and co-ethnic labour; and are struggling to survive in hostile inner-city environments'. There is therefore a tendency for BMEBs to be concentrated in sectors where competition is intense and margins are very low. Specifically in relation to businesses in former City Challenge areas, Oc and Tiesdell (1999) found that many BMEBs have low self-esteem and are low in confidence. Moreover, a large-scale survey comparing BMEBs with a white control group (Ram et al, 2002) found that the BMEBs had a significantly lower propensity to be growth oriented than their white-owned counterparts, with significantly weaker performance in terms of profitability and sales growth.

While the relative lack of growth of BMEB enterprises may reflect the characteristics of the entrepreneurs and the kinds of sectors their businesses are in, research has also indicated that BMEBs encounter various difficulties in accessing the support that is available. Evidence indicates that there are disproportionately low penetration levels of BMEBs by mainstream business support agencies such as Business Link and finance providers (Deakins et al, 2003; Lyon et al, 2007). They have been found to be less likely to access mainstream support, not because of a lack of awareness, but rather because of a lack of understanding of the types of support available, doubts about its relevance, confusion about providers, and lack of trust and confidence in the providers (Fadahunsi et al, 2000). The difficulties of accessing mainstream sources of external finance have also played a part, although such difficulties may be as much perceived as actual. For example, a study of BMEBs in Scotland found that perceived institutional discrimination appeared to be a factor leading to reluctance on the part of BMEB entrepreneurs to approach external sources of finance, leading to a heavy reliance on personal and family sources (Deakins et al, 2005). A Bank of England (1999) report concluded that the problems perceived by BMEB entrepreneurs may be the result of their concentration in highly competitive sectors with high business failure rates rather than any discrimination. Other research indicates a diversity of experience with respect to raising external finance between BME groups, with Chinese businesses having a significantly greater ability to raise formal sources of finance than African- and Caribbean-owned businesses, whereas South Asian-owned businesses had a particularly heavy reliance on informal and family sources (Ram et al, 2002).

The prospects for BMEBs are likely to improve with generational change, resulting in more niche-focused enterprises in sectors such as business and professional services, hospitality and entertainment, information technology and creative industries (Modood et al, 1995). For example, second- and third-generation Asians have been found to be contributing significantly to the vibrancy of London's creative industries (particularly in the arts, music, performing arts, computer software and publishing), setting up businesses that are more knowledge- and skill-based than the lower value-added activities of clothing and retailing that are traditionally associated with Asian business activity (Smallbone et al, 2005). Second-generation entrepreneurs have been found to be more highly educated, more likely to have positive motives for setting up a business, and more likely to seek external assistance than their forebears (Phizacklea and Ram, 1995). At the same time, many of them are operating in mainstream markets and perceive themselves as being part of the mainstream economy, even resenting being categorised as minority ethnic businesses. In these respects, therefore, involvement in enterprise activity has clearly contributed to the social and economic inclusion of the entrepreneurs themselves, although the extent to which these successful second- and third-generation businesses locate within and contribute to the economic revival of deprived neighbourhoods is unclear given a high propensity for successful BMEBs to leave deprived localities once they are in a position to do so. Without more research evidence, it is difficult to know to what extent the 'embeddedness' that has often been seen as an advantage of BMEBs in the context of deprived neighbourhoods extends beyond the first generation of business founders.

Social enterprises

As well as BMEBs, social enterprises are also seen as having the potential to make an important contribution to economic regeneration and the building of social capital within deprived communities, this being achieved through providing services, developing skills and creating employment opportunities (HM Treasury, 1999). From a neighbourhood renewal perspective, the attraction of social enterprises is that they appear to be a way of bridging the economic and social agendas. The government's National Strategy for Social Enterprises (DTI, 2002, p 14) defines them as 'businesses with primarily social objectives whose surpluses are principally reinvested for that purpose in the business or the community, rather than being driven by the need to maximise profit for shareholders and owners'. It maintains that social enterprises 'have a distinct and valuable role to play in helping create a strong, sustainable and socially inclusive economy' (DTI, 2002, p 13). Moreover, it has been argued that social enterprises can make an important contribution to enterprise and jobs in those areas where more traditional 'investment-driven' enterprise structures are not considered viable and contribute to the development of a wider social economy (Amin et al, 2002; EC, 2005; Evans and Syrett, 2007). New Labour's commitment to the growth of the social enterprise sector and to see it operating at the 'heart of society' led to the establishment of the Office of the Third Sector in 2006 (HM Treasury, 2006a). However, in practice this agenda is narrowly focused on seeking to diversify forms of enterprise, particularly in relation to the delivery of public services, rather than any significant development of a social economy.

The mapping of social enterprises in England (IFF Research, 2005) found that they tended to be concentrated in more deprived areas, possibly reflecting the various funding streams and policy initiatives to support social enterprises in deprived areas as a way of providing various services run by voluntary and community organisations. It is interesting to note here that 10% of the businesses that qualified for inclusion in the Inner City 100 between 2001 and 2004 were social enterprises, demonstrating, according to the New Economics Foundation (NEF, 2004), that achieving growth and commercial success can be combined with achieving social and environmental objectives.

While social enterprises have the potential to provide a wide range of services and to contribute to neighbourhood renewal, their impact is currently limited due to their small number and scale of their operations (Amin et al, 2002; Lyon et al, 2002; Henry et al, 2005). They can offer people some experience of enterprise and can help in getting people into, or back into, a work routine that can contribute to longer-term capacity building in the local economy. As such, social enterprises are sometimes associated with the intermediate labour market (ILM) initiatives discussed in the previous chapter, providing waged employment opportunities and experience of the world of work, while at the same time providing local services. However, the counter-argument is that they have a tendency to create low-paid and low-skilled jobs, sometimes relying on voluntary labour in order to be financially viable (Evans, 2001b). The example in Box 4.1 shows the role played by social enterprises in Sunderland in seeking to bring about greater social inclusion and employment generation in deprived communities.

Box 4.1: Social Enterprise Sunderland (SES)

Founded in 1983 as Sunderland's Cooperative Development Agency, Social Enterprise Sunderland (SES) has targeted its activities at the most deprived neighbourhoods within the city, with the formation of social and community enterprises being promoted as vehicles for achieving social inclusion. They are seen as a way of empowering people to take an active part in the regeneration of their communities as well as creating employment and personal development opportunities. For SES, 'social enterprises combine a strong social purpose with the energy and dynamism of enterprise – they experiment and innovate, marrying a strong public service ethos with business acumen' (www.socialenterprise-sunderland.org.uk). Social enterprises assisted by SES employ over 400 people in full- and part-time employment, with a collective turnover exceeding £5 million in 2003. In addition, people from deprived neighbourhoods have been helped to set up over 100 other types of trading businesses. One of the largest social enterprises assisted by SES is a cooperative providing personal home care, having expanded to 150 members/employees.

One of the activities of SES has been to target individuals engaged in informal economic activities and encourage and support them in entering the formal economy. A number of individuals have been helped to establish successful legitimate businesses: for example, according to an interviewed SES advisor, 'there's a guy who now owns probably 20 properties if not more, runs two care homes and started by poaching fish in the middle of the Wear – that's where he got his original capital from'. SES's success in supporting formalisation activity was attributed to their particular approach, the organisation's voluntary sector culture and the close links developed with the area over time. Individuals, such as community activists or welfare rights workers, working with SES had themselves a long history of working in the area and therefore saw themselves as being well placed to understand and gain the trust of local people. Mainstream agencies, on the other hand, were considered to be less well suited for such work, largely because the 'cultural background' of the individuals working for such organisations is too different from that of the people targeted for help.

Many advocates of social enterprise go further than seeing them merely as an intermediary stage between social exclusion and participation in the mainstream economy. Instead, they are seen as a means of empowering communities to develop alternative solutions to local economic problems that rely less on market mechanisms and develop a more socialised economy focused on attaining socially useful and environmentally sustainable benefits. The Local Alchemy initiative in the East Midlands, for example, has been concerned with helping local communities to find solutions to local economic problems that are more self-reliant and capable of achieving economic, social and environmental benefits (NEF, 2002). Developed jointly by the New Economics Foundation and the East Midlands Development Agency,

Local Alchemy aims to challenge existing institutions and agencies to think differently about communities experiencing economic disadvantage and to adopt approaches that harness resources, skills and passions within local communities. By means of employing business coaches and coordinators to engage with local communities and local agencies, Local Alchemy has sought to facilitate the development of 'local economic visions' that are then translated into a wide range of projects on the ground, including the formation of social enterprises that are seen as being particularly suited to the ethos of this approach. For some authors this is the main potential of social enterprises. Amin et al (2002) conclude their review of social enterprises by suggesting that they are never going to become a growth machine or an engine of job generation but rather a symbol of an alternative economy, based on meeting social needs and enhancing social citizenship. Thus, the benefits of social enterprises are frequently of a wider and non-monetary nature, such as building local capacity and social capital, empowering individuals and developing innovative approaches to local problems (Evans and Syrett, 2007).

Informal economic activity

It is frequently alleged that there is a lot more 'entrepreneurial activity' going on in deprived neighbourhoods than is apparent from official figures because many residents obtain income from participating in the shadow or informal economy. Notwithstanding the difficulties involved in defining the scope of the 'informal economy' and in measuring its extent in deprived neighbourhoods, the available research evidence suggests that although the volume of informal economic activity is not any larger in deprived neighbourhoods than in more affluent communities, people living in deprived neighbourhoods have a greater reliance on informal work and enterprise activities to fulfil their needs and wants than those elsewhere (Evans et al, 2006; Williams and Windebank, 1998). In Mansfield, for example, as multiple stakeholders attested, informal economic activities play an important role in sustaining the livelihoods of large numbers of low-income households within the deprived communities, with a highly developed network to supply a range of both legal and illegal goods and services.

While such informal economic activities are important to people 'getting by' on low incomes, they can also reinforce the problems of the poor quality of enterprise activity and low skills within the local economy, adversely affecting the viability of legitimate enterprises. It is sometimes suggested that in those markets characterised by cut-throat competition and low barriers to entry, such as those that many start-up BMEBs enter, there is limited scope for establishing viable enterprises as part of the formal economy, resulting in entrepreneurs cutting corners with respect to taxes and regulations, or employing illegal workers (Kloosterman et al, 1999). However, it would be misleading to explain informal economic activities as being entirely the result of a deliberate cost minimisation strategy. Research on new immigrant entrepreneurs from disadvantaged backgrounds in London draws attention to other factors such as cultural differences, lack of awareness about taxation and regulations, and the difficulties of gaining access to the business and financial support system (Sepulveda and Syrett, 2007).

From a neighbourhood renewal and regeneration policy perspective, policy makers need to be aware of the dilemmas and challenges posed by the existence of informal economic activities as well as their intimate relationship with the formal economy (Sepulveda and Syrett, 2007). Rather than adopting an entirely negative and punitive attitude towards informal economic activities, there is an argument for seeing them in a more positive light in terms of the human assets and skills that can be acquired and their contribution to achieving economic and social inclusion. While not overlooking the fact that much informal enterprise activity reinforces the poor quality of businesses in deprived areas, the pursuit of survival strategies assists the development of various skills often associated with entrepreneurial behaviour, such as self-reliance and initiative. Thus, the skills developed as a result of engaging in informal economic activities could be channelled into more legitimate forms of self-employment and business activity (see Box 4.1). In this respect, the informal economy might be seen 'as a development site for entrepreneurship and ... a positive component in the development of a business-oriented entrepreneurial culture' (Sepulveda and Syrett, 2007, p 97). Similarly, while still emphasising the importance of deterring informal economic activity, the government recognises the need for a persuasive approach that 'sees entrepreneurship in the informal economy as an asset to be harnessed' (DTI, 2005a, p 7).

In recent years there has been a growth in various supply-side policy initiatives aimed at encouraging the self-employed and those running small enterprises within the informal economy to make the transition into the formal economy, via various tax incentives and grants, awareness-raising initiatives and information campaigns (see Box 4.1). These generally see formalisation as a staged process, each stage containing various formalising elements, and delivered using community business advisors who are trusted within the local community and have the necessary culturally specific knowledge and skills (Williams, 2004; Llanes and Barbour, 2007). As noted by Swash (2007, p 398), many voluntary and community organisations are better placed to support the transition out of the informal economy than mainstream enterprise support agencies.

Policy responses

Having discussed the contribution of different types of enterprises to neighbourhood renewal, we now turn to reviewing the policy interventions that have been concerned with encouraging and supporting various kinds of enterprise development in deprived areas. As discussed in Chapter One, there have been a number of distinct conceptualisations of the 'urban problem' over the last 50 years, reflecting various political and ideological shifts, each leading to its own particular approach to intervention and associated policy mechanisms. While a comprehensive discussion of all of these lies beyond the scope of this chapter, the focus here will be on the role that stimulating enterprise and entrepreneurship has played in four principal approaches and the kinds of policy mechanisms associated with each one. This analysis draws on available research evidence, including the results of various evaluative studies that endeavour to measure what the intervention achieved, in order to reflect on the challenges facing policy makers concerning the role that enterprise plays in the regeneration of deprived neighbourhoods.

The area-based property-led approach

This approach, much in vogue during the 1980s and early 1990s, was closely associated with the 'urban entrepreneurialism' favoured by the 'New Right' Conservative governments of the period, with their belief in free-market solutions, the creation of an enterprise culture and a determination to reduce public spending and intervention (Oatley, 1998). Although it was promoted as a private sector-led approach to inner-city regeneration, the approach did in fact involve substantial central government intervention to free up the land and property markets in areas experiencing economic decline. The principal aim was to make these locations attractive to developers, inward investment and business growth. As such, there was a clear focus on the competitiveness and economic growth agenda with little consideration given to the social aspects and the distribution of economic and employment benefits, except in so far as it was assumed that the benefits would 'trickle down' to residents of deprived neighbourhoods.

Two major policies, frequently running in tandem, were concerned with transforming the economies of deprived areas by attracting private investment and stimulating enterprise activities: Urban Development Corporations (UDCs) and Enterprise Zones. Taken together, these were supply-side policies, primarily concerned with freeing up the land market, attracting investment from developers and building new industrial and commercial space as a way of stimulating new enterprise creation, attracting inward investment and enabling the expansion of existing firms.

Urban Development Corporations, accounting for about 30% of urban policy expenditure from 1981 until 1995, were essentially about the physical redevelopment of run-down inner-city areas, often in waterside locations (Imrie and Thomas, 1999). Some of the original UDCs (for example the London Docklands Development Corporation) were strongly criticised (notably by the House of Commons Employment Committee; see House of Commons, 1988) for being too narrowly concerned with the physical aspects of regeneration, to the neglect of the social aspects, leading to calls for the second- and third-generation UDCs to be more focused on ensuring that local people benefit from the physical and economic transformation of the areas. As its name indicates, the Enterprise Zone policy was an area-based initiative (ABI) aimed at stimulating enterprise activities in designated zones by means of a number of incentives to stimulate investment. The main incentives were a 10-year exemption (from the date of designation) from the payment of business rates, and 100% tax allowances on the capital costs of industrial and commercial buildings. Although most Enterprise Zones did not include housing within their boundaries, they were often close to residential neighbourhoods experiencing high unemployment and other forms of deprivation. However, it tended to be an assumption rather than a stated objective of Enterprise Zone policy that those living in nearby neighbourhoods would reap some of the benefits of new investment and job creation, although no specific impact targets or mechanisms for achieving this were ever established.

One of the initial concerns about both UDCs and Enterprise Zones was that they would have a shadow effect on surrounding business areas, resulting in a large number of vacant properties and businesses closing down because of their inability to compete with the 'subsidised' businesses within the zones. The shadow impact of UDCs has been tested by means of research on property chains in Bristol, Leeds and Manchester (Robson et al, 1999) and Cardiff (Francis and Thomas, 2006). Both studies showed that the property chains were generally short and that a lot of properties were being occupied by new rather than existing businesses. It was also found that the spatial reach of property excitation was very limited, indicating a predominance of short-distance relocations. Both studies also found a low level of displacement in the form of vacancies or demolitions, leading to the conclusion that the UDCs had achieved a high level of net additionality for the local economy, with over 70% of the property chains producing net additionality in the case of Bristol, Leeds and Manchester and 57% in the case of Cardiff. This evidence demonstrates that UDCs were successful in reviving local commercial property markets and adding to the stock of local businesses.

This view is corroborated by evidence from the national evaluation of Enterprise Zones (DoE, 1995), which again found little evidence of a negative 'shadow effect' on businesses in surrounding areas. Premises vacated by firms moving into the zones tended to be reoccupied by other tenants at earlier stages of their business development. According to the authors of this government-commissioned evaluation, Enterprise Zones made a significant contribution to local economic regeneration by stimulating local property markets, achieving environmental improvements and encouraging enterprise (DoE, 1995). They estimated that some 1,500 'new' firms (that is, firms that were not in the Enterprise Zones prior to designation) were set up in 22 Enterprise Zones, resulting in 58,000 'new' jobs (that is, when deadweight, displacement and short-term multiplier effects were allowed for).

Although UDCs may have succeeded in terms of attracting investment, stimulating enterprise development and reviving the immediate local economies, there is also strong agreement from the results of studies of specific UDCs that they had limited 'trickle-down' benefits for those living in neighbouring local communities. To quote from the government's own review of the evidence base relating to UDCs, 'the general consensus from the available evidence is that a lasting and sustained economic impact has occurred, although evidence about the longer term impacts on local residents is currently absent' (DETR, 2001, p 82). With regard to detailed research evidence, a study of the Black Country UDC based on a survey of 133 employers found that less than 40% of employees lived within the local authority (Sandwell) in which much of the UDC was located and only one in seven employees lived within one mile of their workplace (Nevin, 1998). One reason put forward for the low level of local recruitment by the surveyed firms was their heavy dependence on word-of-mouth recruiting methods. As well as leading to ongoing racial homogeneity in predominantly 'white' firms, this also led to people from the poorest and most disadvantaged housing estates being bypassed, thereby reinforcing rather than reducing existing exclusion tendencies.

Other studies have produced similar findings. Research on the Sheffield Development Corporation demonstrated that it had considerable success in the attraction of retailing and distribution activities (600 out of 1,100 businesses within the UDC area), much of it concentrated around the Meadowhall shopping centre, which contributed to maintaining employment levels in the area following industrial closures (Dabinett and Ramsden, 1999). However, research by Lawless (1995) indicated that there was a range of institutional, cultural and labour market barriers that stood in the way of unemployed people (particularly men) from the surrounding deprived neighbourhoods benefiting from the employment opportunities in the Sheffield Development Corporation area. Despite the fact that over 1,000 new jobs were created within two kilometres of two deprived housing estates, only 8% of residents were found to have applied for any of these posts, 3% receiving interviews and only 1% being successful. Furthermore, a study of an initiative by Merseyside Development Corporation to target jobs in a discount warehouse specifically at local unemployed people also found that, despite the relatively low-skilled nature of the employment offered, only 11% of the jobs went to local unemployed people (Meegan, 1999).

The area-based property-led approach, linked to financial incentives, undoubtedly succeeded in its aim to stimulate enterprise development in a range of depressed local economies in different geographical contexts and in so doing contributed to the modernisation and improved competitiveness of enterprises in the designated areas. However, one of the main lessons to be drawn is that it cannot be assumed that successful enterprise development in or close to deprived neighbourhoods will transform the employment prospects for those living in these areas, since the majority of additional jobs created and wage income generated 'leaked out' to workers commuting in from other areas. This demonstrates that the proximity of areas of employment growth to deprived neighbourhoods does not by itself guarantee significant improvements to the employment prospects of those disadvantaged in the labour market. It was this realisation and other concerns about the lack of community involvement that led to a shift of policy direction in the early 1990s towards a more comprehensive approach to regeneration, which linked the economic and enterprise dimensions more closely with the social, community, environmental and physical dimensions.

Comprehensive regeneration and enterprise development

This broader and more holistic approach to regeneration, both in terms of the issues covered and the stakeholders involved, was favoured by successive Conservative and Labour governments during the 1990s. Stewart (1994, p 144) coined the term 'new localism' to characterise this approach because of the prominence it gave to a localised bidding process that relied less on the representative democracy of local government and more on the consensual corporatism of local governance comprised of a range of public, private and voluntary partners with overlapping (and at times conflicting) interests. Following the City Challenge initiative of the early 1990s, the Single Regeneration Budget Challenge Fund (SRBCF) became the government's main vehicle for allocating funds for regeneration in England, with six annual bidding rounds between 1994 and 2000, resulting in some 900 programmes worth £5.5 billion in SRB support. One of the distinctive characteristics of the SRB was that it adopted a wide view of what constituted 'regeneration', aiming to break away from the narrow property-led approach to embrace a more comprehensive approach that encouraged community-oriented initiatives and addressed various social issues, such as crime and community safety and community capacity building, as well as employment, training and business support.

Enterprise promotion and development did not feature as strongly within SRB programmes as other aspects of regeneration, such as employment and training in the early rounds and latterly community capacity building. In fact, the SRBCF was criticised for underplaying the potential role of new and existing enterprises in achieving regeneration (HM Treasury, 1999, p 115). The mid-term evaluation of the SRB showed that out of 1,028 schemes in all six rounds, there were 70 thematic schemes (defined as focusing on a particular aspect of regeneration) concerned with economic growth and enterprise, representing only 6.9% of SRB schemes and 6.5% of total spending (DTLR, 2002, Table 7.1, p 114). A study of the 243 SRB schemes in London identified 53 (representing 15% of SRB funding in London) as having a primary concern with aspects of enterprise development (North et al, 2002). The most commonly identified aim of these schemes was to try and realise the enterprise potential among disadvantaged groups and to assist the formation of new businesses, whether on an area, sector or ethnic basis. For example the London Social Exclusion Growth Fund (a successful round five bid) aimed to provide both start-up and growth loans to potential entrepreneurs from excluded groups (that is, minority ethnic groups, women, older people, refugees, disabled people and young people). Other SRB-funded initiatives targeted those kinds of businesses (for example, micro businesses or BMEBs) that had traditionally fallen outside the assistance available from mainstream business support providers such as Business Link.

Some of the dilemmas involved in initiatives aimed at increasing the business start-up rate among disadvantaged groups and in deprived areas are well illustrated by the case study of Brent and Harrow's Business Support scheme in north-west London, featured in the national evaluation of the SRB (Brennan et al, 1999). On the face of it the scheme appeared successful since the £1.5 million of SRB funding spent led to the creation of 600 new businesses providing over 1,000 jobs. In fact, the original targets had to be revised upwards because more new businesses were being formed than originally thought. However, a more detailed study of the scheme's impact showed that the claimed outputs overestimated the survival rates of new businesses because a lot of marginal and potentially vulnerable start-ups were assisted, some of which were displaced by other local firms before they could become fully established. This tends to confirm the 'more means worse' thesis discussed earlier, showing that as business support is extended to include more marginal candidates, non-survival and displacement rates become higher. The net additional number of surviving start-ups was in fact estimated to be a more modest 100 firms, representing a net increase of 1% in the borough's business stock and resulting in a net reduction in unemployment of 0.7%. The authors of the evaluation concluded that 'these contributions to a change in outcomes for the area are quite small – they do not have the critical mass to provide the catalyst for dynamic change which could transform the local economy in the medium and longer term' (Brennan et al, 1999, p 19). Another study of business start-up programmes funded under the SRBCF came to similar conclusions (DfEE, 1998). This questioned the wisdom of supporting marginal business proposals simply because they move someone out of unemployment and argued for a more selective approach focused on quality business start-ups that are more likely to produce enterprises that survive and grow. Looked at from the economic growth and competitiveness perspective, therefore, these findings question the value of broad, indiscriminate policy initiatives aimed at stimulating new business formation among disadvantaged groups and areas.

The promotion of enterprise as part of a comprehensive and balanced approach to regeneration has continued as part of the NDC programme, launched in 1998 by the New Labour government as a 10-year programme aimed at turning around the poorest neighbourhoods through an approach based on community engagement and partnership working. There is some evidence that the lessons drawn from previous attempts to stimulate enterprise activities in disadvantaged areas have led to a more selective and focused approach. The types of initiative to support enterprise taken across the 39 NDC partnerships include the provision of business start-up premises, such as managed workspace schemes, grants to improve the security or state of repair of business premises, the provision of start-up funding for social enterprises and initiatives to raise awareness of self-employment within the local community (CRESR, 2005). The NDC programme in the Brighton case study area provides an example of the kinds of support aimed at encouraging people to consider self-employment and starting a business (see Box 4.2).

Box 4.2: East Brighton Business Support (ebbs)

One of the six strategic themes of NDC in East Brighton (East Brighton for You; eb4u) is developing enterprise. Ebbs started in 2004 to support residents considering self-employment or starting a business as well as existing small businesses in the eb4u area and is run by two staff from the Brighton and Hove Community Partnership. As a way of trying to encourage residents to set up their own businesses, eb4u created a £100,000 business support fund so that those proposing to go into self-employment can apply for grants of up to £5,000 if they are unable to obtain commercial funding by submitting a business plan to a panel of local business people. The business support team also provide help with finding business premises and providing business plans. To date more than 16 new businesses have started with ebbs support, including a growing wastepaper recycling business, which is working with the Youth Offending Team to provide work experience placements. In addition to ebbs, eb4u has established a new business centre comprising small industrial units and offices in Moulsecoomb. Whereas only 72% of offices, workshops and shops were occupied in East Brighton in 2003, this had risen to 94% in 2005, providing some indication that new businesses were setting up and existing businesses remaining.

Strengthening the competitiveness of deprived areas

Since the first New Labour government came to power in 1997, there has been a further noticeable shift in the approach adopted towards the role played by enterprise in the regeneration of deprived areas, resulting in a raft of policy initiatives specifically aimed at fostering enterprise and entrepreneurship among disadvantaged groups and areas. This stemmed partly from a concern that existing regeneration programmes, particularly the SRBCF, were giving insufficient emphasis to encouraging enterprise activity in deprived areas, and that existing forms of mainstream business support – especially those accessed through Business Link – appeared to be having relatively little impact in deprived areas. These concerns combined with the growing influence within government of ideas on promoting inner-city competitiveness, based largely on the influential writings of Michael Porter and apparently supported by evidence of inner-city economic revival in the US (Porter 1995, 1997), which chimed well with New Labour's strong commitment to an essentially neoliberal, market-based approach to the pursuit of competitive advantage at national, regional and local levels.

Porter's 'Initiative for a Competitive Inner City' (ICIC), which started in the US in 1994 as a national, not-for-profit organisation, stimulated a renewed interest in identifying the competitive advantages of deprived areas and inner cities in particular. For Porter, policy makers had for too long viewed urban problems 'through the social rather than the economic lens … if inner-city areas lack a viable economic base and pool of enterprise, all the social initiatives in the world are not going to pay off' (BIC, 2002a, p 30). In arguing that economic regeneration of deprived areas can only happen through private investments based on the pursuit of competitive advantages and not through 'artificial inducements' associated with government interference in business investment and location decisions, Porter's views resonated strongly with those of the Thatcher government during the 1980s. Moreover, it was argued that the only real way to tackle poverty in the inner cities on a sustainable basis was to create the conditions for people to generate an income for themselves, through employment and self-employment, rather than relying on assistance from others.

Drawing principally on US evidence, Porter claimed that inner cities typically have four competitive advantages:

- a strategic location, that is, proximity to high rent business or retail areas, good transport links, and opportunities for back office, support and logistics functions;
- local market demand, that is, large underserved retail markets as well as opportunities to serve the cultural and ethnic needs of inner-city residents;
- clusters of interlinked activities as part of supply chains, which in turn help stimulate new businesses to supply these opportunities; and

- human resources, that is, large working-age populations seeking employment and 'a real capacity for legitimate entrepreneurship among inner city residents' (Porter, 1995, p 62).

These are in many respects the kinds of agglomeration economies that have been recognised by urban economists for a long time, but were skilfully rebranded by Porter. Porter also recognised a number of disadvantages of inner cities as locations for enterprise, including a lack of suitable premises, high crime levels, a deficiency in management and other skills, and the problems that disadvantaged groups have in accessing capital. However, Porter's main contention was that enterprise can flourish in inner cities, thereby creating wealth for inner-city residents, and that the UK is no different to the US in that respect. Inspired by these arguments, the government was able to declare its intention to ensure that there are 'no no-go areas for enterprise in any part of Britain' (HM Treasury, 2005b). Thus, the Inner City 100 initiative discussed earlier had a clear political purpose in helping the government argue that successful, growing businesses are to be found in inner-city locations and they have a beneficial impact on inner-city economies and communities.

Porter's thesis that business interests should be at the heart of economic regeneration, identifying and exploiting the competitive advantages of deprived areas, has been adopted in two principal policy initiatives in recent years. First, drawing on the work of the Initiative for a Competitive Inner City in US inner cities, the government announced its City Growth Strategy (CGS) initiative in 2000 aimed at developing a new approach and mindset to tackling underinvestment and low levels of economic activity in disadvantaged areas. This was heralded as a business-led, market-driven approach to identifying and building on the inherent competitive strengths of particular locations. It involved developing partnerships between representatives of the private sector, including local business leaders, and representatives of public and voluntary sector organisations to produce a business-led strategy based on the analysis of local circumstances. One key criterion used in the selection of the successful bids was that there needed to be clear evidence of the existence of business clusters that could form the main pillars of each CGS. The CGS did not involve substantial new money or new programmes, but aimed to align existing resources around a business-oriented strategy.

Initially four pilot projects were selected (St Helens, Nottingham, Plymouth and London, the last of these being split into four separate projects – City Fringe, Haringey, Heathrow City and London South

Central) with a further 10 areas being added in 2004. It remains to be seen to what extent this 'new mindset' takes root in the selected CGS areas and whether the private sector is willing to invest without the kind of financial incentives that were a feature of previous property-led approaches such as the UDCs and Enterprise Zones. The CGS initiative also assumed that business leaders would be willing and able to take actions that go beyond their short-term profit maximisation interests in the interests of the longer-term development of the local economy. However, it appears unlikely that the CGS will prove any more capable than previous approaches of solving the persistent problem of linking areas of opportunity with areas of need, given the disjuncture between the place of residence of poorer people and the location of much business activity (that is, on business parks and in town centres) apparent in a number of first-round CGSs (Convery, 2006, p 323), and the absence of any clear mechanisms to ensure that increases in business activity will benefit marginalised groups (Bertotti, 2008).

The second government policy initiative based on a business-led approach to economic regeneration takes up the notion that underserved retail markets exist in many deprived urban economies. Launched in 2002, the 'Under-Served Markets' (USM) project aims to use private investment in various consumer service sectors as a catalyst for the economic regeneration of deprived inner-city communities, based on successful US examples. The most quoted of these include the Magic Johnson theatre complexes, which have been successfully developed in low-income inner-city areas in Atlanta, Los Angeles and New York, and the Pathmark grocery store chain, which has pursued a strategy of using relatively low-cost sites in inner-city areas to develop a product mix customised to the particularities of inner-city consumers (Porter, 1997; Cobb, 2001; BIC, 2002a). In the UK context there are a number of examples of the involvement of private sector companies in regeneration schemes, the best known being the investment of Tesco in Seacroft (Leeds) and Sainsbury's in Castle Vale (Birmingham) (BIC, 2002b). The USM project involves securing the support of brand retailers, developers and financiers to take the lead in investing in a deprived area to provide goods and services for residents of all incomes and backgrounds and in so doing, creating employment opportunities for the disadvantaged within the labour market (Dunford, 2006). The increase in customer numbers (footfall) is then expected to benefit other businesses in the locality, in what has been described as a 'halo effect' (BIC, 2005). The USM project also assumes that 'inward investment' in the form of property and retail development will stimulate endogenous investment via various mechanisms, such as giving local small businesses greater confidence to invest in the area and creating local supply-chain and procurement opportunities. These assumptions are somewhat counterintuitive, given that large retail chains and superstores frequently force smaller retailers out of business and result in profits and spending being transferred out of the local economy (Dixon, 2005).

After conducting research on the market potential of various deprived localities, four pilot USM projects were selected in 2003: Bradford, Oldham, and both Lewisham and Waltham Forest in London. In the case of Oldham, the USM project aims to support the local council's efforts to revitalise the town centre as well as contributing to the regeneration of a district retail centre in Failsworth, a deprived neighbourhood, where the intention is that a new Tesco food store becomes the catalyst for further private sector investment. There is to date no clear evidence as to the positive economic impacts of the investments in these four pilot projects, especially in the longer term. However, fundamental concerns do remain as to whether markets within deprived neighbourhoods in UK inner-city areas offer the same potential market attractions as those in the US, given that levels of private sector disinvestment are rarely as extreme.

Social inclusion and enterprise policy

A central strand of thinking under successive New Labour governments has been a belief in the enterprise potential of deprived communities and the need to remove the barriers that stand in the way of people going into self-employment or starting a new business venture. While it is quite common for people to have to overcome various obstacles to starting a new business or self-employment, those living in deprived communities invariably face additional barriers, some of which are specific to the circumstances of particular social groups while others may be more pervasive, for example lack of confidence or lack of awareness of the support that is available. Table 4.3 identifies the barriers that different social groups typically face as well as some of the positive attributes contributing to their enterprise potential. It is the case that the nature and strength of these barriers and the factors influencing enterprise potential will also be influenced by specific local circumstances. For example, the lack of an 'enterprise culture' in former coalfield areas acts to compound existing barriers to entry into self-employment compared with some inner-city locations where a tradition of small business and entrepreneurial activity provides greater encouragement. Similarly, workless people living in deprived rural areas may face greater barriers to starting a business in the form of low population densities and limited local markets than those living in coastal towns that attract large numbers of visitors.

Within the government's vision that it is possible to release the productivity and economic potential of deprived neighbourhoods by means of animating entrepreneurship in places that have a weak

Table 4.3: Factors affecting the entrepreneurial potential of disadvantaged groups and communities

Disadvantaged group	Barriers	Positive attributes
BME groups	• Access to finance (especially Afro-Caribbean groups) • Cultural/religious barriers (some Muslim groups) • Tendency to concentrate in crowded sectors	• Particular skills/ qualifications • Social capital (supportive networks) • Tradition of enterprise (especially some Asian groups)
New in-migrants	• Language barriers • Access to finance • Lack of familiarity with UK regulatory requirements	• Strong work ethic, ambitious and energetic • Previous experience of self-employment • Usually young/healthy • Particular skills/ qualifications • Prepared to take risks
Lone parents	• Childcare responsibility • Lack of capital • Isolation	• Resilience/initiative required to raise children alone • Attracted by flexible working arrangements
Long-term unemployed	• Lack of capital • Lack of employability • Lack of confidence and motivation • Isolation from social and business networks • Benefits trap	• 'Latent' skills
People with disabilities (physical and mental)	• Disability and related prejudice/social stigma • Access to finance • Benefits trap • Lack of specific support provision	• Flexibility of working from home • Motivated not to be held back by disability and related discrimination
Ex-offenders	• Criminal record • No capital • Lack of skills/ qualifications	• Possible entrepreneurial skills developed in the informal/illegal economy

enterprise culture, the agendas of enterprise development and social inclusion have become inextricably linked (Blackburn and Ram, 2006). A Department of Trade and Industry (DTI) report (Small Business Service, 2004, p 54) set out the government's position:

> The government's main objective in encouraging more enterprise in disadvantaged communities and under-represented groups is to increase the overall rate of business start-up and growth. This objective forms part of a wider government agenda to address social exclusion, whether this is caused by lack of access (disadvantage) or a lack of resources (deprivation).

In other words, by focusing on enterprise development in deprived areas the government is aiming to address both its economic competitiveness and social inclusion agendas simultaneously. One of the government's key Public Service Agreement (PSA) targets thus became the creation of 'more enterprise in deprived areas' (DTI PSA 6iii), aimed at bringing levels of new business formation in the most deprived areas closer to the national average. Regional and local bodies (particularly Regional Development Agencies, local authorities and Local Strategic Partnerships [LSPs]) were urged to identify and realise the enterprise potential of deprived communities, to remove the barriers to enterprise and to provide better access to business support and finance. HM Treasury emerged as a particularly strong proponent within government of the enterprise agenda in deprived areas, even to the extent of designating 1,997 of the most deprived wards in the UK as 'Enterprise Areas' in 2002 – a designation that reflected government aspirations rather than the reality in most of these areas. As Enterprise Areas they were eligible for various incentives to encourage enterprise, notably exemptions from Stamp Duty to stimulate local property markets, fast-track planning, and the Community Investment Tax Relief to improve access to finance.

Certain central government initiatives have sought to specifically address and promote this relationship between enterprise and social exclusion (HM Treasury, 1999). One of the first was the creation of the Phoenix Development Fund (PDF) in 1999, with the aim of encouraging innovative ideas to promote and support enterprise among disadvantaged groups and in deprived areas. The PDF, which ran until 2006, supported 95 projects over its first four years, which purported to encourage experimentation and to spread best practice. Many of the projects involved 'outreach' to particular BME groups, mentoring and coaching, client contact and follow-up, networking and training. The 95 PDF projects claimed to have helped 12,101 individuals to think about setting up in enterprise, of whom 2,770 had actually started and 3,175 had been helped to expand their enterprise, most of these being micro enterprises (GHK, 2004). Social enterprises featured prominently in many of the projects and accounted for a large share of the employment that was generated, although much of it was part time or unpaid. A further element of the PDF was the provision of £20 million of support to Community Development Finance Institutions, which were addressing market imperfections in the provision of finance to new and existing enterprises, particularly those run by entrepreneurs from disadvantaged groups.

However, despite multiple initiatives giving greater prominence to an enterprise-led approach to regeneration from the late 1990s, the government became concerned that too little attention was being paid to this aspect at the local level. In an effort to stimulate a greater commitment to supporting enterprise on the part of local authorities and other local stakeholders, a further initiative was launched in 2005 to stimulate enterprise activity in the most deprived areas. The 'Local Enterprise Growth Initiative' (LEGI) had the stated aim of releasing 'the productivity and economic potential of our most deprived local areas and their inhabitants through enterprise and investment – thereby boosting local incomes and employment opportunities' (HM Treasury, 2005a, p 47). This translated into three specific outcomes:

- to increase total entrepreneurial activity among the population in deprived local areas;
- to support the sustainable growth, and reduce the failure rate, of locally owned business in deprived local areas; and
- to attract appropriate inward investment and franchising into deprived areas, making use of local labour resources.

The government originally committed £50 million to LEGI in 2006/07, rising to £150 million per year by 2008/09, although this was subsequently cut back as part of the government's 2007 spending review. Unlike several previous initiatives to stimulate enterprise in deprived areas, LEGI gives local partners the freedom to best determine local needs, options and targeted solutions for enterprise development, this being consistent with the aim to devolve the lead role and responsibility for much business and skills development towards local government (Convery, 2006, p 322). The 10 local authorities that successfully applied for LEGI in the first round received up to £10 million to spend on local enterprise development projects.

Analysis of the successful first-round LEGI bids shows the kinds of activities that were being proposed to stimulate enterprise in deprived areas (Tables 4.4 and 4.5). All 10 successful bids proposed giving advice and support to existing businesses and all but one to new start-up businesses as well. Initiatives aimed at developing enterprise awareness and an enterprise culture were common as were those directed at enterprise education, with all 10 bids including initiatives targeted at children and young people. Other initiatives concerned improving access to finance, the provision of space, and supporting local procurement. A common feature of many of the projects was that they involved outreach activities and provided 'grassroots' support at the neighbourhood scale, making explicit reference to targeting underrepresented groups such as women or various minority groups. Given the aim for initiatives to be appropriate to specific local contexts, it is significant that 'the best bids, especially in low employment areas, were those demonstrating a good connection to the labour market and to plans for growing local employment in addition to boosting enterprise' (Convery, 2006, p 324). This relation to local context is well illustrated by the LEGI programme relating to the three district councils of Ashfield, Bolsover and Mansfield in the East Midlands (see Box 4.3).

Table 4.4: Types of intervention in successful Round 1 LEGI bids

	Enterprise education	Enterprise awareness/culture	Business advice/support: new starts	Business advice/support: existing businesses	Provision of business premises	Access to finance	Training provision	Supporting local procurement/supply chains	Attract inward investment	Target sectors/clusters	Access to employment/skills	Travel to work	Place marketing	Franchising
Ashfield, Mansfield, Bolsover	✓	✓	✓	✓	✓	✓		✓			✓	✓		
Barking and Dagenham	✓	✓	✓	✓	✓	✓								✓
Bradford	✓	✓	✓	✓	✓	✓								
Coventry	✓	✓	✓	✓	✓	✓	✓	✓	✓		✓			
Croydon	✓	✓	✓	✓	✓	✓		✓			✓		✓	✓
Durham County	✓	✓	✓	✓	✓	✓		✓		✓				✓
Great Yarmouth	✓		✓	✓		✓	✓	✓	✓		✓		✓	
Hastings and Bexhill		✓	✓	✓	✓		✓	✓		✓				
St Helens	✓	✓	✓	✓		✓		✓	✓			✓	✓	
South Tyneside		✓		✓										
Total	8	9	9	10	7	8	3	7	3	2	4	2	3	3

Table 4.5: Social groups targeted in successful Round 1 LEGI bids

	Young people/ children	Refugees	Women	Schools/teachers/ governors	Ethnic minorities	Disabled	Incapacity Benefit claimants	Workless families/ unemployed	Under 30s and over 50s
Ashfield, Mansfield, Bolsover	✓		✓			✓			
Barking and Dagenham	✓		✓	✓	✓	✓	✓		
Bradford	✓		✓	✓	✓	✓	✓	✓	✓
Coventry	✓							✓	
Croydon	✓		✓		✓	✓			
Durham County	✓		✓			✓		✓	
Great Yarmouth	✓			✓					
Hastings and Bexhill									
St Helens	✓		✓			✓			
South Tyneside	✓								
Total	10	1	7	3	5	6	3	4	2

Box 4.3: Ashfield, Bolsover and Mansfield LEGI

These three district councils made a successful bid for LEGI funds under Round 1 of the government's programme, receiving £7.2 million in 2006 to be spread over a six-year period. The programme is based on two principal concepts, these being the delivery of neighbourhood level outreach support to new and already established businesses to link local people to new employment opportunities, and the creation of longer-term benefit through developing a new culture of local enterprise. Using the umbrella title 'The Alliance Enterprise Exchange', initiatives were organised into five workstreams (Smith, 2006):

(1) *Promoting an entrepreneurial ethos* aims to reverse the area's lack of an enterprise culture resulting from its historic dependency on the coalmining and textile industries. A key initiative here is a 'Virtual Enterprise Academy' aimed at linking business with young people in schools, developing enterprise skills among 14- to 19-year-olds, and raising the aspirations to start an enterprise among residents of deprived neighbourhoods. The Academy acts as a hub for tutors to work closely with outreach and mentoring workers.

(2) The *Making the Connection* initiative aims to link employers such as inward investors and expanding businesses with local people, via training and access initiatives, in an effort to widen employment opportunities in deprived neighbourhoods and to reduce levels of worklessness.

(3) *Business and Social Enterprise Support* aims to enhance the performance of new and existing businesses and social enterprises and includes a one-to-one business counselling service based on the successful 'Bizfizz' business coaching programme that had run in Bolsover. This involves outreach business support tailored to the needs and potential within particular deprived neighbourhoods. Support in the form of assisting small businesses with access to finance comes in the form of two new Community Development Finance Initiatives.

(4) *Business Realm* is concerned with the physical infrastructure to support new and small enterprises, including the provision of suitable business properties via the development of property accommodation ladders in deprived neighbourhoods.

(5) *Procurement* involves the creation of a local supply-chain network to enable smaller businesses to compete more effectively for public sector procurement contracts.

Conclusions

There are significant spatial variations in levels of enterprise activity and business start-up, with deprived areas demonstrating lower levels of start-up and survival. Reducing the enterprise gap between deprived areas and more affluent areas is seen by government as essential to achieving national and regional economic growth targets and reducing regional disparities. Yet seeking to foster enterprise and entrepreneurship and place it at the heart of the neighbourhood renewal process produces a number of dilemmas for policy makers. Not least of these concerns is how to embed and retain indigenous and exogenous enterprise within a deprived area in a manner that produces sustainable benefits to its residents.

A central feature of the current enterprise policy agenda with respect to disadvantaged areas is the attempt to simultaneously pursue both economic and social objectives underwritten by significantly different, and often competing, rationales for intervention. Whereas some previous policy approaches were single-minded in their pursuit of enterprise development and private sector investment in order to revive run-down inner-city economies, recent government policy has sought to stimulate enterprise activities and release entrepreneurial talent both as a way of reviving the economic competitiveness of marginalised economies and combating social and economic exclusion. Yet as the discussion of various types of enterprise activity in relation to deprived neighbourhoods has shown, ambiguities and tensions between these objectives often arise, making it difficult to arrive at unequivocal conclusions about the impact and utility of policy interventions.

The joint pursuit of economic growth and social inclusion objectives can be achieved in certain circumstances, as for example where growing minority ethnic enterprises embed themselves in deprived communities and draw their labour and supplies from them, rather than relocating elsewhere. Yet there are also frequent cases of conflict, as for example where recruitment practices of enterprises moving into an area prevent local people accessing newly generated jobs, or where the creation of marginal, low value-added enterprises in highly competitive sectors has the effect of pushing others out of business and into unemployment. Such conflicts reflect fundamental differences in principles informing policy development. Whereas the pursuit of inner-city competitiveness (for example via the CGS) is rooted within a neoliberal model of pro-business market-led growth, the rationale for the development of social enterprises is rooted within varying conceptions of the social economy. Positions here range from those that see social enterprise as an effective means of meeting social needs through providing socially useful products and services, to those that view social enterprise as a core component of a different model of socialised, self-reliant local economic development, which eschews conventional forms of economic development. Consequently, it is important to clarify and differentiate these various positions and their relation to different types of enterprise activity before embarking on a particular course of policy.

In seeking to use enterprise within deprived areas as a means of promoting economic competitiveness, past and current practice demonstrates a number of important points. First, the economic development of deprived areas achieved by interventions promoting inward investment have, in the past, provided only limited benefits to the population living in these areas. However, given the lack of indigenous business within deprived areas and the problems of stimulating its development, drawing in business from outside remains an attractive policy option. It is notable in this respect that despite the emphasis of government policy on indigenous development, initiatives such as CGS, USM and LEGI all recognise roles for inward investors. In policy practice there is considerable potential to develop mechanisms that better root incoming enterprises into the local economy through requirements to recruit and source locally, but to date these remain underdeveloped and in their absence the majority of the economic benefits from incoming business will continue to leak out of the local economy.

Second, one of the key conclusions arising from research on new and small enterprises in deprived areas is the need to generate better-quality enterprises, run by people with the entrepreneurial qualities to be successful in business. A disproportionate number of those going into self-employment or setting up a business in deprived neighbourhoods are pushed into it by the difficulties of accessing mainstream employment, including facing overt discrimination, and do little more than imitate existing businesses rather than starting something that is innovative, niche focused and capable of growth. A key policy challenge is therefore to stimulate better-quality and more innovative enterprises capable of growth in deprived areas but this is largely conditional on changes at the level of individuals and households. This requires making improvements in educational attainment, skill development and entrepreneurial awareness, particularly among the younger generation who have not traditionally been targeted under past initiatives. In this respect, successful enterprise development in deprived localities cannot be divorced from other aspects of the renewal of deprived neighbourhoods and their residents.

With regard to the use of enterprise to tackle social exclusion and promote cohesion, it is important to recognise that enterprise activity in deprived neighbourhoods can exacerbate social problems, through the provision of low-quality goods, services and working conditions, or the negative impacts on confidence and income of business failure. However, aside from providing a source of income, employment and skills, there are clearly many wider social and community benefits that flow from enterprise and entrepreneurial activity – from building the confidence of individuals through to the development of community networks and social capital. Narrow policy evaluations frequently fail to capture these wider benefits. The fact that a new business only survives for a year may be regarded as a 'failure' from a strictly economic perspective, yet it may have contributed to the development of human and social capital within the local population if those involved gain skills, experience and networks that help them in a later business venture or make them more employable. Furthermore, the time period over which any evaluation of impact takes place is also crucial, given that entrepreneurs and business owners frequently experience initial failures, which provide the learning necessary for subsequent success.

The governance arrangements and policy delivery mechanisms for enterprise-based interventions in deprived neighbourhoods display two characteristics worthy of comment. First, all interventions feature an attempt to get business and the private sector either to lead the development process, or at least to be centrally involved. Although the private sector has responded positively to ABIs oriented around a strong economic growth agenda with clear benefits to business (such as the property-led developments of the 1980s), where the policy agenda seeks to engage business around a wider social benefit, engagement is more limited, often restricted to a relatively small number of larger firms.

Second, the constant stream of ABIs again displays recognition by central government of the relative failure of mainstream business support to reach disadvantaged neighbourhoods and individuals. However, the parachuting of these locally targeted central government initiatives into deprived areas – in a number of cases via policy transfer from the US – has meant that they frequently struggle to adjust to local circumstances. Alternative approaches, such as the Local Alchemy project in the East Midlands, demonstrate a more bottom-up strategy for stimulating enterprise activity, and the LEGI initiative does mark a move towards an approach where local authorities are charged with developing their own priorities on the basis of local economic analysis. Certainly, the more successful enterprise support initiatives within deprived areas have demonstrated the importance of outreach activity, operating through community-based advisors who are sensitive to different community groups and recognise the particularities of the local business context (Swash, 2007). The possibilities and constraints for developing a more locally sensitive governance framework with regard to the economic development of deprived neighbourhoods is the focus for the next chapter.

Notes

[1] An important proviso in the use of VAT registration rates to measure business formation is that it excludes at least half of new businesses because it is confined to those that are above the VAT payment threshold (a sales turnover of £67,000 in 2008/09). Thus, new business formation in the most deprived areas is likely to be underrepresented by this analysis as the business population comprises a higher proportion of very small businesses than is the case elsewhere.

[2] There is a conceptual debate as to what constitutes BMEBs and whether they should be defined on the basis of sole ownership, shared ownership, the ethnicity of the majority of workers, the types of products and markets and so on. In most of the studies referred to here,

BMEBs are those businesses that are substantially owned by members of one or more BME communities, irrespective of their workers and their customer base for the product or service being offered.

[3] The GEM focuses on the role played by individuals in the entrepreneurial process in order to calculate an index of total entrepreneurial activity for each country. This comprises people thinking of starting an entrepreneurial venture, those involved in setting up an enterprise, new business owners (that is, businesses in existence for up to 42 months) and established business owners and managers (that is, businesses in existence for more than 42 months).

[4] *The Brixton Disorders 10–12 April 1981, Report of an Inquiry by the Rt Hon the Lord Scarman*, Cmnd 8427 (HMSO, 1981).

FIVE

Institutions and governance: integrating and coordinating policy

Introduction

The previous two chapters have analysed an array of labour market and enterprise policy interventions that have developed in relation to deprived neighbourhoods and demonstrated their often limited effectiveness. In seeking to better understand the reasons why these policies have had only a restricted impact, part of the explanation relates to the nature of the governance structures and institutional arrangements responsible for their development and implementation. In this respect, progressing and delivering effective policy to tackle the economic problems of deprived neighbourhoods generates particular challenges. First, tackling multiple and reinforcing elements of deprivation concentrated within a given locality requires integrating multiple policy objectives and agendas often characterised by significant differences and tensions. Second, as the economic problems of deprived areas are rooted within processes operating at wider spatial scales but also require responses tailored and implemented with sensitivity to local difference, policy responses need to be coordinated across and within different spatial levels.

This chapter explores the governance and institutional terrain within the British context to explore how these two related factors – integration of differing policy agendas and coordination across and within spatial levels – have influenced the nature and effectiveness of the policy response. First, the chapter outlines the institutional structures and governance arrangements responsible for delivering economic development to deprived neighbourhoods. Consideration then turns to the issues raised by integrating differing rationales and policy agendas related to economic interventions in deprived neighbourhoods set out in Chapter One, and the extent of coherence and tension within these agendas is examined in relation to the role of different government departments and mainstream policies. Second, the chapter turns to consider the issue of different levels of intervention, examining the rationales for intervention at different spatial scales and how different types of activities have been pursued at varying neighbourhood, local, subregional, city-regional and national levels. The chapter then moves on to specify the principal barriers to policy integration and coordination and how these vary locally, and concludes by identifying key issues related to governance arrangements and policy delivery in relation to the economic development of disadvantaged areas.

The institutional and governance context: complexity, fragmentation and decentralisation

Central features of the governance structures and institutional arrangements in relation to subnational economic development and regeneration activity in the British context are their complexity and constant evolution. This situation generates deep-seated problems of fragmentation, duplication and instability. The complex governance and institutional context partly relates to the multidimensional nature of the challenges posed by the economic and related problems of deprived neighbourhoods but also reflects the particular evolution of the economic and urban governance system since the early 1980s. Successive government reports have argued for the need for greater clarity and simplification over such arrangements, most recently in the publication of a major review by the Treasury (HM Treasury et al, 2007). Yet a notable feature of the period of New Labour government is that rather than reducing complexity, the array of policy initiatives outlined in earlier chapters, and the development of different scales and forms of governance, have reproduced and further added to institutional complexity.

The multidimensional nature of the economic challenge presented by concentrated deprivation requires the involvement of a number of different government departments and institutions (see Figure 5.1). In the British context, this includes a role for the Department for Business, Enterprise and Regulatory Reform (DBERR) (formerly the Department of Trade and Industry) with overall responsibility for issues related to enterprise and inward investment, the Department for Work and Pensions (DWP) and the Department for Innovation, Universities and Skills (DIUS) with responsibility together for skills, employment and post-16 education, and the Department of Communities and Local Government (DCLG) with responsibility for local government and subnational governance in cities and regions as well as planning and housing.[1] In addition, at various points over time, the Prime Minister's

Strategy Unit has taken a lead interest in social exclusion and the neighbourhood renewal agenda, and the Treasury has taken an active interest in relation to enterprise and employment within deprived areas. Other government departments have also had varying degrees of involvement in the economic development of disadvantaged areas, in particular issues of transport, education, health and community cohesion (for example, the Department of Transport [DoT], the Department for Children, Schools and Families [DCSF], the Home Office and the Department of Health). Each of the main government departments has developed its own set of mainstream and area-based policies and associated funding arrangements, which has led to the existence of multiple funding streams within local areas. This not only creates considerable local-level complexity but also real potential for a lack of coordination between agencies and the duplication of services.

The evolution of governance arrangements with respect to economic development and regeneration within Britain reflects wider changes in the nature of governance. The development of urban policy in the 1980s and early 1990s saw a shift towards a model that combined strong central government control with an emphasis on local delivery involving an ever-expanding range of locally and regionally based non-elected actors (see Chapter One). This was characterised by a proliferation of quasi public/private sector organisations (such as the Training and Enterprise Councils and Business Links) and partnership-based delivery of economic regeneration policies that were increasingly organised around a competitive bidding process (for example, City Challenge, the Single Regeneration Budget [SRB], European Union [EU] Structural Funds). With the power of local government attacked and reduced by Conservative governments in the 1980s, a system of 'competitive localism' emerged, with contestation between local and central government and between local authorities and a variety of quasi-governmental agencies involved in economic regeneration, which led to increased fragmentation in provision (Robson et al, 1994; Stewart, 1994).

In response to the lack of coordination and strategic capacity of these governance arrangements and their limited legitimacy and accountability, the incoming New Labour government set about introducing a wider programme of constitutional reform. This aimed to ensure that functions were carried out at the appropriate level and that regions were better able to respond to the particular opportunities and challenges they faced (Cabinet Office and DTLR, 2002). The new settlement that has been put in place in the UK since 1997 has seen a strongly unitary and centralised state devolve varying degrees of power

Figure 5.1: Governance structure relating to enterprise, employment and neighbourhood renewal, 1997–2007

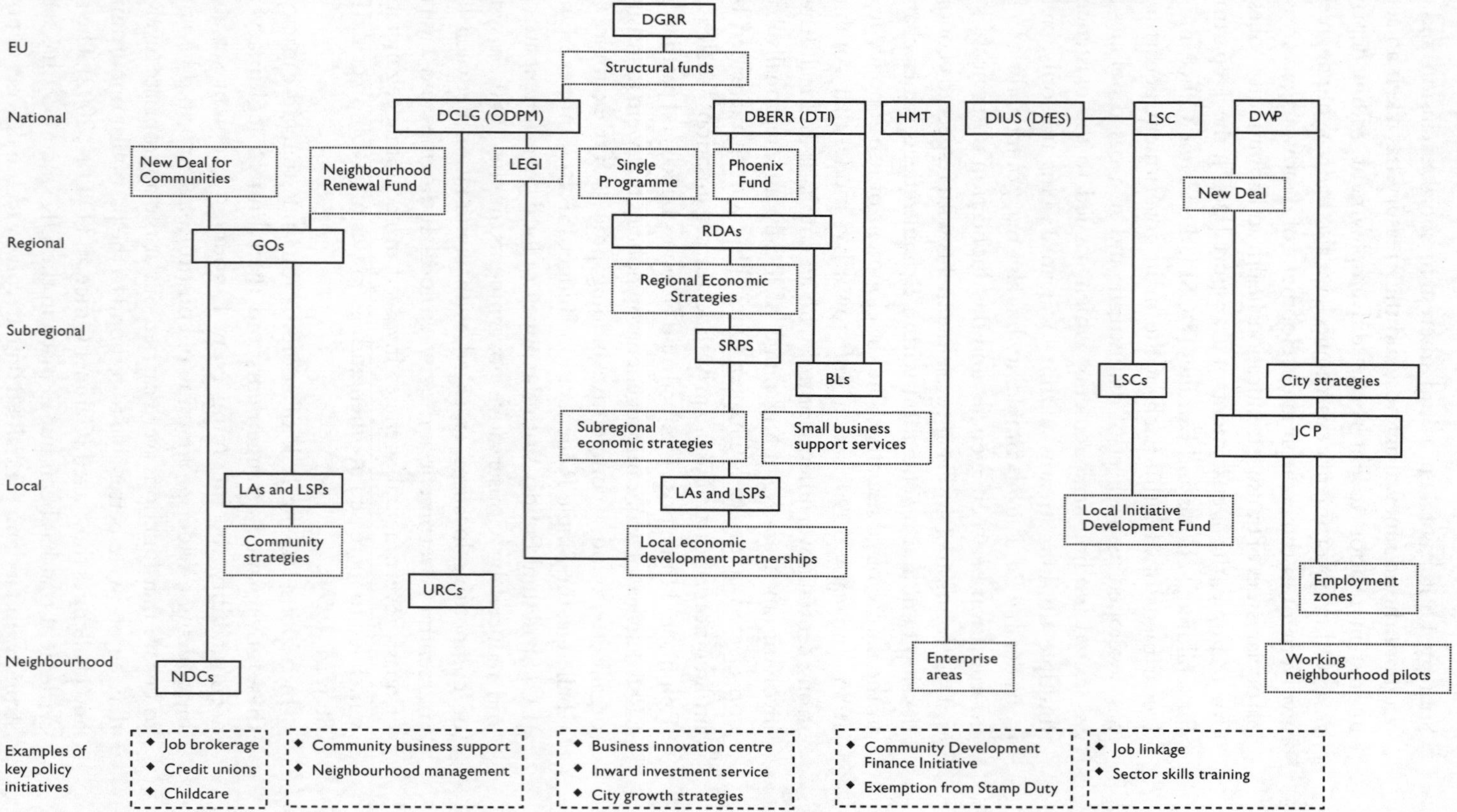

to an elected Parliament in Scotland, and elected Assemblies in Wales and Northern Ireland, and an elected Mayor and Assembly in London. The government also introduced a limited decentralisation of administrative functions and decision-making power to the English regions, notably through the development of Regional Development Agencies (RDAs) with their primary duty to improve regional competitiveness (North et al, 2007). Furthermore, local government reforms have sought to promote greater responsiveness of local government to the needs of local communities through the development of various forms of neighbourhood management (Smith et al, 2007).

These processes of change since the 1980s have produced complex sets of subnational economic governance arrangements, which extend both horizontally and vertically and involve private, voluntary and community and public sector activities, often with limited levels of democratic accountability (Robson et al, 2000). The level of complexity has further been exacerbated by the pace of change, with a constant introduction of new and variant governance forms and institutional entities, and the lack of co-terminosity of boundaries. In this latter respect, different government departments and policies continue to operate to differently delimited geographical areas while the workings of local, city and regional economies rarely map well onto existing institutional boundaries.

The scalar relationships between various spatial levels of governance and the main agencies, programmes and policies relating to economic development and neighbourhood renewal are illustrated in Figure 5.1. This complex institutional context does provide spaces for proactive local institutions to mobilise resources from an array of sources, but it also presents challenges for the integration of policy agendas and the coordination of interventions across and within different spatial levels, and these issues will be considered in more detail in the following sections.

Integrating the policy agenda

Despite a much-vaunted commitment to 'joined-up' government by successive New Labour administrations, the experience of policy development and implementation with respect to disadvantaged neighbourhoods has demonstrated considerable constraints in delivering this in practice. These constraints are rooted both in the problems of integrating policies that display inherent contradictions rooted in conflicting rationales for intervention, as well as the problems of integrating action across multiple government departments and institutions that are pursuing their own interests and policy agendas.

Rationales for intervention: tensions and contradictions

At the heart of the New Labour political project has been an attempt to couple the pursuit of a pro-market, neoliberal-inspired economic growth model that seeks to develop a strong national economy capable of competing successfully within a highly competitive global economy, with a commitment to promoting an inclusive and cohesive society through tackling the multiple bases of social exclusion. For deprived neighbourhoods this has produced differing rationales for intervention related to economic efficiency and competitiveness, social justice, and community engagement and cohesion (see Chapter One), which generate inherent contradictions – as the discussion of work- and enterprise-related interventions in Chapters Three and Four clearly illustrated. Although the national economy has performed relatively well in terms of macro-economic indicators of growth, particularly in the wider South East, this liberalised, market-based growth model has led to widening social inequality reflected in, and constituted by, spatial inequalities, including areas of concentrated deprivation. The 'success' of this economic growth model has therefore been predicated on the bypassing of certain sections of the population that lack the skills, qualifications, experience and attitudes necessary to secure employment and on the existence of a large section of the workforce being willing to work for low pay in low-skilled and normally insecure employment, principally in the service industries.

Set within this context, policies of neighbourhood renewal that prioritise tackling social exclusion and promoting social equity have been constrained to agendas that seek to ameliorate the situation (for example by improving the competitive position of those not in work within the labour market), and guaranteeing basic levels of welfare provision (for example, in terms of income, public services, quality of the environment and so on). Further contradictions are also apparent with regard to the pursuit of sustainability (where the pursuit of private sector profitability consistently fails to factor in the wider costs and benefits of particular investments within a given area) and community cohesion (where attracting migrant workers to meet labour demands produces challenges of integration both for incoming migrant populations and pre-existing communities).

In recognising the contradictions inherent in the current dominant economic growth model critics argue that in order to tackle social and spatial deprivation more fundamentally, an alternative model of economic development is required. Such alternatives argue that economic development should be seen as a means to an end, rather than an end in itself (Mayo, 1996; Sen, 1999), variously outlining a more localised economic development process focused on achieving a better quality of life and improved social well-being through providing opportunities for personal and community development in an environmentally sustainable manner (Mayo, 1996; Haughton, 1999; Canzanelli, 2001; Williams and Windebank, 2001; Pike et al, 2006b). Fundamental to such social–economy perspectives is thinking about how the economy can serve the interests of society rather than social goals being subsumed by the pursuit of economic growth. Current approaches to tackling concentrated deprivation with their emphasis on entry into formal employment and increased productivity via enterprise are clearly based within the latter view.

Institutional constraints: silos and 'joined-up' working

Beyond the inherent tensions of the current development model that informs policy development are practical difficulties related to attempting to 'join up' the workings of a number of different government departments, operating with different levels of power and pursuing their own policy agendas, targets and interests. Despite the introduction by government of a series of Public Service Agreement (PSA) targets to coordinate activity within and across government departments, the prevalence of a 'silo' mentality remains. The practical problems of 'joining up' activity are evident both within and between departments in Whitehall itself, and in bringing activity together at regional, local and neighbourhood levels. This is evident from the level of strategy formation through to policy delivery in relation to a lack of shared planning, target/outcome setting and resourcing in tackling the problems of deprived localities.

Much of the decentralisation of central government activity in England has been to the regional Government Offices (GOs), originally created in 1994 and given an enhanced role from 2000 onwards, with 10 central government departments establishing a presence within them. The GOs have an important role in improving coordination of government programmes at the regional level, especially those with a strong territorial impact, and have responsibility for most policies and funding streams related to the social and community aspects of regeneration directed at deprived localities. Yet in terms of power, Whitehall departments have retained control over resources and key policy decisions and the GOs operate within the constraints of national divisions between departments (Marsh et al, 2003; Musson et al, 2005). Similarly, at the local and neighbourhood level, where economic development and regeneration activity is largely reliant on funding from mainstream programmes and area-based initiatives (ABIs) emanating from various central government departments, local actors have little choice but to operate within the constraints of these funding streams, linking up activity where they can via local partnership working.

These problems of integration with regard to the economic problems of concentrated deprivation are particularly evident in terms of the relationship between the economic growth and social inclusion agendas, and the development of policy activity in the related fields of employment, skills, enterprise and physically based economic development. Difficulties are also apparent where economic-oriented activity needs to be integrated with other related policy areas, such as housing, education, transport and spatial development. Thus, the DoT is frequently isolated from the regeneration agenda in spite of the importance of transport in connecting people to jobs. Similarly, the Department for Education and Skills (DfES) (now DCSF) with responsibility for school education has had little involvement in issues of neighbourhood renewal, even though school-age education has a fundamental role to play in changing the opportunity structures of young people living in deprived neighbourhoods.

Integration of economic development and social inclusion agendas

Within existing governance arrangements in England, economic competitiveness-focused national and regional economic strategies are developed by the DBERR/DTI and the RDAs, while responsibility for the area-based social exclusion agenda, as exemplified by the National Strategy for Neighbourhood Renewal, lies with the DCLG and regionally through the GOs. In the devolved administrations of Wales and Scotland, similar divisions are evident as both countries have grappled with developing appropriate institutional arrangements and strategies capable of integrating national economic growth agendas with more locally based social inclusion ones. In all cases, the extent and manner of integration between strategies for economic development and social inclusion demonstrates a limited and variable concern towards deprived areas within the array of regional, subregional and national strategies that exist within England, Scotland and Wales (North et al, 2007).

At the regional level within England, Regional Economic Strategies (RESs), first produced in 1999–2000 and subsequently revised, set the direction and priorities for economic development by the RDAs and other key stakeholders. The primary focus of successive RESs has been on how to promote economic and business competitiveness, performance and growth within the region/subregion, with only a marginal concern as to whether more disadvantaged groups and communities directly benefit from this growth. The desire to be market facing and attract and retain private sector involvement for business development and larger regeneration projects has limited the attention paid to issues of community and social benefit. In many respects, thinking has been dominated by notions of 'trickle down' that assume that any benefits of economic and employment growth within the wider regional/subregional economy will work through markets for labour, goods and services to provide opportunities for those living in more deprived areas (see Box 5.1). Justification of this position – not only from the RDAs but also from a range of other actors – is that, given limited resources, RDAs should be single-minded in their objective to improve regional economic performance and competitiveness, leaving distributional questions to other organisations.

Box 5.1: Deprived areas and Regional Economic Strategies and Employment Frameworks in the North East

In the previous versions of the RES for the North East region of England, the main focus was not on deprived areas in the region but on 'opportunity' areas where growth potential could be exploited. As one officer from One NorthEast stated:

> 'In the past the RDA essentially said that the thing we can do for the people of the North East is to improve their economic opportunities and to grow the economy – as we have limited resources the priority is to get more jobs and businesses and more economic activity and let somebody else worry about who benefits from that and all the social issues.'

In the revised RES entitled *Leading the way* (One NorthEast, 2006) there now appears to be a greater focus on deprived areas:

'In focusing on strategic activity to drive up economic participation rates in the region, we must not rely on "trickle down" economics. Rather concerted efforts will be made to link areas of opportunity with areas of disadvantage, and to work with communities to overcome the barriers they face in economic engagement.' (One NorthEast, 2006, p 16)

Significantly, alongside the RES the North East has also developed a Regional Employability Framework (REF), which aims to achieve a more coordinated approach to employment services and a better alignment of funding in efforts to reduce barriers to employment and increase employability. In the North East, the REF focuses on a number of clusters of the most deprived Super Output Areas (SOAs) with the highest levels of economic inactivity.

Regional and related subregional economic strategies have to date predominantly focused on creating a 'knowledge economy', based on high-skilled, high-value-added sectors while routinely ignoring lower-value-added, low-skill service sectors that are crucial to enhancing labour market participation among marginalised groups. For these groups it is the numbers and quality of entry-level jobs and the subsequent possibilities of career progression within these jobs that is important. For those engaged in developing neighbourhood renewal strategies and seeking to deal with problems of worklessness, the high-skill/value-added focus of the economic development strategy provides little basis with which to integrate their activity.

The initial failure of RESs to address the economic needs of deprived areas led to pressure from central government on RDAs to give greater priority to this issue (PMSU, 2005, p 84). The resulting government guidance for the revision of RESs stated that as a framework for the spatial targeting of public investment the RES 'should identify areas or communities with significant problems such as deprivation, inequalities and social exclusion and identify the main social, environmental and economic factors which underlie these issues' (DTI, 2005b, section 29). As a result, much greater attention to deprived areas and the need to reduce intraregional inequalities was apparent in the revised RESs for the English regions produced in 2006. In addition, there is increased recognition from a range of actors within the regions that RESs cannot rely only on 'trickle-down' economics, and that more concerted efforts are needed if economic growth is to benefit areas of disadvantage (see Box 5.1). Yet, given performance to date, there remain doubts among many stakeholders as to how deep this commitment runs. As one respondent from the East Midlands noted: 'If you look at the RES there are lots of good words about social equity, sustainability and communities, but a lot of this is lip service, to be honest – the main thrust of emda [East Midlands Development Agency] is economic development'.

Employment, skills and worklessness

A major challenge for integrating economic and social agendas for those living in deprived neighbourhoods relates to coordinating strategy development and policy delivery in relation to economic development, employment, skills and training at regional and local levels for those not currently in work. Principal responsibility for this agenda lies outside of the DTI/DBERR and DCLG (see Figure 5.1). The DWP takes lead responsibility for employment issues and for Jobcentre Plus, the institution charged with providing help to people to find paid work, while responsibility for training for those over 16 years of age is delivered by the Learning and Skills Council (LSC), formerly part of the DfES and now under the control of the DIUS.

A lack of joint working between these departments nationally and at regional/local levels through RDAs, LSCs and Jobcentre Plus has been evident both at strategic and delivery levels. In this respect the Leitch Review (HM Treasury, 2006b) identified the lack of coordination between the employment and skills agendas and the fragmented service that people receive at the subnational level as major problems. The development of more spatially sensitive strategies has been hampered by the traditional lack of concern for issues of spatial development within many departments. The focus of DWP activity has traditionally been on delivering mainstream employment policies to individuals, with little concern for geographical variations in labour market conditions. Such an approach has made it poorly positioned to respond to local economic differences and link up with local and regional economic development strategies.

In response to these problems there is evidence of evolution in governance arrangements and institutional structures. The government's renewed emphasis on increasing levels of economic and employment participation, driven by the objective of achieving an 80% employment rate nationally, has refocused attention on localised concentrations of people of working age who are out of work and the need to better coordinate labour market responses. The recent production of REFs in several English regions provides evidence of attempts to improve regional strategic coordination of labour market supply- and demand-side issues. At the local level the Leitch Review (HM Treasury, 2006b) recommended the development of a locally integrated employment and skills service capable of developing a full range of support to people in recognition of rapidly changing labour market conditions. Furthermore, the launch of the previously discussed DWP City Strategy Pathfinders initiative in 2006 (see Chapter Three) aimed to better integrate the provision of employment and skills in a manner that was flexible and responsive to the needs of deprived areas.

Yet, despite this shift towards a greater strategic focus at the national, regional and subregional level on concentrated worklessness, to date the delivery of effective initiatives has been limited and sporadic. On the one hand, national policies in relation to employment and skills have struggled to reach the most marginalised populations and places, while on the other, neighbourhood initiatives better placed to reach marginalised groups have remained poorly integrated with mainstream provision. At the same time the delivery of related policy areas – housing, transport and childcare – frequently demonstrates little or no integration with the employment agenda. The difficulties in joining up top-down national policies with localised initiatives sponsored by programmes such as neighbourhood renewal or the New Deal for Communities (NDC) are apparent in all the case study areas (see Box 5.2). Larger regeneration projects frequently fail to include any meaningful attempt to link to the needs of deprived areas, and where there is attention to issues of deprived areas and populations the policy focus is almost exclusively on employability and supply-side interventions. More positively there is evidence that an increasing number of local and subregional initiatives are seeking to put in place concrete mechanisms to link residents and businesses in deprived areas to new development opportunities.

Box 5.2: Oldham: joining up local and neighbourhood-level programmes

The government's evaluation of the NDC programme drew attention to the critical importance of the relationship between local authorities and NDC partnerships (CRESR, 2005). Not only does the link with local authorities ensure an element of local accountability, but the delivery of the NDC partnership's policies is likely to depend on the actions of various local government departments. Local authorities are also in a good position to foster partnerships with other organisations, including Local Strategic Partnerships (LSPs). However, there has often been a difficult and tense relationship between local authorities and LSPs, on the one hand, and NDC partnerships, on the other, although the evidence points to improving relationships across the programme as a whole (CRESR, 2005).

Oldham illustrates the difficulties of achieving joined-up working between the local authority and the NDC. From a local government perspective, the Hathershaw and Fitton Hill NDC partnership has been perceived as being 'out on a limb' and somewhat parochial, paying little regard to the strategies of the LSP, whereas for their part, the NDC officers have encountered a number of difficulties in relating to the local governance and management structure. While the NDC partnership wanted to be autonomous from the Council, it found that it was unable to deliver projects without the Council's support and skills (for example in relation to land and physical environment issues). For its part, the Council has been much happier with the organisational structure for the Housing Market Renewal Fund programme as it has more involvement (for example a seat on the Board) and feels that its structure fits in better with the LSP and community partnership working.

Whether a more integrated and spatially sensitive agenda in tackling worklessness can emerge in the English context in the future remains open to question. In delivery terms, although there is now better appreciation of what works in tackling worklessness in deprived areas (see Chapter Three), a shift towards more locally based personalised delivery will require additional resources to the routine delivery of mainstream services. At the same time as the DWP is supporting a more locally sensitive way of operating under its City Strategy initiative, it is also cutting back frontline staff within Jobcentre Plus in order to reduce costs and moving towards the provision of employment-related services via large private sector providers, as recommended in the Freud Report (DWP, 2007a).

At the strategic level the lack of integration between national-level policies towards tackling worklessness, on the one hand, and the pursuit of national economic growth, on the other, has real consequences for the development paths of deprived neighbourhoods and their residents. This is well exemplified by the national strategy of 'managed migration' to address skill deficiencies and fill labour shortages in order to improve national economic competitiveness (Home Office, 2005). This approach has focused on the positive economic impacts of immigration as a cheap and effective means of maintaining economic growth through expanding the labour supply. However, despite these net national-scale economic benefits, large-scale in-migration has created strong competition for entry-level jobs, which has in certain local economies made it more difficult for the least competitive in the labour market to gain access to low-wage employment (Gordon et al, 2007; Green et al, 2007).

Coordinating spatial levels of intervention

In the UK, the development of a complex, multilayered governance structure and a range of public and quasi-public organisations has ensured that the issue of different levels of governance and their responsibility for economic development policy has become a central concern of government (HM Treasury et al, 2007). Debate relates not only to identifying the most appropriate level at which to formulate and deliver various economic development functions, but also to clarifying what organisations at each level are seeking to achieve in terms of tackling the economic problems of deprived neighbourhoods, their means of achieving it and the extent of their legitimacy and accountability.

Identifying appropriate levels of intervention

As the underlying economic processes that lead to concentrated deprivation predominantly operate at higher spatial scales, the development of a range of policy interventions at the level at which different markets (for example, for labour, investment and so on) function is required. Yet attempting to develop a policy framework that neatly relates different spatial scales with different types of intervention is problematic. Economic processes operate within and through space. Local processes constitute wider national and global processes so attempting a simple scalar reading of economic change is neither possible nor desirable. The contextual nature of economic development and concentrated deprivation means that there is neither an 'optimal' level for any particular intervention nor only one way in which different governance levels can develop and implement spatially informed economic policies.

Despite these limitations, there is clearly a need within policy development and implementation for greater thought concerning the manner in which economies operate across spatial scales and at what level interventions are best developed and implemented. This is important not only to clarify the potential scope and impact of such interventions but also to provide a basis against which to evaluate critically the confusion of current policy initiatives. Table 5.1 sets out different spatial scales and the economic development interventions most appropriate at these scales. In the absence of any simple relationship between scale and types of intervention there is necessarily considerable overlap between different types of activity at different spatial levels. However, with regard to certain activities – such as active engagement with workless populations at the neighbourhood level, or the pursuit of innovation policy at national and regional levels – there is greater clarity concerning the most appropriate intervention level. Also of critical importance is the extent to which the different levels identified actually relate in any meaningful way to the operation of local, subregional, city and regional economies. In practice, the inflexible formalised spatial units of subnational governance normally have only a limited relationship with the operation of constantly evolving and overlapping economically functional areas. However, where there is a degree of 'fit', this provides greater scope for meaningful economic action.

The relationship between different spatial levels and their relationship to different types of economic activity raises a number of issues for consideration with regard to tackling the economic problems of deprived neighbourhoods. The first issue relates to the overall capacity of these different levels to tailor economic policies to the particular economic needs of very different deprived neighbourhoods. Even where policy development may be more appropriate at a higher spatial level (for example at the level of the subregion or city with regard to labour markets), the implementation and delivery of such policies still need to be tailored to particular local needs (for example via employability programmes). The second issue relates to the potential for negative externalities, displacement effects and the promotion of place-based competition to result from interventions pursued at different spatial levels, which may have negative impacts on wider local, regional or national interests. For example, the pursuit of inward investors by multiple localities within the same region, or indeed by multiple regions within the same country, can lead to a 'zero-sum game' leading to a wasteful duplication of resources where the success of one area is only at the expense of another. Third, economies of scale and scope exist in the implementation of policy responses, with higher levels of government able to offer access to more specialised and knowledgeable staff and realise cost savings through delivering large volumes of public goods and services. For example, the development of high-quality educational and training materials or a highly professional inward investment service is more likely to be achieved at a national/regional level. In contrast, multiple localised initiatives related to such areas may produce lower-quality materials or services while also wastefully duplicating activity. Finally, where there are multiple interventions across different spatial scales, the capacity of the governance system to coordinate and integrate these effectively becomes a major issue.

Table 5.1: Levels of economic intervention

Neighbour-hood	Engagement with diverse populations and 'marginalised' groups; development of social economy; development of community-based economic capacities
	• *employment/skills*: outreach/engagement role; personalised and accessible information and support; making job ready; basic skills; job brokerage; intermediate labour markets
	• *enterprise*: outreach/engagement role; personalised and accessible information and support; self-employment; formalisation initiatives; community/social enterprises; credit unions; Local Exchange Trading Systems (LETS).
Local	Local economic intelligence particularly related to supply and demand; engagement with diverse populations and 'marginalised' groups; coordination of economic development programmes with social provision; engagement with local employers (particularly in key economic sectors); engagement with voluntary and community sector; physical regeneration including land development, planning and infrastructure provision
	• *employment/skills*: delivery of employment policy; coordinate and regulate local training providers; integrate employment and skills provision; oversee outreach/engagement role; basic skills provision; job brokerage; intermediate labour markets;
	• *enterprise*: delivery of enterprise policy; local business support via information and advice; provision of land and premises; incubation units for start-up businesses; oversee local outreach/engagement role; enterprise initiatives with local schools; community/social enterprise; formalisation initiatives; LETS; supply chains.
Sub-regional	Demand/supply issues particularly related to local labour markets/travel to work areas and deprived areas; skills/sectoral forecasting; job-creation activity (business parks; regeneration projects); engagement with local employers; coordination with planning, housing and transport policy; cluster/sector policy; place promotion; major events
	• *employment/skills*: labour market intelligence; coordination of employment and skills policies; engagement with local employers (eg, training needs); initiatives related to local labour market conditions (eg, sector specific)
	• *enterprise*: land and property provision; business parks; business retention; enterprise development; inward investment activity; supply chains.

Table 5.1: Levels of economic intervention (continued)

Regional	Strategy development; forecasting of skills/employment needs and business needs; innovation and technological development for key clusters/sectors; job creation via major physical development and regeneration projects and inward investment; coordination with transport, planning and housing strategy/policy • *employment/skills*: labour market intelligence (supply and demand); coordination of employment and skill policies; engagement with major employers; development of appropriate vocational qualifications; engagement with universities • *enterprise*: inward investment; place promotion; provision of major business sites; innovation support; access to finance (eg, regional venture capital funds).
National	National frameworks for economic development, economic inclusion and social justice • *employment/skills*: policy frameworks for employment, education and skills; National Minimum Wage; benefits policy; employer regulation; migration policy; national frameworks for prioritising investment; approval of qualifications and standards; Higher Education provision • *enterprise*: innovation policy; trade policy; mobile investment; regulation and competition policy; national frameworks for enterprise support policy.

The next section looks in more detail at how economic interventions related to deprived neighbourhoods have developed at different scales in the UK context, before considering in more detail the barriers to, and spatial variation in, integration and coordination. The various levels of intervention are illustrated by a series of policy maps relating to two of the case study areas – Mansfield and Newham. For each locality these have been split into interventions relating to enterprise and business investment (Figures 5.2 and 5.5), employment and skills (Figures 5.3 and 5.6), and area and community regeneration (Figures 5.4 and 5.7).

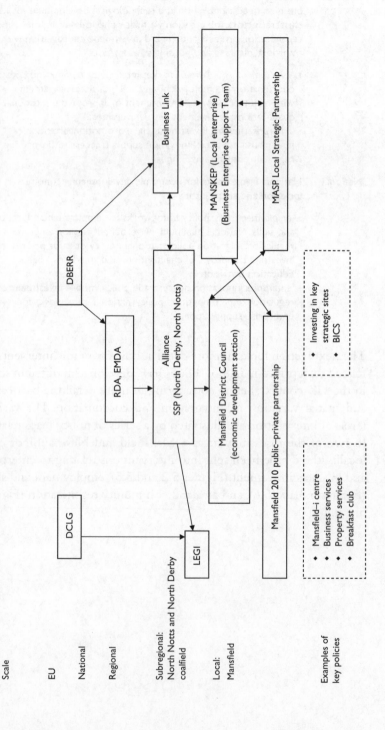

Figure 5.2: Mansfield local economic development policy map: enterprise and business investment

Figure 5.3: Mansfield local economic development policy map: employment and skills

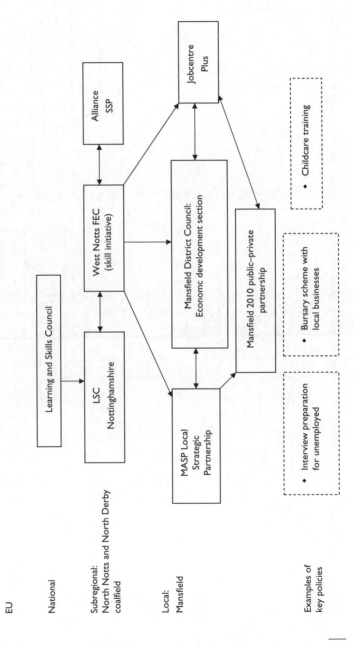

Figure 5.4: Mansfield local economic development policy map: area and community regeneration

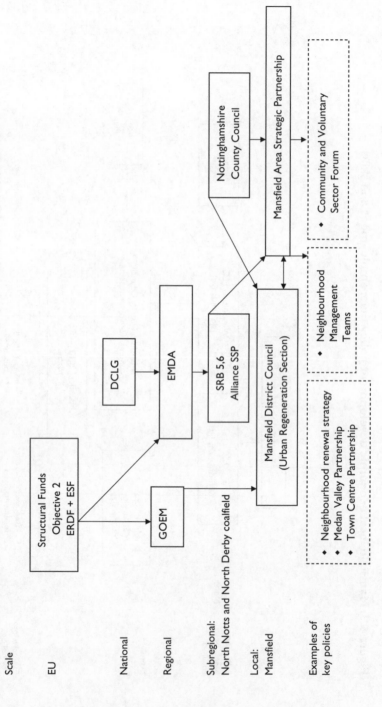

Figure 5.5: Newham local economic development policy map: enterprise and business investment

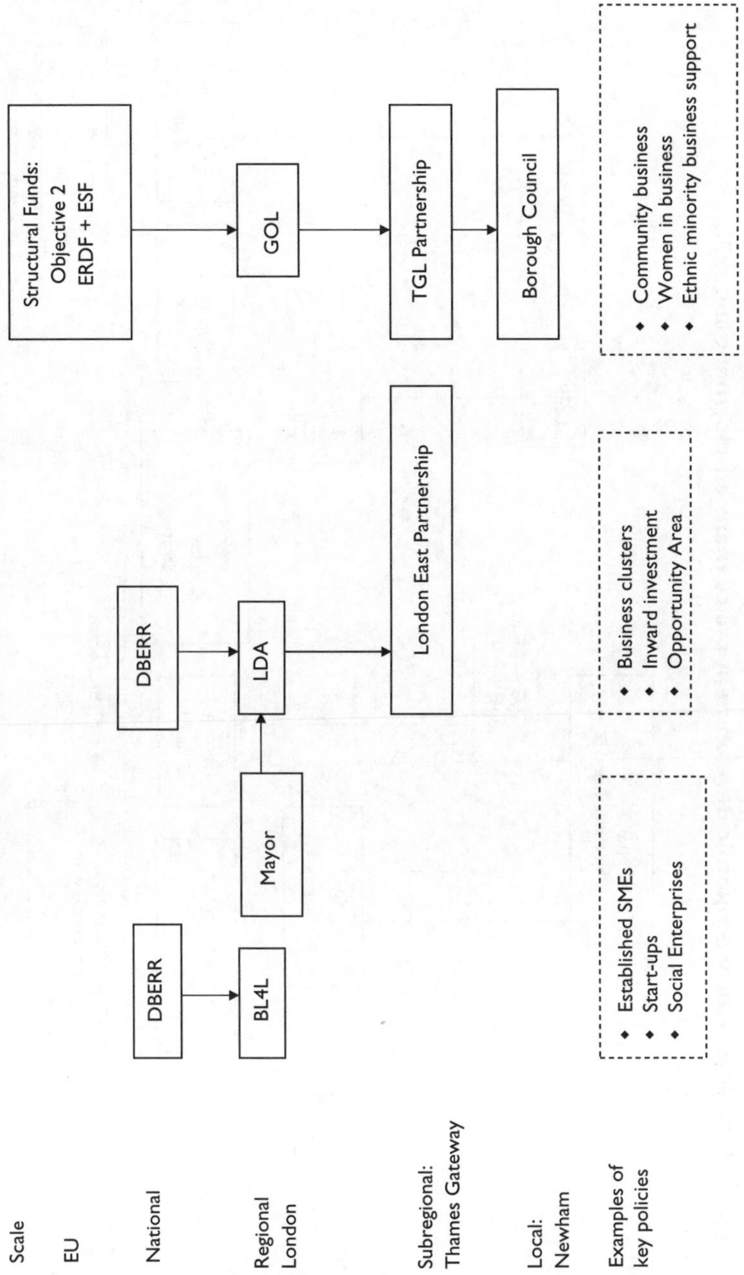

Scale				
EU				Structural Funds: Objective 2 ERDF + ESF
National	DBERR	DBERR		GOL
Regional London	BL4L	Mayor	LDA	TGL Partnership
Subregional: Thames Gateway			London East Partnership	Borough Council
Local: Newham				

Examples of key policies
- Established SMEs
- Start-ups
- Social Enterprises

- Business clusters
- Inward investment
- Opportunity Area

- Community business
- Women in business
- Ethnic minority business support

Figure 5.6: Newham local economic development policy map: employment and skills

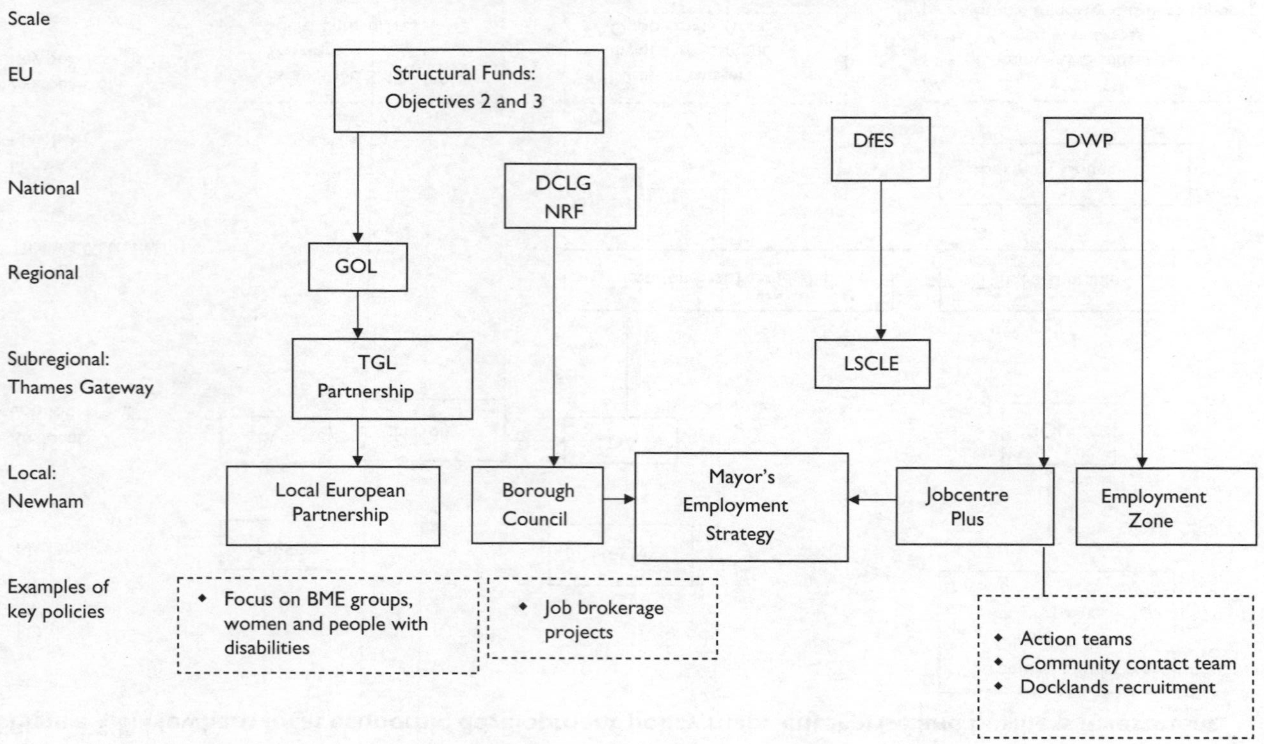

Scale		
EU	Structural Funds: Objectives 2 and 3	
National	DCLG NRF / DfES / DWP	
Regional	GOL / LSCLE	
Subregional: Thames Gateway	TGL Partnership	
Local: Newham	Local European Partnership / Borough Council / Mayor's Employment Strategy / Jobcentre Plus / Employment Zone	
Examples of key policies	• Focus on BME groups, women and people with disabilities / • Job brokerage projects	• Action teams • Community contact team • Docklands recruitment

Figure 5.7: Newham local economic development policy map: area and community regeneration

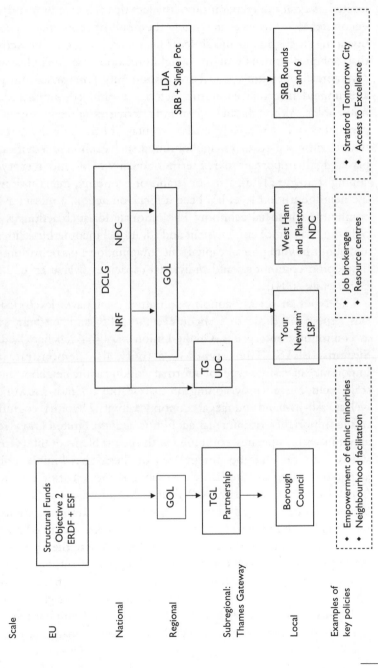

Levels of intervention in the UK context

Neighbourhood level

Economic interventions at the neighbourhood scale have been limited in extent in recognition of the fact that the economic realities encountered at this level are largely the result of economic processes operating at higher spatial scales. The sphere of economic activity that operates primarily at the neighbourhood level includes small commercial operations, social and community enterprises and paid and unpaid informal economic activity within communities and households. Although such economic activities are responsible for generating only a relatively small percentage of the employment and wealth within a particular neighbourhood, such economic activities can play a highly important role in terms of quality of life and in everyday coping strategies. Thus, a major strand of economic interventions at the neighbourhood level has been a focus on actions to develop the community or social economy. The rationale for such actions is not only the creation of employment and additional income, but critically also about building social capital, encouraging local participation and developing community and individual capacities (Mayo et al, 2003; Burns et al, 2004).

The types of social economy initiatives that have developed in this respect are those that encourage mutuality and self-help, such as community enterprises, Credit Unions, Local Exchange Trading Systems (LETS). These types of activity also demonstrate the importance of various types of informal working at the neighbourhood scale, including self-provisioning, mutual aid, unpaid informal work, as well as cash-in-hand and illegal economic activity. Despite recognition of the importance of informal economic activity, limited knowledge about how this operates, combined with the problems of intervening where activities may be unregulated or illegal, has limited policy activity related to this area largely to sporadic formalisation initiatives (Small Business Council, 2004; Williams, 2004; Evans et al, 2006) (see Chapter Four). Generally, initiatives promoting enterprise activity at the neighbourhood level have been limited given constrained market opportunities and the skills of local residents. Where they have been developed the focus has been on the development of self-employment and social enterprises oriented towards particular local needs.

The second major strand of interventions at the neighbourhood scale relates to the development of the skills and employability of residents to aid their integration into the wider labour market. Initiatives here comprise a range of active labour market measures to raise the competitiveness of neighbourhood residents within the wider labour market (for example, through improving basic skills and improving preparation for employment), as well as actions that seek to remove local barriers to work and improve access to external markets (see Chapter Three). These might include the subsidisation of transport and childcare costs or the development of agreements with local employers to encourage workplace integration and recruitment from deprived areas.

As part of their integrated approach to tackling neighbourhood disadvantage both NDCs and the neighbourhood renewal programme have been expected to include actions related to issues of employment and economic development; however, in practice this dimension has remained relatively weak (SEU, 2004; CRESR, 2005). In part this reflects that local residents and agencies have often prioritised 'crime and grime' initiatives, but more broadly it reflects recognition of the limited ability to intervene meaningfully at this level given the wider constitution of labour markets and local economies. Consequently, much of the neighbourhood renewal agenda has focused on public service delivery and often has been only weakly integrated into wider local economic development agendas. Where neighbourhood-level interventions have developed these have been predominantly in relation to supply-side labour market actions. Employment-related actions at the neighbourhood scale have enabled better access to so-called 'hard-to-reach groups' via delivery from more accessible and trusted local agencies often based in the community and voluntary sector. However, such 'one-off' initiatives have been frequently criticised in relation to their quality, longer-term impacts and lack of coordination with mainstream provision. Attempts to develop such coordination are frequently frustrated by the lack of flexibility evident in key agencies of central government such as Jobcentre Plus and the LSCs to respond to their specific neighbourhood agendas.

Local level: local authorities and local strategic partnerships

The local scale has been the principal focus for the development of subnational economic policy in the UK. This is largely because over the last 40 years the local authority has been the key subnational governance level and often has had a central role in delivering national programmes and developing local strategies, particularly in the absence of stronger regional and subregional governance structures. As a result, local authorities and related partners have at times become involved in interventions that may have been more appropriately carried out at higher spatial levels, such as the attraction of inward investors and the promoting of innovation and industrial clusters.

Local–level economic interventions over the years have been wide-ranging, including a focus on promoting economic development (for example, sectoral policies; the development of local supply chains and clusters); business development (for example, support for business start-ups and self-employment as well as developing the local business community, retaining businesses and attracting new ones); physical regeneration (for example, land acquisition and development, property development, the planning and development process and the provision of infrastructures such as transport and communications); labour markets (for example, identifying skills need; education and training provision) and community economic development (for example, support for the development of community enterprises, the voluntary sector and self-help initiatives) (Audit Commission, 1999).

Since the late 1980s, the limited power, funds and statutory functions related to economic intervention gave these activities a lower priority within local authorities, and their subsequent ability to link into and inform regional and subregional strategies has remained limited. At the local level in England, the introduction of LSPs, with their requirement to develop Community Strategies that address the needs of deprived areas, has been characterised by the weakness of their activities in relation to 'economic well-being' relative to other areas of their activity (ODPM, 2005). There is, however, considerable variety between LSPs and local authorities in their relative engagement with local economic activity and they remain key actors, not only through their role in the delivery of neighbourhood renewal policies but also due to their power and legitimacy, derived from being elected bodies in contrast to other subnational organisations (see Boxes 5.3 and 5.4). The principal local authorities associated with the major UK cities remain powerful political actors in the absence of strong regional-level leadership. In London the key relationship remains, as it has done historically, that between the London boroughs and the city-wide Mayor and Greater London Authority, with subregional groupings of minor significance politically.

Although the long-term trend has been towards a decline in their economic development functions, in England, the introduction of Local Area Agreements (LAAs), the Area-Based Grant (ABG), the Working Neighbourhoods Fund (WNF) and the Local Enterprise Growth Initiative (LEGI) marks a significant shift in direction. Local authorities are set to have an enhanced role with regard to local economic development and there are renewed incentives for local authorities to give greater priority to issues of employment and enterprise and to strengthen policy coordination locally and within the sub/city-region. As yet there is limited evidence of stronger and meaningful vertical integration between local authorities/LSPs and regional and subregional bodies, although certain city-regions (such as Manchester) are actively taking forward this agenda. More routinely, as a scrutiny review by the Regional Assembly (EMRA, 2006) in the East Midlands noted, the RES did not substantially recognise LAAs, and their link with the objectives of the RES needed to be more apparent in a formal sense. Proposed changes within the subnational review will change this situation, requiring a redefined and more closely integrated relationship between local authorities and RDAs than has existed to date.

Box 5.3: Local authority approaches: the case of Mansfield

The governance structure relating to economic development and regeneration in Mansfield is set out in Figure 5.2. The key institutions involved in the strategic development and delivery of local economic development and neighbourhood renewal within Mansfield are Mansfield District Council and the Mansfield Area Strategic Partnership (MASP). These two bodies work closely together and with a number of other key local institutions in the development of strategy and delivery. These include Mansfield 2010, Mansfield, Sutton and Kirkby Enterprise Partnership (MANSKEP), Business Link and Jobcentre Plus, as well as the Community and Voluntary Sector Forum and West Nottinghamshire College. In 2006 Mansfield along with two neighbouring local authorities put in a successful bid for Local Enterprise Growth Initiative funds (see Chapter Four)).

Mansfield District Council has both an economic development section and an urban regeneration section. The economic development section has responsibility for developing and implementing the authority's economic development strategy. Its key areas of activity comprise innovation (through the Mansfield-i centre), investment, business support, business services and property services. The urban regeneration section focuses on three main areas: neighbourhood regeneration (Neighbourhood Renewal Fund [NRF]-based programmes), heritage regeneration, and urban regeneration projects, particularly related to infrastructure projects and town-centre renewal.

The LSP – MASP – evolved out of a broad-based Mansfield area-based partnership drawing partners from the public, private, voluntary and community sectors, and was originally formed in 1999. MASP has eight partner groups covering the key issues and services, including one for economic development.

Mansfield 2010 was set up in 1990 in response to the decline in the textile and coal industries to provide a collective voice to promote socially and environmentally sustainable economic development for the north Nottinghamshire coalfield area. Mansfield 2010 is a public–private partnership of local businesses (currently over 150) and a range of public sector organisations such as Mansfield District Council, Nottinghamshire County Council and West Nottinghamshire College. It aims to help the private and public sectors to work together in the pursuit of economic development through lobbying for national and EU funds for transport and physical infrastructures and promoting networking activities. Mansfield 2010 works closely with MANSKEP (Business Enterprise Support Team), a local enterprise agency charged with raising awareness of new business opportunities and providing support to new and existing businesses to survive and grow via advice and mentoring. MANSKEP and Mansfield 2010 also work closely with the local Business Link, and all three operate out of the same building.

Box 5.4: Local authority approaches: the case of Newham

As one of London's most disadvantaged boroughs, Newham has had a strong commitment to economic and social regeneration over many years. Since 1997 when Newham Council set out its long-term vision of Newham as a major business location where people will choose to live and work, the borough has obtained significant public resources from central government to support this vision, including Stratford City Challenge (completed in March 1998), 12 SRB Partnerships, a Pathfinder for the NDC, and the NRF. In addition, Newham has been in receipt of European Regional Development Fund (ERDF) and European Social Fund (ESF) resources as part of the Lower Lea Valley Objective 2 programme and will benefit substantially from investment related to the London 2012 Olympics.

Newham Council's last Economic Development Plan (1999/2000) had the principal aims to:

* attract new investment;
* retain income and economic activity within the borough;
* retain and attract aspiring residents; and
* improve access to employment for the borough's residents.

Its approach to economic development has been multidimensional, including strategic development projects in the Docklands and the Lower Lea Valley, developing shopping centres, supporting business development, equipping local people with the skills needed to compete for local jobs, community regeneration, and anti-poverty and welfare rights.

Much of the borough's economic development activity is now encompassed by the 'Your Newham' LSP, with 'employment' being one of six workstreams, which includes a focus on barriers to employment; employment in the public sector; and enterprise and local procurement. The delivery of the Council's employment strategy is in the hands of the 'Access to Jobs Partnership', which comprises a wide range of partner organisations within the borough (including Jobcentre Plus, the LSC, various training providers, the further education college, key employers such as City Airport, and voluntary sector organisations). Existing actions include working with contractors on major developments to prioritise the use of local labour; setting up customised training schemes linking local people to jobs; a job brokerage service to help local people obtain permanent jobs in health and social care; initiatives to link school children into opportunities resulting from the renewal of Newham; and providing support for voluntary sector training providers in developing projects that successfully move people into employment.

Subregional scale

Although the subregional level is commonly identified as of central importance in terms of addressing many local labour market issues and in integrating economic development activity with transport, housing and planning policy, institutionally it is a governance level that is weakly and variably developed. Across the regions of the UK a variety of forms of subregional/city economic governance structures have developed, even though not formally required, partly to respond to the realities of how particular spatial economic units function, but also as a practical means of linking wider regional strategies, which cover disparate areas, with smaller-scale local authority areas (see Box 5.5). Generally, these subregional economic development structures are weak in terms of resources, staff and decision-making powers given their reliance on local/regional stakeholder cooperation, and this fundamentally limits their role and effectiveness.

Existing economic-related subregional partnerships (SRPs) reflect a number of different types and origins. While many SRPs were created/developed by RDAs to take forward their regional economic development agenda, others reflect past partnership working (for example around EU-funded Objective 1 programmes), the development of national enterprise and employment–related policy initiatives (for example, City Strategy Pathfinders and LEGIs) or a focus on physical development interventions (for example Urban Regeneration Companies and Urban Development Corporations [UDCs]). The variation that characterises SRPs is apparent along a number of dimensions including geographic scale (from localised cooperation between two or more local authorities through to major city-regions); their principal types of activity (for example from wider strategic economic development to more focused activity in relation to labour markets, enterprise or physical regeneration); the role of different partners (for example from public sector-led and dominated partnerships to those that are private sector-led, independent companies); their history and length of time they have been operating; the balance in their role between strategic and operational activity; and critically, the power and resources with which they operate.

Box 5.5: Subregional differences and partnerships in the East Midlands

The East Midlands lacks cohesion as a region both in terms of its geography and in the absence of any clear sense of identity. It ranges from its southern part, which is heavily linked into the wider South-East labour market, through to the quite different challenges presented by the former coalfield areas in the north, the three major cities of the centre and the rural coast of Lincolnshire. Despite the region's improved economic performance, there remain many places with high levels of deprivation and low economic activity, especially in the main urban centres.

As a consequence of its internal subregional variation the RDA – emda (East Midlands Development Agency) – has pursued various strategies to develop subregional working in order to develop and implement its RES. Interestingly, while emda initially pursued a relatively high level of decentralisation to its SRPs it subsequently drew power back from these bodies, reducing the amount of funding directly spent by them.

Currently, emda recognises seven SRPs (which it terms Subregional Strategic Partnerships [SSPs]), which comprise Alliance SSP (North Derbyshire and North Nottinghamshire), Northamptonshire Enterprise Ltd, Greater Nottingham Partnership, Leicester Shire Economic Partnership (LSEP), Derby and Derbyshire Economic Partnership (DDEP), Lincolnshire Enterprise, and the Welland SSP. These are set up as companies with limited guarantee and operate on the basis of an appointed Board, with a key role to formulate subregional economic strategy and coordinate its delivery. It is also important to recognise that other bodies with interests in economic development also operate at the subregional level, not least six county councils (Derbyshire, Leicestershire, Lincolnshire, Northamptonshire, Nottinghamshire and Rutland).

The relationship between SSPs and local authorities exhibit a number of tensions, with some local authorities sceptical about the role and relevance of the SSPs, seeing them merely as another layer of bureaucracy between local and regional levels. This was certainly the case initially with regard to Mansfield District Council and its subregional body – the Alliance SSP – as the SSP struggled to develop a strong, effective and legitimate subregional presence.

The development of the city-region agenda and the anticipated development of City Development Companies (CDCs) in the three major cities of Derby, Leicester and Nottingham appear set to lead to major changes in the organisation and roles of subregional bodies in the East Midlands. While the SSPs currently formally oversee local economic development activities across all city and county authorities, the formation of new partnerships that will give city authorities a more powerful role will necessitate further evolution in subregional arrangements, particularly in relation to other towns (including, for example, Mansfield) and rural areas.

In the implementation of regional/subregional economic initiatives that regenerate deprived areas, the subregional level is clearly of critical importance as it is this level that relates most meaningfully to Travel to Work Areas (TTWAs) and economically functional areas that relate issues of supply and demand (for example, in terms of labour, housing, transport and so on). However, the performance of SRPs remains strongly variable: ranging from an ineffective and unnecessary level of bureaucracy, through to being a significant actor linking economic and social agendas. This variability reflects the ability of SRPs to operate effectively, their credibility with local stakeholders and the degree of clarity over their role and purpose vis-à-vis other local, subregional and regional bodies. In general there remain problems related to SRPs linking up with other subregional and local bodies. In part this is due to a lack of co-terminosity of boundaries. For example, in England the recent reorganisation of the LSCs and Jobcentre Plus towards a regional scale of operation has further constrained the development of subregional collaboration. Locally, the business–led nature of some SRPs has at times acted as a barrier to wider inclusion and stakeholder buy–in to their strategies, especially from the voluntary and community sector and certain public bodies who question their transparency and legitimacy.

A major outcome of the subnational review is a move towards attempting to strengthen the subregional level with respect to economic development and regeneration (HM Treasury et al, 2007). The review promotes the development of a so-called 'variable geometry' of subregional arrangements, notably through the creation of city-regions and the new institutional form of CDCs. This flexible approach is designed to permit the development of SRPs appropriate in form and function to local/subregional economic conditions. While this is a positive response to the need for improved subnational coordinated working, such changes will also reinforce the complexity of governance arrangements and their variability in effectiveness.

Regional scale

Intervention at the regional level in the UK has traditionally been seen to serve two main purposes: to help implement national economic strategy in a manner that is sensitive to regional economic variation; and to reduce levels of economic imbalance between different regions within the national space. While regional-level economic planning was pursued strongly in the 1960s, this level of intervention fell out of favour across the 1970s and 1980s. However, it returned on a limited basis with the establishment of regional GOs in 1994, and on a more significant scale with the incoming New Labour government in 1997, which pursued its plans for devolution and regional administrative decentralisation, leading to the creation in England of RDAs and an expanded role for GOs, but not the envisaged elected Regional Assemblies.

The purpose of regional-level economic activity as led by the RDAs (according to the 1998 Regional Development Agencies Act) has been to improve the economic performance of their respective regions through their responsibilities for economic development and regeneration; promoting business efficiency, investment and competitiveness; promoting employment; enhancing the development of skills; and contributing to sustainable development. Regional Development Agencies were established not only to strengthen national economic performance and competitiveness, but also to reduce disparities both between and within regions (Robson et al, 2000). Since 2002, the RDAs have been accountable to the Secretary of State for the DTI (now DBERR) although most of their funding comes from the DCLG. Board membership of the RDA is drawn principally from business, although there are representatives from trades unions, the voluntary sector, higher education and local government. Over time the RDAs have seen their responsibilities and resources increase, including acquiring new responsibilities relating to business support, skills, tourism and rural policy. The government therefore sees the RDAs as the main agencies of decentralised economic governance in England, albeit strongly tied to central government accountabilities and performance incentives (HM Treasury et al, 2003).

Regional Development Agency activity has focused on preparing RESs and coordinating with a range of partners to oversee their implementation. Regional-level activities have been particularly focused on promoting innovation and technological development, particularly in relation to key economic clusters and sectors, attracting inward investment and retaining major companies, overseeing the development of a suitably skilled workforce, and developing major transport and communication infrastructures and large-scale physical investments and events that will have a far-ranging economic impact on the wider region.

Despite administrative regional decentralisation, structures such as the RDAs and regional GOs within England remain relatively powerless in relation to the wider economic forces driving processes of regional change and the powers of the central state. The budgets of RDAs remain very small in relation to the bulk of public spending (see Table 5.2). Thus, the vast majority of mainstream and area-based public spending related to deprived areas comes from central government programmes (for example, DCLG, DfES, DWP, DoT), only some of which is channelled through the regional GOs.

The RDAs have to date had a limited impact relating to the needs of deprived areas because of a lack of control and coordination with key agencies and issues (for example, employment and training, education, housing, planning and transport), restricted resources, and as discussed earlier, their primary focus on promoting regional economic competitiveness (North et al, 2007). A lack of clarity over the role of RDAs plus problems of dealing with issues of public accountability have weakened further the legitimacy of RDAs with regard to other stakeholders, particularly at the local level (Audit Commission, 2007). In practice, RDAs have struggled to operate effectively and retain credibility given their limited agenda-setting and leadership capacity and lack of direct engagement with local and neighbourhood bodies. Furthermore they operate across economically highly diverse regions, the boundaries of which bear limited relation

Table 5.2: RDA spending compared with total government spending in English regions, 2005–06

	Total central government and public corporations expenditure[1] 2005–06 (£m)	Total local authority expenditure[1] 2005–06 (£m)	Total RDA allocations[2] 2005–06 (£m)
East	22,744	10,107	129
East Midlands	18,921	7,799	156
London	37,491	23,885	373
North East	14,136	5,855	240
North West	36,054	15,161	382
South East	33,717	14,943	157
South West	23,270	9,156	153
West Midlands	25,294	10,962	272
Yorkshire and the Humber	24,840	10,348	295
England	236,466	108,216	2,157

Notes: [1] HM Treasury, Public Spending by Country and Region, 2007
[2] Department for Business Enterprise and Regulatory Reform

to the operation of labour markets and subregional and city economies (see Box 5.5).

The regional GOs have a key role, albeit one constrained by their lack of power in relation to central government departments, in terms of the regional administration of the regeneration agenda and ensuring that the interests of deprived areas are taken account of in various regional strategies (including RESs). Since the creation of the RDAs, there has been a clear tension resulting from the GOs' regional control of important elements of the regeneration agenda, despite the fact that the RDAs were given a lead role in economic development and control over the administration of the SRB. Although a *modus vivendi* has developed between the RDAs and GOs within the English regions given the necessity for them to work together, tensions continue to resurface, as was the case concerning regional coordination of LEGI, which was placed under GO control, despite the fact that responsibility for small business support through Business Link rested with the RDAs.

Factors constraining policy integration and spatial coordination

Barriers to coordination

It has been argued that in seeking to tackle concentrated area-based deprivation, the need to integrate economic development and social inclusion agendas and operate across spatial levels provides a challenging agenda for governance. On the basis of the preceding discussion a number of fundamental barriers can be identified that limit the extent of compatibility and coordination between economic interventions aimed at tackling the problems of deprived neighbourhoods.

Complex, fragmented and changing systems of governance

As demonstrated in this chapter, throughout the UK the governance arrangements and systems of policy delivery related to economic development, regeneration and neighbourhood renewal are characterised by a high level of complexity resulting from the existence of numerous agencies operating at a variety of scales. In consequence, there is often considerable overlap and duplication in functions and a lack of clarity over respective roles and responsibilities and appropriate scales for intervention, all of which militates against effective coordination and communication. In England, the development of policies and institutions at the regional and neighbourhood level since New Labour came to power has added to this complexity.

The high level of change in economic development and regeneration-related institutions and policies since 1997 has produced an environment in which settled, long-term working relationships necessary for effective coordination are difficult to develop and maintain. The continuation of short-term funding for many projects and bodies similarly militates against the development of long-term objectives and relationships, particularly where there are high levels of staff turnover. This context of change and pursuit of multiple initiatives has also resulted in a lack of clear direction in UK central government policy on key issues such as the devolution of power to local government and the role of city-regions. This reflects a changing balance of government priorities related to economic competitiveness, social inclusion and community cohesion as well as the absence of clear thinking over the most appropriate local and regional arrangements for delivering improved economic performance in more deprived areas.

Central–local relations

A recurrent complaint heard from those working subnationally is: 'how are we expected to join activities up at the local level when this is not being done at the level of central government departments?'. This lack of joined-up working is rooted within the contradictions in national policy agendas and the problems of joint working across multiple government departments pursuing their own interests and policy agendas. Despite territorial restructuring leading to increased multilevel nature of governance and a dispersal of power and authority to various levels of governance, the central state retains a dominant role vis-à-vis the variety of arrangements at the subnational level that have developed to 'fill in' the spaces produced by the reconfigured role of the central state (Goodwin et al, 2005). Central government departments still exercise significant power through their control of agenda setting, policy development and budgetary functions. The limited development of regional-level institutions has been accompanied by a failure to significantly devolve power to local government. While current proposals indicate that local government will be given a more central and flexible role in the local economic development and neighbourhood renewal agenda in the future (HM Treasury et al, 2007) this is unlikely to be accompanied by any significant devolution of power under current local government reforms (DCLG, 2007a). This situation ensures that the economic development role at the local level remains highly circumscribed and demonstrates the marked reluctance of central government to permit local authorities and other local stakeholders to pursue strategies that might lead to greater variability in approaches and outcomes.

Power inequalities in partnership working

The emphasis on partnership working within the current governance system related to the economic development of deprived neighbourhoods fails to acknowledge the power inequalities and differing agendas of actors. Despite the move towards greater community involvement, many local actors demonstrate limited trust in a system that often lacks transparency and accountability, remains dominated by central government targets and agencies, and locally, by the interests of local government. This is strongly evident within representatives from the community and voluntary sector and neighbourhood-level organisations, which often feel undervalued, particularly at a time when there is considerable uncertainty over future funding of this sector. However, it is also apparent in the private sector. Here the benefits of engagement often remain unclear to business and this is combined with what is often a considerable level of distrust of public sector interventions derived from past experiences. Within partnerships (such as LSPs and SRPs) partners often pursue their own objectives to the detriment of the wider partnership objectives, although the introduction of mechanisms such as LAAs is intended to ameliorate this situation.

Spatial variations in joined-up governance

The nature and extent of these barriers are, however, spatially variable, with certain localities and regions achieving a much better level of integration between strategies and policies and coordination across spatial scales than others. In explaining this variability, a number of factors are clearly influential.

Traditions of partnership working

Where subnational integration and cooperation exist, this normally has its roots within a history of partnership working between certain agencies built up over a number of years, often via involvement in past initiatives (for example, EU Objective 1 and 2 regions, SRB and so on). Such institutional evolution can lead to greater clarity over the roles and responsibilities for differing organisations through practical experience and results in differentiated capacity at the local/regional level. However, many areas lack a history of cooperation at regional, subregional and city level – indeed, the history may be one of conflict and active competition – which provides a difficult context for any current attempts at more integrated activity.

Socioeconomic context

The particularities of any given socioeconomic context play into the extent of integration in different ways. In areas where there is strong economic growth, market conditions provide greater scope for policy interventions that seek to link areas of growth to deprived areas (for example, via employability and job brokerage programmes or procurement practices). This is perhaps most notable when economic growth is producing labour market shortages, which may impede future growth and hence there is a strong rationale for interventions aimed at improving employment rates and workforce skill levels (for example in Newham and Brighton in London and the South East). In areas where there is weak labour demand, the policy focus is often primarily on attracting investment and stimulating economic development, with the issue of who benefits from these jobs seen as a lesser priority.

The presence of large regeneration/development projects that have significance at the subregional, regional or even national level (for example the Olympics in the case of Newham) can provide a strong basis around which to mobilise and coordinate activity. Cooperation across spatial levels is often a basic requirement for the successful realisation of such projects and their high profile provides a strong political imperative for success. Certainly, RDAs have a tendency to focus their efforts and resources on a limited number of large capital/ property investment, 'flagship' projects. While these have traditionally been weak in linking the needs of residents of deprived areas into their strategies, there is evidence of growing recognition of the need to build in social inclusion objectives from the outset. Yet this is by no means unproblematic. The high profile of such projects creates an imperative to deliver on time and sometimes at the expense of social benefits that are still viewed as 'add-ons' by certain partners. Furthermore, the realisation of large projects inevitably produces a high level of controversy and local political battles that can erode trust and cooperation.

Political decentralisation and devolution

The political priority afforded to issues of economic development and deprivation reflects the particularities of local and regional political contexts and changes in political control. Devolution has had some impact here and, locally, certain local authorities have stronger traditions of local and neighbourhood economic activity.

The extent to which greater devolution of power has made a substantial difference to the operation of economic governance arrangements in relation to deprived areas and populations remains difficult to assess. Certainly, the political process in devolved areas and its link to the electoral process has impacted to provide leadership, agenda-setting capacity and legitimacy for action with regard to issues of economic development and social justice in Scotland, Wales and London (North et al, 2007). In these cases the higher political priority afforded to issues of social justice and deprivation reflected the nature of the left-of-centre political control that predominated in these areas after devolution, as well as the existence of deep-seated social problems and that disadvantaged groups were an important section of the electorate. This was reflected in Scotland's 'Social Justice' and Wales' 'Communities First' strategies, and London's Economic Development Strategies. In contrast to other English regions, London's first Mayor, Ken Livingstone, used his elected position to argue for, and gain, more powers in the economic development and regeneration fields throughout his period in office (2000-08) (Syrett, 2006). Despite limited resources Mayor Livingstone used his strong agenda-setting powers to take the lead in social areas related to economic development (for example, equality, social housing, childcare, the 'living wage' campaign) and to take potentially controversial decisions (for example, the precept for the Olympics and Congestion Charging).

Despite the presence of strong political and policy commitment to issues of deprivation in the initial period after devolution, there remained problems with regard to the extent and nature of the integration of this agenda with that of economic development policy and its delivery. There was little evidence to suggest that an increased strategic focus was translated into significant impacts in terms of delivery. Clear tensions were evident between an emphasis on the economic promotion of the wider nation/city and the extent of a strong spatial strategy informed by concentrated deprivation. In the case of Scotland and Wales the particular devolution settlement continues to limit the scope for action, a notable anomaly being that employment and labour market policy is not a devolved responsibility. In London, the lack of influence in the areas of employment and training was the basis for Mayor Livingstone's successful lobbying for a greater strategic role and the creation in 2007 of the 'London Skills and Employment Board' chaired by the Mayor. In this respect, the evolutionary nature of the devolution process ensures that governance arrangements related to economic development are similarly set to evolve further.

Leadership

The presence of an individual or group of individuals who provide strong leadership, energy and commitment and act as a catalyst to stimulate action is often an important factor in overcoming the constraints inherent in a highly complex and fragmented governance system. Leaders, based at a variety of spatial levels, but effective at operating across them, can play a key role in exploiting the spaces for action inherent in such a system, including identifying opportunities and tapping into various funding streams. For individuals capable of providing strong leadership and with an entrepreneurial and creative attitude, the features of the current governance system can provide considerable scope for action through the existence of different spatial levels of intervention and access to multiple funding streams.

In fact, analysis of successful economic initiatives related to deprived neighbourhoods demonstrates that effective coordinated action is possible, although often in spite of governance arrangements rather than because of them (North et al, 2007). In these cases committed teams and strong individuals are able to make governance arrangements work, through getting key local agencies to work together to deliver common objectives and outputs, often in an innovative and risk-taking manner, which contrasts with the risk-averse and rule-bound culture that dominates in the regeneration and renewal field.

Conclusions

In examining how governance arrangements and the institutional and policy environment impact on the development and delivery of economic policy in relation to deprived neighbourhoods, a number of issues become apparent. The highly complex, fragmented and often unaccountable nature of governance arrangements provides a context that militates against the integration and coordination necessary for effective economic intervention at the neighbourhood level. This complexity, allied to a high level of change, produces high transaction costs and often prevents the maturing and realisation of the high trust relations required for effective working at the subnational level across and between local, subregional and regional levels. Policy integration is limited too by the contradictions emanating from the policy agenda and the institutional constraints arising from the need to work across a number of different government departments and policy networks. These difficulties are particularly evident in relation to issues of fundamental importance to the economic development of deprived neighbourhoods, namely the integration of the economic development and social inclusion agendas and the integration of employment, skills and enterprise policies.

The coordination of economic interventions across different spatial levels is problematic due not only to a lack of conceptual clarity over what is the most appropriate level for different types of intervention but also to the nature of governance capacities and institutional development at different levels within the UK context. As a result there is a lack of precision over the roles and responsibilities of institutions operating at different spatial levels, which contributes to confusion and duplication, as well as a lack of capacity, most notably at the subregional/city-region level – a level important to the functioning of subnational economic units and TTWAs – but also at the local level. In addition, there are tensions between different spatial levels, with neighbourhood and local institutions often feeling marginalised from the workings of regional and national agencies pursuing a narrow agenda predominantly focused on economic competitiveness and economic inclusion.

Current practice is characterised by regional, local and temporal variation, reflecting how constraints and opportunities for coordination are realised within specific contexts and develop over time. Where power has been devolved in Scotland, Wales and London, a greater strategic focus on issues of social justice and spatial concentrations of deprivation is apparent although there is little evidence that this has yet delivered significant concrete benefits. Despite the recent moves towards devolution and regional decentralisation, the UK state remains a highly centralised form of network governance, which struggles to provide the necessary sensitivity to local difference that effective interventions related to deprived neighbourhoods require. Furthermore, given the operation of wider processes of economic and labour market change and the current levels of powers and resources of subnational bodies, these are only ever likely to have a modest impact on the problems of widespread and longstanding localised concentrations of deprivation and their integration into wider city and regional contexts.

Note

[1] Following the change from the Blair to the Brown government in July 2007 the Department of Trade and Industry was renamed the Department for Business, Enterprise and Regulatory Reform (DBERR) and the responsibilities of the Department for Education and Skills (DfES) were transferred to the Department of Innovation, Universities and Skills (DIUS) and the Department for Children, Schools and Families. Throughout this chapter we use the title of government departments as they applied at the time of the research.

SIX

Deprived neighbourhoods: future prospects for economic intervention

Introduction

Concentrations of poverty rooted within particular neighbourhoods are a longstanding and persistent feature of evolving urban landscapes. The challenges faced by such neighbourhoods are multifaceted and the policy responses many and varied. In this book we have focused on the economic dimension of the problems of poor neighbourhoods, exploring how these areas are integrated within wider economic development processes in such a way that the benefits flowing from dominant models of economic growth routinely bypass their residents. In analysing the nature of the policy response, the book has considered the development of UK policy, evaluating critically an array of policy actions that have aimed at addressing issues of work, enterprise and governance in relation to deprived neighbourhoods, principally in the period since the New Labour government came to power in 1997.

Successive New Labour governments have placed the 'neighbourhood' at the forefront of the social exclusion, urban development and civic renewal policy agendas, with a particular focus on tackling concentrated deprivation in order to reduce the gap in income and living standards between the poorest neighbourhoods and the rest. The neoliberal-inspired model of urban regeneration that has informed policy development has sought to simultaneously promote economic competitiveness, social inclusion, community cohesion and improved governance, underwritten by a generalised commitment to notions of 'sustainability'. The evolution of this policy approach to neighbourhood renewal was also informed by the perceived failings of past urban regeneration and social policies aimed at tackling concentrated deprivation. These included the lack of a comprehensive approach that simultaneously tackled the multiple and reinforcing dimensions of exclusion, the need for longer-term responses that recognised the deep-seated nature of problems, and the imperative of involving the local community actively in the development process and ensuring resources were targeted effectively to the most deprived areas.

In terms of tackling the economic dimension of the challenges faced by deprived neighbourhoods, three key elements apparent in policy – work, enterprise and improved governance – have been the focus of this book.

- *Work:* Moving workless people of working age into employment has been one of the main objectives of New Labour governments over the last 10 years. This has led to a succession of welfare-to-work programmes and active labour market policy initiatives – many of them targeted at those living in the most deprived neighbourhoods – as well as various changes to the benefits system to ensure that unemployed recipients seek work. Labour market participation through obtaining paid employment has been seen as the main means by which individuals can better themselves and an essential element of the process of neighbourhood renewal. Yet, it is also clear that the causes behind concentrations of long-term unemployment and economic inactivity are invariably complex. There are multiple barriers that prevent people from entering the labour market including a range of influences on employers' demand for labour, the personal and household characteristics that affect attitudes to work and the ability to compete for jobs, as well as various institutional practices and failures that make it difficult for individuals to access employment. There are also important differences between places in terms of the mix of barriers that people face in obtaining employment, demonstrating the need to develop solutions that are sensitive to specific situations.
- *Enterprise:* The role that new and small enterprises can play in the regeneration of deprived areas has been given increased emphasis under New Labour governments. While this has been driven largely by economic considerations in terms of the role that enterprise can play in strengthening the economic competitiveness of places and regions, there have been important social motives too, such as developing social capital and combating social exclusion. Yet, encouraging endogenous enterprise within deprived areas has proved a challenging task, especially in those regions and localities that historically have been dependent on employment in large-scale industries and have lacked anything approaching an 'enterprise culture'. Encouraging entrepreneurial activity and self-employment in such localities is constrained by a number of factors, not least a lack

of relevant skills and experience, knowledge of operating in particular markets and capital to invest in nascent business ventures.

• *Governance:* In attempting to provide a more integrated and 'joined-up' approach to policy delivery within deprived neighbourhoods, New Labour governments have made a number of changes to institutions and governance arrangements with the objective of promoting greater devolution and decentralisation. At the local and neighbourhood level this has seen the development of an enhanced 'place-shaping' role for local government as well as the development of Local Strategic Partnerships (LSPs) and neighbourhood management. At the regional level, Regional Development Agencies (RDAs) have been created to take forward the economic competitiveness agenda, and more variably, at the level of cities and subregions, a range of institutions and arrangements have developed to try to connect deprived areas to wider city/subregional economies. Despite multiple reforms, governance arrangements in relation to the economic development of deprived neighbourhoods are still highly complex and fragmented, characterised by limited business engagement and the continued dominance of central state structures and policy agendas.

The considerable policy attention directed towards promoting employment, enterprise and better governance with respect to poor neighbourhoods has to date provided only limited evidence of success. Although individual initiatives have had significant localised impacts, policy interventions have struggled to make a difference beyond the margins and address the economic basis of the problems faced by deprived areas in a comprehensive manner.

The absence of clear evidence as to the effectiveness and outcomes of neighbourhood-oriented policies aimed at tackling concentrated deprivation in part results from the inherent constraints in evaluating such interventions (Lawless, 2007; Griggs et al, 2008). The complex interaction of mutually reinforcing processes makes it difficult to identify simple causal relationships. The challenge of understanding the nature of the interaction between employment change, housing markets and population turnover within any given specific context, and the direction and nature of causality within these relationships, is but one example. In addition, the lack of robust baseline data and the differences between local contexts make it difficult to establish the 'counterfactual' of what would have happened in the absence of intervention. The impacts of displacement effects are also difficult to evaluate given that these may be far reaching, extending out across local, subregional and regional scales in the case of labour markets and investment decisions. In respect to interventions that seek to effect long-term fundamental change, evaluations may often be undertaken too early to pick up important changes. Developing a more entrepreneurial local business culture or changing cultural attitudes towards employment and education are subtle long-term processes, which are likely to be characterised by contradictory elements that evolve temporally through stepped change rather than by neat linear relationships. In fact, much policy evaluation is fundamentally constrained by the nature of the original policy targets set and the operation of political and policy cycles, factors that limit the scope of policy activity and its subsequent evaluation (NEF, 2008).

Beyond the considerable problems of evaluating policy interventions targeted at economically improving conditions within poor neighbourhoods, a number of key issues are apparent in relation to considering the effectiveness of the current policy agenda and the changes that could be made to ensure a greater impact in the future. In this final chapter we return to these central issues, identified in the introduction and developed through subsequent chapters in this book, to identify what can be learnt from recent policy practice and what the prospects are for more effective interventions in relation to current policy agendas and alternative paths of local economic development.

Spatial difference

In seeking to understand and respond to the economic needs of deprived neighbourhoods, place matters. Spatial differences present different economic challenges and require different mixes of interventions tailored and delivered to meet local needs. As the case study neighbourhoods analysed in this book demonstrate, deprived neighbourhoods differ significantly in terms of the presence of different types of human, financial, physical and social capital, differences that play into the nature and scope of their integration into wider local and regional economies. The particular composition of individual and family characteristics of local residents (for example, in terms of age, ethnicity, health and mobility) and the extent of human capital development in relation to levels of work experience, education and skills are of central importance in this respect. However, population characteristics also need to be understood in terms of their rootedness in a variety of place-based factors, such as accessibility, the quality of the local physical environment and levels of service provision, as well as neighbourhood effects related to the extent of social networks, the availability of role models and area-based discrimination. These place-based factors vary across neighbourhoods and help shape the opportunity structures and lifecourses of residents of deprived neighbourhoods through incremental and compounding effects.

The fundamental relationship of poor neighbourhoods to the wider local/urban economy within which they are situated was a neglected feature in New Labour's initial neighbourhood renewal agenda (North and Syrett, 2008). Although current national policy directions are now seeking to address this issue, there remains a need to confront the recurring finding from evaluations of the impact of various types of regeneration programmes that only a very small minority of the unemployed and jobless living in deprived neighbourhoods have benefited from the jobs being generated in nearby employment growth areas. The evidence shows that the much-vaunted trickle-down benefits have turned out to be, at best, a 'slow drip'. Over time the boundaries of local labour markets have become more porous, such that employers no longer look solely to local sources of labour and may sometimes actively discriminate against using local labour in favour of, for example, migrant labour. Yet, those who are out of work and living in deprived neighbourhoods have more restricted spatial search and commuting horizons, as well as limited occupational mobility.

Policy responses to the lack of benefit flowing to residents of deprived areas from new job opportunities exist both in terms of improving linkages between these residents and available job opportunities and seeking to develop indigenous self-employment and enterprise within the local area in order to diminish reliance on external employment generation. In the case of the first of these, research evidence demonstrates that the linking of areas of opportunity with nearby areas of need cannot be left to unfettered market forces but requires various intervention mechanisms in order to help local people compete for the jobs that are on offer within a reasonable commuting distance. Establishing such linkages requires much closer working between new and existing employers and those working with disadvantaged groups in poorer areas, to increase their access to such jobs. In the case of larger regeneration projects, economic inclusion objectives need to be built in from the start and ways found to ensure that local people are aware of future job opportunities and equipped through employability initiatives with the skills that employers are seeking. This also means persuading employers of their local social responsibilities and guaranteeing that local residents will take a certain proportion of jobs.

In this respect the London Olympics provides a unique opportunity to learn from the mistakes of previous large regeneration projects. Much of the case for attracting the 2012 Olympics to London related to the opportunities it would create for the regeneration of East London, providing thousands of employment opportunities for the residents of some of London's most deprived boroughs, such as Newham, not only in the construction of the site and the staging of the Games themselves, but also through more lasting jobs generated by investment attracted into the area. The London Development Agency has predicted a 77,000 reduction in the number of workless people in London as a result of the 2012 Olympics (London Assembly, 2007), yet to achieve this in a manner that will benefit the residents of deprived areas requires a focused and systematic targeting of coordinated interventions that link the workless to job opportunities on a scale that has not been achieved in the past.

The second major strategy of building indigenous enterprise and employment within deprived neighbourhoods must confront notable challenges. The evidence demonstrates that enterprises created within deprived areas are subject to a high rate of failure and are unlikely to make any significant impact on levels of unemployment and worklessness. Because those in disadvantaged areas and social groups are more likely to be 'pushed' into self-employment or setting up a new enterprise by the lack of alternative employment, they often lack the market knowledge, self-belief and innovative capacity necessary to make the business venture a success. Consequently, disillusionment can easily set in, resulting in the early closure of the business and possibly financial insolvency. Moreover, it has been shown that efforts to increase the number of new enterprises in deprived localities can simply result in poorer-quality enterprises (that is, 'more means worse'), many of which end up undercutting and forcing existing enterprises to relocate or close down completely (Greene et al, 2007). On the basis of much of the research evidence, therefore, the economic gains of stimulating more enterprise creation in deprived localities are at best fairly small.

However, doubts about the short-term economic benefits of encouraging residents of deprived neighbourhoods to start enterprises need to be considered within wider and longer-term approaches to local development. Encouraging independent and entrepreneurial activity has a crucial role to play in terms of developing locally rooted responses that build confidence and capacity and avoid the reproduction of relations of dependency and associated cultures. Such activity can play an important role in plugging gaps in the provision of local goods and services as well as helping develop skills and capabilities of local residents, which may assist with the transition to employment. These arguments point towards the importance of valuing a range of different forms of entrepreneurial and enterprise activity, including social and community-based enterprises, which are rooted in local needs and provide services to particular areas or social/ethnic groups that remain unmet by existing commercial operations. Although the economic impact of such enterprises may be marginal in terms of conventional economic criteria, they frequently fulfil important social and community roles, as well as providing training and personal development for those involved in their operation.

In the longer term, achieving a step change in the level of entrepreneurship and enterprise will depend on influencing the attitudes and ambitions of young people towards seeing self-employment or starting a business as a career option. This is becoming the focus of a number of national and regional-level initiatives aimed at nurturing future entrepreneurs. The important role played by education in developing an understanding of enterprise and fostering entrepreneurship skills within deprived areas is increasingly recognised, as evidenced by the fact that initiatives directed at school-age children and young people were a central feature of all the successful Local Enterprise Growth Initiative (LEGI) bids in 2005. Yet, this remains an underdeveloped area of policy intervention that will need to operate over a significant time period if it is to change embedded cultures towards entrepreneurship and self-employment.

People *and* place

The importance of place to understanding the nature of concentrated deprivation is fundamental to the nature of any policy response, whatever the informing rationale. That much recent policy debate has been advanced on the basis of an opposition between people- *versus* place-based approaches has created an unhelpful and oversimplified dichotomy that at times has become a barrier to addressing the problems of deprived areas and their residents. Conceptually, any attempt to disentangle a person or group of people from the context in which they live, work and play is profoundly problematic given the simultaneous influences acting between people and places. It is perhaps not surprising, therefore, that many of the analyses or evaluations that have attempted to make such a separation have failed to produce clear or convincing evidence. Despite this difficulty, there is a strong need to specify as precisely as possible the nature of the relationships between different disadvantaged individuals and groups disproportionately present within poor neighbourhoods, the particularities of a given place, and how a specific policy intervention is seeking to address this relationship. Certainly, an ongoing limitation of much recent neighbourhood-related policy has been a lack of clarity over the nature and direction of such relationships and whether policy is primarily focused on residents, neighbourhoods or a combination of the two. In this respect, the indiscriminate and sometimes conflated use of the terms 'community' and 'neighbourhood' has frequently contributed to such confusion.

Policy interventions in relation to deprived neighbourhoods need to combine the concerns of people *and* place and in a more effective manner than has been achieved to date. The rationale for forms of area-based intervention remains strong given the importance of differences between neighbourhoods and their integration into the wider local and regional economy. A focus only on developing the skills, employability and entrepreneurial capacities of those individuals living within deprived areas may increase their social mobility but fails to develop either the necessary housing, services and environmental conditions that make a place attractive to live in or the locally rooted social networks and communal resources that will endure even when individuals 'get on and move out'. The persistence of concentrated poverty also provides an ongoing justification for a strategic and targeted focus on these areas. Deprived neighbourhoods and their residents may receive substantial flows of public resources through benefit payments, but very little of this money is spent on providing better routes out of deprivation through improved education and training. Governance arrangements and mainstream policy development and delivery within what is still a highly centralised British state similarly necessitate certain area-based interventions in order to address local particularities and neighbourhood effects, and shape mainstream policy responses to spatial difference.

Yet, as the evidence presented in this book demonstrates, area-based work and enterprise interventions are constrained not only by their relationship with mainstream provision and wider governance arrangements, but also more fundamentally by the scale of the wider socioeconomic processes that are manifested through, and constituted within, deprived neighbourhoods. The processes of deindustrialisation, labour market polarisation and rising social and income inequalities that underpin the socioeconomic problems of deprived neighbourhoods operate nationally, and increasingly internationally, and need to be addressed by economic and welfare policies developed and implemented at the appropriate spatial level. As the evaluations of the New Deal for Communities (NDC) programme indicate, while neighbourhood-level interventions have produced significant outcomes in relation to place-based environmental, liveability, crime and community cohesion initiatives, they have been much less effective in terms of producing positive outputs in relation to longer-term, people-based issues related to employment, education and health (Lawless, 2007). In part this difference may be due to people-based outcomes being more difficult to sustain and identify at the neighbourhood level because of the movement of people away to better areas and the problems of identifying the benefits of people-based interventions in area-based surveys (DCLG, 2008b).

Making mainstream policies sensitive to spatial difference and delivering them with localised flexibility presents a considerable challenge. Those living in the most deprived areas who are seeking to enter the labour market or start up businesses face multiple barriers, which mainstream policies, either on their own or in combination, struggle to address. Those moving into self-employment or business ownership, for example, invariably face additional barriers connected with where they live, their background, lack of skills and lack of starting capital as well as the general challenges associated with starting a business. And as with making the transition into employment, the movement into self-employment or starting an enterprise by those who have been out of work for a long time is likely to require intensive and ongoing support through a number of stages, responsive to the particular needs of the individual and knowledgeable about the context within which they are operating. Consistently, mainstream employment and training policies or business support policy, such as those provided by Jobcentre Plus or Business Link, have been shown to be ineffective in this respect.

In contrast, localised employment and enterprise initiatives have demonstrated what is possible. Proactive and more person-centred support tailored to the needs of particular social and ethnic groups, delivered locally by motivated advisors, has been successful in reaching individuals and supporting them into employment, self-employment or business creation, where mainstream policies have failed. Successful enterprise-promotion projects, such as the 'Bizfizz' initiative, have combined business coaches with a particular focus on the pre-start and start-up phases of enterprise formation and a wider range of training and support (covering areas such as basic skills, language and financial literacy) than normally provided to those starting an enterprise.

The challenge is how to translate such initiatives into the mainstream in a manner that retains the commitment, enthusiasm and focus central to their success, and ensures that they are properly resourced. Such personalised support initiatives are necessarily more expensive than the delivery of standardised services in the short term, although they may produce significant savings in the longer term through reduced health, social and benefits costs. Unfortunately, while individual projects supported by the National Strategy for Neighbourhood Renewal may have been successful, there is as yet little evidence that this strategy has had a major impact on its principal target, which was to get mainstream funds substantially more focused on the needs of the most deprived areas.

In practice, effective and sometimes inspirational localised economic initiatives that 'make a difference' to places and people's lives often remain as islands within the sea of regeneration practice. Integrating innovative initiatives with wider provision is rare, as is feeding into the policy mainstream good local practice and effective learning from successful initiatives. Such difficulties of policy learning and rollout are partly rooted within the contextually dependent nature of individual initiatives, but also in the complexity, institutional instability and differing agendas of government departments and the unequal power relations between different agencies, institutions and levels of governance. Certainly, the lack of spatial sensitivity evident in the agendas of many central government departments with a key role to play in tackling the economic problems of deprived neighbourhoods, remains a considerable limitation.

Rationales for intervention

The particular discourse of urban development that has informed New Labour's approach to deprived neighbourhoods is characterised by a number of different, and sometimes competing, rationales for intervention. Although it has delivered certain positive outcomes within individual deprived neighbourhoods, it has made limited impact on the nature and scale of the overall problem of concentrated deprivation. This inability of current policy approaches to engage with the structural nature of problems of intense spatial inequality inevitably raises questions as to whether fundamental changes are needed in the informing rationale for policy intervention and the substantive regeneration and renewal industry that has grown up in the UK over recent decades. Critiques of the current rationale for intervention come from three broad positions, summarised simply in terms of the need for more market, more state or more self-reliant development.

More market

Those promoting a liberalised free market position maintain that the economic difficulties of deprived neighbourhoods are still rooted in an insufficient exposure to the operation of market mechanisms. This position argues that tackling concentrated deprivation requires a stronger focus on business-led approaches that maximise the opportunities (cheap land, property and labour) provided by spatial inequality, accepting social and spatial inequality as inevitable and ultimately non-problematic as long as economic growth is taking place. The lack of success of interventions to date is attributed in large part to their public sector-dominated conception and delivery. Instead, it sees a limited role for the state in providing a business-friendly environment, basic infrastructural provision and a minimum level of social welfare provision necessary to ensure political and social stability. Yet, as the analysis in this book has demonstrated, there is little evidence that a more liberalised, pro-market growth model will benefit deprived neighbourhoods and their residents. The success of the London and South East of England economies demonstrates that concentrated deprivation can exist within, and contribute towards, rapid regional economic growth, with low-cost neighbourhoods playing a significant role in reproducing the labour necessary for the growing number of low-wage service jobs. More fundamentally, the acceptance of a local economic development model that systematically marginalises certain social groups and spaces offends basic commitments to social justice and raises questions about its longer-term sustainability.

More state

This critique argues that instead of a proliferation of costly and wasteful localised initiatives, stronger action is needed, principally by the central state, to strengthen welfare provision and reduce social inequality. Specifically in terms of the economic conditions related to deprived neighbourhoods, major improvements are required in mainstream education and training provision to improve the life chances and mobility of those born into marginalised places and social groups, and in the regulation at the bottom end of the labour market, to improve basic levels of pay, working conditions and workforce development. The primary rationale for intervention here is centrally focused on the pursuit of improved social justice, arguing that what is required to effect real change is a fundamental commitment to the reduction of social inequality, the redistribution of wealth and the protection of marginalised groups. Certainly, the pursuit of social justice through mainstream social and economic policies and the associated redistribution of spending by the central state have to be a key component of any response to spatially concentrated deprivation.

Yet, it is also the case that mainstream policies have in the past routinely demonstrated an inability to reach the poorest residents living in the poorest neighbourhoods.

More self-reliant development

This position argues for the pursuit of a more self-reliant model of local economic development that questions the basis of the dominant economic growth paradigm. Alternative local economic development models that promote greater economic self-reliance are informed by diverse notions of social solidarity, equality, tolerance, local autonomy, self-development and environmental sustainability (Frankel, 1987; Harvey, 1996). While presenting a range of analyses from differing ideological standpoints, these approaches commonly critique the fundamental assumptions that underwrite existing economic growth models. These include arguing that the purpose of economic growth is a means to an end rather than an end in itself; that the economy should serve the needs of society rather than social goals being subsumed by the economic imperative; that the physical environment provides limits to growth, which makes current development paths unsustainable for future generations; and that the need for individuals to gain meaning, satisfaction and self-development within their lives and communities is hindered by consumerist ideologies and the alienation of much paid employment (Mayo, 1996; Gorz, 1999). These viewpoints routinely emphasise justice, equality, solidarity, democracy, fairness and environmental sustainability as the informing principles for any model of local development. They also provide a significantly different set of rationales to inform policy intervention with respect to deprived neighbourhoods than those that currently predominate.

The pursuit of autonomous strategies is for most localities heavily restricted in an era where global interactions and interdependencies are ever increasing. However, there do remain possibilities for self-reliant models of development that are outward looking and combined with a degree of external openness (Pike et al, 2006a). At the current time, it is increasing concerns about the environmental sustainability of current economic growth models that is generating the greatest impetus for developing alternative visions of local development. To date, notions of 'sustainability' have been much abused in UK local economic development and regeneration policy, being used in a diverse and generalised way, predominantly to justify existing development practice. Yet, a genuine commitment to rethink the current resource-intensive consumerist model of development in order to drastically reduce current and future environmental impacts, inevitably includes a recasting of localised development models. Shifts towards people living closer to their places of work, the local sourcing of products and the development of localised services and supply chains provide possibilities for a local economy oriented more directly to the needs and resources of the local population. For deprived neighbourhoods that may have been blighted by the loss of local shops and services, and their residents who often have limited travel options and are less involved in commuting over longer distances given the predominantly lowly paid nature of their employment, a reinvigorated localised economic sphere provides a series of new possibilities largely absent from recent local economic development trajectories.

Refocusing on the economic: work and enterprise

These diverse critiques of the New Labour approach to the economic development of deprived neighbourhoods suggest the need for a re-evaluation of its core elements. A positive element of New Labour's overall approach has been an emphasis on a holistic approach, recognising the multidimensional nature of the problem of deprived neighbourhoods arising from interlocking and reinforcing cycles of decline. However, recent moves towards the prioritisation of getting people into employment and the introduction of the Working Neighbourhoods Fund (WNF) to replace the Neighbourhood Renewal Fund (NRF) mark a shift away from this holistic vision and associated broad-based policy actions and its replacement with a narrower emphasis on employment, enterprise and skills. While a strengthened economic dimension to neighbourhood-oriented policy is to be welcomed, this needs to be in addition to, rather than instead of, a wider holistic approach.

At the heart of a renewed economic focus is a strengthened emphasis on formal employment as the principal route out of poverty, with self-employment and enterprise as supporting elements. Although localised supply-side initiatives developed over recent years have demonstrated that it is possible to improve the integration of people living in deprived areas into the formal labour market, the success of such initiatives is strongly concentrated on those groups who are already 'closest' to the labour market. Given relatively high employment rates nationally, policy attention has become directed increasingly to those groups who are more 'distant' to the labour market, such as those claiming Incapacity Benefit (IB) or the long-term unemployed. This provides an ever more challenging agenda, particularly as the recent phase of employment growth appears to be coming to an end. Integrating these groups into the labour market is a long-term, resource-intensive process that requires the development of pre-employment skills, the provision of transitional working environments (such as intermediate labour markets; ILMs) and appropriately structured welfare support. However, even then, it is likely that a significant proportion will still not enter into stable, long-term formal employment.

A local economic development policy for deprived neighbourhoods narrowly focused on getting people into paid employment faces fundamental challenges. The lack of priority on building up enterprise and entrepreneurial activity means a continuing reliance on jobs generated elsewhere. Moreover, there has been too little attention paid thus far to the quality and prospects provided by the types of jobs being created that those living in deprived areas are most likely to access. Low-wage, low-skill, low-status, unstable jobs with limited future opportunities provide limited incentives to enter into formal employment. For many, particularly for those living in high-cost areas, the insecure low-wage jobs on offer fail to provide a living wage (Butler and Watt, 2007; TUC Commission on Vulnerable Employment, 2008). In these circumstances the alternative of not working and claiming benefit payments may for some households provide a higher and more stable level of income. For other groups, such as certain young people or minority ethnic groups with no (recognised) qualifications, alternatives such as engagement in informal economic activity may provide similar, or indeed much higher, levels of income, while also offering a more attractive lifestyle through providing a higher status among peers and/or less engagement with state authorities.

The emphasis on 'work first' initiatives for those living in poor areas has contributed to the development of a low-wage, flexible work culture, encouraging or compelling the most deprived to take jobs, whatever these may be. The high level of in-migration has also played a key role in allowing the continuance of this policy, with a ready supply of workers willing to take on the low-grade service, manufacturing and agricultural jobs that existing residents are not willing to do. Recent policy directions have begun to recognise the limitations of this approach and the need to develop what are termed more 'sustainable' jobs, in a bid to reduce the constant 'churning' at the bottom end of the labour market. The aim here is to better integrate employment and training provision to promote workers developing their skills and employers their workforces and to ensure that those entering the labour market stay in employment longer and have opportunities for career advancement. The provision of genuine chances for employment progression for those taking up entry-level jobs is central to providing a more positive environment for labour market entry. However, the effectiveness of such strategies is reliant on employer commitment and past practice suggests a deep-seated reluctance of many UK employers to invest in workforce development.

In contrast, there has been virtually no attention paid to the equally important aspect of improving the pay and working conditions at the bottom end of the labour market. Here national-level regulation is central, but aside from the introduction of the National Minimum Wage by New Labour, there has been a notable lack of political will to improve further regulation related to pay, conditions and security for low-wage workers. Policy responses related to labour market regulation and training need to be pursued predominantly at the national level but the more localised operation of labour markets also ensures the need for the active engagement of local stakeholders. It is notable, for example, that the campaign in London to achieve a higher minimum 'living wage' better aligned to the capital's living costs has been led by civil society-based organisations, with subsequent backing from the Mayor of London.

Interventions of this type, alongside localised employment initiatives that have succeeded in connecting the most marginalised to the labour market, illustrate the need for active engagement with employers to enable the development of more positive relationships between business, local agencies and workers. This is required not only to develop appropriate education and training initiatives via local colleges and schools to fulfil skills needs and enable genuine workforce development but also to improve the quality of the employment on offer. Unfortunately, to date, Regional Economic Strategies (RESs) and other city/subregional strategies have largely paid little or no attention to the development of the low-wage, low-skill element of the labour market, fixated instead on the development of high-tech, high-skill jobs. Ultimately, it will only be through improving demand-side conditions, relating to the quality of the employment on offer, as well as labour market supply to make marginalised workers more competitive, that residents from deprived areas – notably young males and certain minority ethnic groups where a lack of labour market integration is particularly apparent – will successfully enter the labour market.

However, there is a more fundamental critique of the employment-led renewal agenda that relates to the development of broader notions of economic and social well-being, individual self-development and the development of stronger community and social solidarity. The current policy emphasis on paid employment necessarily downgrades the importance of economic activity, paid or unpaid, that takes place outside of this sphere, whether in the home, family or community. Yet, for many residents of deprived areas, work and life outside of paid employment dominates and is central to their well-being. Recognising and building on the positive aspects of this work – whether this is in the form of entrepreneurial, voluntary or caring activity – becomes an important complement to paid employment. Important here too is the stimulation of entrepreneurial activity, not just for its economic benefits, but also for wider social and community purposes, as it encourages proactive development of individual and community activities rather than a dependency on existing unstable and short-term paid jobs.

In developing a wider notion of economic well-being, not only is there a need to recognise the value of a full range of economic activity, but also to value and promote the self-development of individuals within their wider communities of place and interest. The lack of self-worth, ambition, and indeed hope, apparent in some individuals and groups living in deprived neighbourhoods reinforces processes of social exclusion and negatively impacts on overall well-being and quality of life. Low self-esteem emanates from socioeconomic marginalisation, limited opportunities and lack of social mobility often over long periods of time. Much of the low-grade entry-level employment currently on offer provides limited prospects for improving self-esteem or gaining job satisfaction, and where it necessitates working long or unsocial hours to ensure a living wage, it also limits the possibilities to gain satisfaction in activities outside of the workplace.

In this respect, alternative models of local economic development put at their centre promoting an environment where individuals and the communities they are a part of can pursue worthwhile working lives through paid employment, self-employment or other forms of unpaid work that offers possibilities for personal satisfaction and a decent quality of life. Critical here is the development of work activities that are rooted within local social and environmental needs, to develop a socialised economy that is more small scale, community based and socially useful. Important too is the role of education, not in the narrow sense of preparing individuals for paid employment that increasingly predominates in regeneration practice, but in a wider sense of self-development and realisation, which opens up personal horizons and provides the capacities and confidence for individuals to participate actively in all aspects of social, economic and political life.

The governance challenge

A recurring issue central to the success of economic initiatives related to tackling concentrated deprivation is the nature and scope of governance arrangements. Operating in an integrated and coordinated manner across a range of different agencies, policy domains and spatial scales provides a particular challenge whatever the prevailing governance arrangements. Over the last 25 years the governance of economic development and policy delivery in relation to deprived areas within the UK has evolved to display a high level of complexity and instability alongside a well-established lack of devolved power at the local level. Recent governance change towards devolution and administrative decentralisation has acted to reinforce this complexity, by developing additional spatial scales of operation at the regional and subregional level, and has contributed towards an environment in which constant change in institutions, policies and governance arrangements has become the accepted norm.

For relationships between agencies to become better established and mature into effective working arrangements, simpler structures and funding regimes, greater stability and increased clarity over the roles and responsibilities of different agencies are required. The *Review of subnational economic development and regeneration* undertaken in England (HM Treasury et al, 2007) recognised many of these points, as do associated reforms such as the creation of the new Homes and Community Agency and the development of an enhanced 'place-making' role for local government. The introduction of the Area-Based Grant (ABG) in 2008 to simplify multiple funding streams and provide greater localised discretion to local authorities over priorities provides one example of such changes. Yet the implementation of the subnational review also initiates a further round of reform of institutions and governance arrangements, with proposals for changes in the relationships between regions and local authorities and the development of subregional and city-region working through the creation of Multi Area Agreements and City Development Companies (CDCs). The danger exists that another round of reform of institutional arrangements is as likely to reproduce past complexity and instability as it is to resolve it.

In fact, it is important not to become fixated on constant revisions of governance structures and arrangements. There is a real danger that the major challenges posed by economic restructuring and labour market polarisation become redefined as a problem of management failure (Jones and Ward, 2002). Given current dynamics of urban and regional change, the very notion of what constitutes 'good governance' needs to be reopened for critical debate. Within a rapidly changing global economic system that is characterised by increasing mobility, openness and interpenetration, economic processes of change operate across scales and boundaries at a speed and force that often leaves national and subnational agencies with only limited room for meaningful action (Gore and Fothergill, 2007). In recognising these fundamental constraints, certain key elements of the current governance discourse require particular attention in relation to the economic development of deprived areas.

Business engagement

A central tension within dominant market-based approaches to local economic development is that although the private sector is the motor of this process, business remains cautious, if not sometimes hostile, to greater involvement in the governance and delivery of policy interventions. Although some larger companies have seen benefits in engagement with local communities as part of wider strategies of corporate social responsibility, the majority of UK businesses, particularly smaller businesses, which often predominate within deprived areas, feel disinclined to engage with a neighbourhood renewal agenda they feel is dominated by public sector interests and delivery mechanisms that operate slowly and stifle initiative, enterprise and risk-taking. Significantly, initiatives such as the City Growth Strategies that aimed to put business at the heart of the agenda in deprived areas have had little success, while the work of much of the LSPs and neighbourhood renewal strategies is dominated by public sector agencies and their agendas and they have struggled to achieve any meaningful private sector engagement.

The challenge of achieving routine and meaningful involvement of employers and business interests therefore remains significant. Effective engagement has tended to take place around focused interventions where the private sector can see a clear and immediate benefit. This has been evident with respect to property developers' involvement in large regeneration schemes or local businesses improving their retail environment within Business Improvement Districts. Yet, in other central aspects engagement has remained limited. The majority of businesses remain reluctant to take on those who have been out of the labour market for long periods of time, or to invest significantly in workforce development for low-skilled jobs, citing that once trained, such workers are likely to move on to benefit other employers. In this respect the dominant policy emphasis on consensual partnership working and the pursuit of win–win solutions struggles to deal with fundamental differences of interest and ways of working evident within different private, public and third sector agencies.

Taking forward employer involvement in relation to deprived areas needs to proceed from a recognition of areas of conflict (for example in relation to the perpetuation of low-wage and low-level working conditions) as well as those of mutual interest. Certainly, the potential exists to build stronger positive relationships with employers in areas such as workforce development, corporate social responsibility and environmental sustainability, where progressive businesses can identify benefits within an increasingly competitive environment. Public sector employers too represent a major, but often underutilised, resource given that they are often some of the largest employers within deprived areas, and are potentially well placed to engage with local communities and other stakeholders.

Spatial levels of intervention

The argument developed throughout this book is that the economic problems of deprived neighbourhoods cannot be tackled effectively at highly localised levels in a context increasingly dominated by liberalised markets. In this respect, bottom–up models of urban regeneration, such as the 'transforming of big places through small spaces' ideal put forward by Power and Houghton (2007), have basic limitations when applied to the economic realm. This is not to deny that scope exists for building more locally based, self-reliant economies. Economic interventions at neighbourhood and local levels can be developed and strengthened in various ways through diverse initiatives ranging from asset-based community trusts through to social enterprises and transitional labour markets. Yet, such interventions cannot of themselves significantly reduce high levels of worklessness and increase low levels of financial investment within deprived neighbourhoods. In this respect, neighbourhood and community-based interventions need to be coordinated and integrated with interventions operating across local, subregional, regional, national and international spatial scales.

Past policy practice has not been informed by clear thinking as to what the optimum levels of intervention are for different types of economic development activity. In practice, a spatial division of policy interventions has emerged over recent years, as detailed in Chapter Five, and current policy practice is to attempt to clarify further the role of different spatial levels (DCLG, 2008c) as part of the subnational review (HM Treasury et al, 2007). What is apparent is that effective intervention requires active consideration of the needs of deprived neighbourhoods across all spatial levels of governance in a manner that has not happened to date, given that the pursuit of economic development at national and regional levels has been narrowly focused on promoting economic competitiveness. In this respect the subregional and city-region scale is important as it is this functional level at which labour markets (particularly in relation to lower-skilled jobs) operate and at which there is considerable scope for improved integration of economic development and social inclusion agendas. Yet, thus far within Britain, this governance level remains variably developed and its future development is likely to be an area of contestation between existing local authorities and regional-level bodies.

Devolution

The highly centralised British state system continues to struggle with accommodating the local differences so important to the constitution of concentrated deprivation. Policy responses towards employment, skills, education, enterprise and social inequality are largely dictated by government at the national level. The differing policy agendas and priorities of central government departments become particularly evident at the local level when attempting to develop integrated responses. Significantly, the attitudes and actions of New Labour towards devolution and decentralisation have displayed strong contradictory tendencies. Despite devolving varying degrees of power to Scotland, Wales and London and recognising that further devolution would be beneficial to economic development and social well-being, in practice it has consistently backed away from further devolution of power to subnational authorities. The failure to more radically reform local government, advance elected Regional Assemblies or, to date, significantly develop city-regions, provides evidence of a national government seemingly fearful of a loss of central control and the emergence of differentiated spatial responses.

In this context the devolution of genuine power to the local level in terms of agenda setting, budgets and policy development marks the only means of escaping the straightjacket of central control that has hindered the pursuit of locally based economic strategies over many decades. The development of a more autonomous local-level sphere with greater community empowerment is a defining characteristic of alternative models of local economic development, as are decentred models of urban development that place stronger neighbourhood and local management at the centre of city transformation (Power and

Houghton, 2007).Yet, it is also important to recognise that a process of political devolution does not necessarily lead to a greater concern for the needs of the most deprived neighbourhoods or indeed more efficient policy responses. Within any given local political context deprived areas and their residents are open to potential marginalisation by other dominant local interests, while neighbourhood-level structures would lack the resources to respond to economic problems rooted in wider economic structures.

But the development of more politically and financially autonomous local and neighbourhood spheres would provide a stimulus to participatory democratic practice, particularly important within areas where long-term deprivation has reinforced political cultures of apathy and dependency, and permit the development of a range of economic and social initiatives better attuned to locally identified priorities and circumstances. The evidence of devolution within the UK to date does suggest that distinct national and city economic and social agendas have emerged within Scotland, Wales and London in relation to deprived areas (North et al, 2007). Although these have often yet to be translated into concrete outputs, the development of political devolution has put in place a context within which there is a stronger political imperative to understand and respond to urban and regional change and its relationship to area-based deprivation.

Final thoughts

This book has demonstrated the possibilities and limitations of current policy approaches to improving the economic conditions that currently exist within deprived neighbourhoods. Over many years, much of the activity aimed at deprived neighbourhoods has been dominated by 'gesture' policy and politics, offering short-term palliatives in response to particular instances of social and political unrest, rather than any consistent and fundamental commitment to alleviating the poverty embedded within these neighbourhoods. The New Labour governments have shown a commitment to placing the issue of localised deprivation at the centre of their policy agenda. However, the resulting impact on improving the economic life of deprived communities and the people who live within them has been hampered both by the wider discourses that have informed policy development and the practical problems of developing integrated delivery mechanisms.

Any future development of the policy context needs to be informed by the basic issues discussed in this chapter. Policy interventions need to be responsive to and rooted within an understanding of unevenly developed local and regional economies and to effectively combine mainstream responses with area-based initiatives (ABIs). Responses need to demonstrate clarity over the rationale for intervention and the centrality of social justice, and develop governance arrangements that provide genuine levels of local-level autonomy as a basis for meaningful integration and coordination of activity across and within spatial levels.

More broadly there is a need for a critical questioning of the informing rationale for policy intervention in order to improve the economic realities for those living in deprived neighbourhoods. In light of the continued presence of deprived neighbourhoods and the limitations of past policy practice to meet the needs of many of those people living and working within such areas, careful consideration of alternative prescriptions of local economic development alongside existing mainstream approaches is necessary if we are to avoid a future that merely reinvents and recycles past policy practice. Rather than the development of an ever more narrow focus on getting people into formal employment, what is needed is a wider vision that places responses to deprived neighbourhoods within an approach to local economic development that is genuinely inclusive and sustainable.

References

Adams, J., Greig, M. and McQuaid, R.W. (2002) 'Mismatch in local labour markets in Central Scotland: the neglected role of demand', *Urban Studies*, vol 39, no 8, pp 1399-416.

Ambrose, P. (2003) *Love the work, hate the job: Low cost but acceptable wage levels and the exported costs of low pay in Brighton and Hove*, Brighton: Health and Social Policy Research Centre, University of Brighton

Amin, A. and Thrift, N. (1994) 'Living in the global', in A. Amin and N. Thrift (eds) *Globalization, institutions and regional development in Europe*, Oxford: Oxford University Press, pp 1-22.

Amin, A., Cameron, A. and Hudson, R. (2002) *Placing the social economy*, London: Routledge.

Amion Consulting (2007a) *National strategy for neighbourhood renewal: Evidence on progress and value for money* (unpublished), Liverpool: Amion Consulting Ltd.

Amion Consulting (2007b) *People and places: Draft phase one report* (unpublished), Liverpool: Amion Consulting Ltd.

Atkinson, R. (2007) 'Under construction – the city-region and the neighbourhood: new actor in a system of multi-level governance?', in I. Smith, E. Lepine and M. Taylor (eds) *Disadvantaged by where you live? Neighbourhood governance in contemporary urban policy*, Bristol: The Policy Press, pp 65-82.

Atkinson, R. and Carmichael, L. (2007) 'Neighbourhood as a new focus for action in the urban policies of West European states', in I. Smith, E. Lepine and M. Taylor (eds) *Disadvantaged by where you live? Neighbourhood governance in contemporary urban policy*, Bristol: The Policy Press, pp 43-64.

Atkinson, R. and Kintrea, K. (2001) 'Disentangling area effects: evidence from deprived and non-deprived neighbourhoods', *Urban Studies*, vol 38, no 12, pp 2277-98.

Atkinson, R. and Moon, G. (1994) *Urban policy in Britain: The city, the state and the market*, London: Macmillan.

Audit Commission (1999) *A life's work: Local authorities, economic development and economic regeneration*, London: Audit Commission.

Audretsch, D., Thurik, R., Verheul, I. and Wennekers, S. (2002) *Entrepreneurship: Determinants and policy in a European–US comparison*, Boston/Dordrecht/London: Kluwer Academic Publishers.

Bailey, N. and Livingston, M. (2007) *Population turnover and area deprivation*, Bristol: The Policy Press.

Bank of England (1999) *Finance for small firms – a sixth report*, London: Bank of England.

Bauder, H. (2001) 'Work, young people and neighbourhood representations', *Social and Cultural Geography*, vol 2, no 4, pp 461-80.

Beatty, C. and Fothergill, S. (2002) 'Hidden unemployment amongst men: a case study', *Regional Studies*, vol 36, no 8, pp 617-30.

Beatty, C. and Fothergill, S. (2003) 'The detached male workforce', in P. Alcock, C. Beatty, S. Fothergill, R. MacMillan and S. Yeandle (eds) *Work to welfare: How men become detached from the labour market*, Cambridge: Cambridge University Press, pp 79-110.

Beatty, C. and Fothergill, S. (1996) 'Labour market adjustment in areas of chronic industrial decline: the case of the UK coalfields', *Regional Studies*, vol 30, no 7, pp 627-40.

Beatty, C., Fothergill, S. and MacMillan, R. (2000) 'A theory of employment, unemployment and sickness', *Regional Studies*, vol 34, no 7, pp 617-30.

Beatty, C., Fothergill, S., Houston, D., Powell, R. and Sissons, P. (2007) 'A gendered theory of employment, unemployment and sickness', Paper presented at the Regional Studies Association Working Group on Employability and Labour Market Policy in European Perspective, Napier University, Edinburgh, October.

Berthoud, R. (2003) *Multiple disadvantage in employment: A quantitative analysis*, York: Joseph Rowntree Foundation.

Bertotti, M. (2008) 'Economic competitiveness and governance in deprived urban areas: the City Growth Strategies in two London areas', Unpublished PhD thesis, Middlesex University, London.

BIC (Business in the Community) (2002a) *Business investment in under-served markets: An opportunity for businesses and communities?*, London: Department of Trade and Industry.

BIC (2002b) *Neighbourhood renewal: Case studies in corporate social responsibility*, London: BIC.

BIC (2005) *Under-served markets: Preliminary research findings*, London: BIC.

Birch, D. (1979) *The job generation process*, Cambridge, MA: MIT Programme on Neighbourhood and Regional Change.

Blackaby, D., Leslie, D., Murphy, P. and O'Leary, N. (2002) 'White/ethnic minority earnings and employment differentials in Britain: evidence from the LFS', *Oxford Economic Papers*, vol 54, no 2, pp 270-97.

Blackburn, R. and Ram, M. (2006) 'Fix or fixation? The contributions and limitations of entrepreneurship and small firms to combating social exclusion', *Entrepreneurship and Regional Development*, vol 18, no 1, pp 73–89.

Boddy, M. (ed) (2003) *Urban transformation and urban governance: Shaping the competitive city of the future*, Bristol: The Policy Press.

Boddy, M. and Parkinson, M. (2004) 'Competitiveness, cohesion and urban governance', in M. Boddy and M. Parkinson (eds) *City matters: Competitiveness, cohesion and urban governance*, Bristol: The Policy Press, pp 407-32.

Bonjour, D., Knight, G. and Lissenburgh, S. (2001) *Evaluation of New Deal for Young People in Scotland: Phase 2*, Edinburgh: Central Research Unit, Scottish Executive.

Brennan, A., Rhodes, J. and Tyler, P. (1999) *Evaluation of the Single Regeneration Budget Challenge Fund: First final evaluation of three SRB short duration case studies*, Discussion Paper 111, Cambridge: Department of Land Economy, University of Cambridge.

Brennan, A., Rhodes, J. and Tyler, P. (2000) 'The nature of local area social exclusion in England and the role of the labour market', *Oxford Review of Economic Policy*, vol 16, no 1, pp 129-46.

Bright, E. (2003) *Reviving America's forgotten neighborhoods*, New York: Routledge.

Bristow, G., Munday, M. and Gripaios, P. (2000) 'Call centre growth and location: corporate strategy and the spatial division of labour', *Environment & Planning A*, vol 32, no 3, pp 519-38.

Brooks-Gunn, J., Duncan, G., Klebanov, P. and Sealand, N. (1993) 'Do neighbourhoods influence child and adolescent development?', *American Journal of Sociology*, vol 99, no 2, pp 353-95.

Bruttel, O. (2005) 'Are employment zones successful? Evidence from the first four years', *Local Economy*, vol 20, no 4, pp 389-403.

Buck, N. (2001) 'Identifying neighbourhood effects on social exclusion', *Urban Studies*, vol 38, no 12, pp 2251-75.

Buck, N. and Gordon, I. (2004) 'Does spatial concentration of disadvantage contribute to social exclusion?', in M. Boddy and M. Parkinson (eds) *City matters: Competitiveness, cohesion and urban governance*, Bristol: The Policy Press, pp 237-54.

Buck, N., Gordon, I., Hall, P., Harloe, M. and Kleinman, M. (2002) *Working capital: Life and labour in contemporary London*, London: Routledge.

Buck, N., Gordon, I., Harding, A. and Turok, I. (eds) (2005) *Changing cities: Rethinking urban competitiveness, cohesion and governance*, Basingstoke: Palgrave Macmillan.

Burgess, S., Gardiner, K. and Propper, C. (2001) *Growing up: School, family and area influence on adolescents' later life chances*, CASE Paper No. 49, London: London School of Economics and Political Science.

Burns, D., Williams, C.C. and Windebank, J. (2004) *Community self-help*, Basingstoke: Palgrave.

Burns, P. (2007) *Entrepreneurship and small business* (2nd edition), Basingstoke: Palgrave.

Butler, T. and Watt, P. (2007) *Understanding social inequality*, London: Sage Publications.

Bynner, J. and Parsons, S. (1997) *It doesn't get any better: The impact of poor basic skill attainment on the lives of 37 year olds*, London: The Basic Skills Agency.

Cabinet Office and DTLR (Department of Transport, Local Government and the Regions) (2002) *Your region, your choice: Revitalising the English regions*, London: The Stationery Office.

Cantle, T. (2005) *Community cohesion: A new framework for race and diversity*, London: Palgrave Macmillan.

Canzanelli, G. (2001) *Overview and learned lessons on local economic development: Human development and decent work*, Geneva: International Labour Office.

Carley, M., Kirk, K. and McIntosh, S. (2001) *Retailing, sustainability and neighbourhood regeneration*, Bristol/York: The Policy Press/Joseph Rowntree Foundation.

Casebourne, J., Davis, S. and Page, R. (2006) *Review of Action Teams for Jobs*, Research Report 328, London: DWP.

Champion, T. and Fisher, T. (2004) 'Migration, residential preferences and the changing environment of cities', in M. Boddy and M. Parkinson (eds) *City matters: Competitiveness, cohesion and urban governance*, Bristol: The Policy Press, pp 111-29.

Chell, E. (2007) 'Social enterprise and entrepreneurship: towards a convergent theory of the entrepreneurial process', *International Small Business Journal*, vol 25, no 5, pp 5-23.

Cheshire, P., Monastiriotis, V. and Sheppard, S. (2003) 'Income inequality and residential segregation: labour market sorting and the demand for positional goods', in R. Martin and P. Morrison (eds) *Geographies of labour market inequality*, London: Routledge, pp 83-109.

CIC (Commission on Integration and Cohesion) (2007) *Our shared future*, London: CIC.

Cobb, C. (2001) 'Zip code 10027 – lookin' good in Harlem', *National Geographic*, vol 199, no 4, pp 120-4.

Cochrane, A. (2007) *Understanding urban policy: A critical approach*, Oxford: Blackwell Publishing.

Cole, I., Lawless, P., Manning, J. and Wilson, I. (2007) *The moving escalator? Patterns of residential mobility in New Deal for Communities Areas*, Research Report 32, London: Department for Communities and Local Government.

Conscise (2003) *The contribution of social capital in the social economy to local economic development in Western Europe*, Final Report, Brussels: European Commission.

Convery, P. (2006) 'Local enterprise growth initiative', *Local Economy*, vol 21, no 3, pp 316-27.

Coombes, M. and Raybould, S. (2004) 'Finding work in 2001: urban–rural contrasts across England in employment rates and local job availability', *Area*, vol 36, no 2, pp 202-22.

Coombes, M., Champion, T. and Raybould, S. (2007) 'Did the early A8 in-migrants to England go to areas of labour shortage?', *Local Economy*, vol 22, no 4, pp 335-48.

Coulson, N. and Fisher, L. (2002) 'Tenure choice and labour market outcomes', *Housing Studies*, vol 17, no 1, pp 35-49.

Cowling, M. and Hayward, R. (2000) *Out of unemployment*, Birmingham: Research Centre for Industrial Strategy, University of Birmingham.

Cox, K., Irving, P., Leather, J. and McKenna, K. (2002) *Evaluation of Action Teams for Jobs*, ESOTEC, Research Report WAE 114, Sheffield: Employment Service.

CPP (Centre for Property and Planning) (1998) *Attracting private finance into urban regeneration*, Coventry: RICS/JRF.

CRESR (Centre for Regional Economic and Social Research) (2005) *New Deal for Communities 2001–05: An interim evaluation*, Neighbourhood Renewal Unit Research Report No 17, London: ODPM.

Cummins, S. and Macintyre, S. (2002) 'A systematic study of an urban foodscape: the price and availability of food in Greater Glasgow', *Urban Studies*, vol 39, no 11, pp 2115-30.

Dabinett, G. and Ramsden, P. (1999) 'Urban policy in Sheffield: regeneration, partnerships and people', in R. Imrie and H. Thomas (eds) *British urban policy and the Urban Development Corporations*, London: Paul Chapman Publishing, pp 168–85.

Dale, I. and Morgan, A. (2001) *Job creation, the role of new and small firms*, London: Trends Business Research and Small Business Service.

DCLG (Department of Communities and Local Government) (2007a) *Place-shaping: A shared vision for the future of local government* (The Lyons Report), London: DCLG.

DCLG (2007b) *Communities and local government economics paper 1: A framework for intervention*, London: DCLG.

DCLG (2008a) *The English Indices of Deprivation, 2007*, London: DCLG.

DCLG (2008b) *New Deal for Communities: A synthesis of new programme wide evidence: 2006–07*, NDC National Evaluation Phase 2, Research Report 39, London: DCLG.

DCLG (2008c) *Planning and optimal geographical levels for economic decision making – the sub-regional role*, London: DCLG.

DCLG and DWP (Department for Work and Pensions) (2007) *The Working Neighbourhoods Fund*, London: DCLG.

de Souza Briggs, X. (1998) 'Brown kids in white suburbs: housing mobility and the many faces of social capital', *Housing Policy Debate*, vol 9, no 1, pp 177–221.

Deakins, D. and Freel, M. (2006) *Entrepreneurship and small firms* (4th edition), Maidenhead: McGraw-Hill Education.

Deakins, D., Ram, M. and Smallbone, D. (2003) 'Addressing the business support needs of ethnic minority firms in the United Kingdom', *Environment and Planning C: Government and Policy*, vol 21, no 6, pp 843–59.

Deakins, D., Ishaq, M., Smallbone, D., Whittam, G. and Wyper, J. (2005) *Minority ethnic enterprise in Scotland: A national scoping study*, Final Research Report, Edinburgh: Scottish Executive.

Dean, J. and Hastings, A. (2000) *Challenging images: Housing estates, stigma and regeneration*, Bristol: The Policy Press.

DETR (Department of the Environment, Transport and the Regions) (2000a) *Social exclusion and the provision of public transport: Main report*, London: DETR.

DETR (2000b) *City challenge: Final national evaluation*, London: DETR.

DETR (2001) *A review of the evidence base for regeneration policy and practice*, London: DETR.

Devins, D. and Hogarth, T. (2005) 'Employing the unemployed: some case study evidence on the role and practice of employers', *Urban Studies*, vol 42, no 2, pp 245–56.

Dewson, S., Casebourne, J., Darlow, A. and Krishnan, S. (2007) *Evaluation of the Working Neighbourhoods Pilot: Final report*, Research Report 411, London: DWP.

DfEE (Department for Education and Employment) (1998) *Review of business start-up activities under the Single Regeneration Budget*, Research Report RR58, London: DfEE.

DfEE (1999) *Jobs for all: Report of the Policy Action Team on Jobs*, London: DfEE.

Dickens, W. (1999) 'Rebuilding urban labour markets: what can community development accomplish?', in R. Ferguson and W. Dickens (eds) *Urban problems and community development*, Washington, DC: Brookings Institute Press, pp 381-436.

Dixon, T. (2005) 'The role of retailing in urban regeneration', *Local Economy*, vol 20, no 2, pp 168-82.

DoE (Department of the Environment) (1995) *Final evaluation of Enterprise Zones*, Cambridge: PA Cambridge Economic Consultants/DOE/HMSO.

Dorling, D. (2006) 'Inequalities in Britain 1997-2006: the dream that turned pear-shaped', *Local Economy*, vol 21, no 4, pp 353-61.

Dorling, D., Rigby, J., Wheeler, B., Ballas, D., Thomas, B., Fahmy, E., Gordon, D. and Lupton, R. (2007) *Poverty, wealth and place in Britain 1968 to 2005*, Bristol: The Policy Press.

DTI (Department of Trade and Industry) (2002) *Social enterprise: A strategy for success*, London: DTI.

DTI (2005a) *Government response to the Small Business Council report on the informal economy*, London: The Stationery Office/DTI.

DTI (2005b) *Guidance to RDAs on regional strategies*, London: DTI.

DTLR (Department for Transport, Local Government and the Regions) (2000) *The English Indices of Deprivation, 2000*, London: DTLR.

DTLR (2002) *Lessons and evaluation evidence from ten Single Regeneration Budget case studies*, Mid-term report, London: DTLR.

Duffy, B. (2000) *Satisfaction and expectations: Attitudes to public services in deprived areas*, CASE Paper No 45, London: London School of Economics and Political Science.

Dunford, J. (2006) 'Under-served markets', *Local Economy*, vol 21, no 1, pp 73-7.

DWP (Department for Work and Pensions) (2007a) *Reducing dependency, increasing opportunity: Options for the future of welfare to work* (The Freud Report), London: DWP.

DWP (2007b) *In work, better off: Next steps to full employment*, London: DWP.

EC (European Commission) (2003) *Entrepreneurship in Europe*, Green Paper, EM5765/03COM (03) 27, Brussels: EC.

EC (2005) *Importance of social economy enterprises*, Brussels: Enterprise and Industry DG, EC.

Eisenschitz, A. and Gough, J. (1993) *The politics of local economic policy: The problems and possibilities of local initiative*, London: Macmillan.

Ellen, I. (2000) 'Race-based neighbourhood projection: a proposed framework for understanding new data on racial segregation', *Urban Studies*, vol 37, no 9, pp 1513-33.

Ellen, I. and Turner, M. (1997) 'Does neighbourhood matter? Assessing recent evidence', *Housing Policy Debate*, vol 8, no 4, pp 833-66.

EMRA (East Midlands Regional Assembly) (2006) *Linking it up locally? A scrutiny review into local area urban regeneration, partnership working and delivering the RES*, Nottingham: EMRA.

Engels, F. (1987) *The condition of the working class in England*, London: Penguin.

Equalities Review (2007) *Fairness and freedom: The final report of the equalities review*, http://archive.cabinetoffice.gov.uk/equalitiesreview/

Evans, M. (2001a) 'Britain: moving towards a work and opportunity-focused welfare state?', *International Journal of Social Welfare*, vol 10, no 4, pp 260-6.

Evans, M. (2001b) *Community enterprise and regeneration in North London: The prospect in four boroughs*, London Regeneration Paper No 3, London: Middlesex University.

Evans, M. and Syrett, S. (2007) 'Generating social capital? The social economy and local economic development', *European Urban and Regional Studies*, vol 14, no 1, pp 53-72.

Evans, M., Eyre, J., Sarre, S. and Millar, J. (2003) *New Deal for Lone Parents: Second synthesis report of the national evaluation*, Research Report W163, Sheffield: DWP.

Evans, M., Syrett, S. and Williams, C. (2006) *Informal economic activities and deprived neighbourhoods*, London: DCLG.

Fadahunsi, A., Smallbone, D. and Supri, S. (2000) 'Networking and ethnic minority enterprise development: insights from a North London study', *Journal of Small Business and Enterprise Development*, vol 7, no 3, pp 228-40.

Fainstein, S. (2001) *Competitiveness, cohesion and governance: A review of the literature*, ESRC Cities Initiative, Swindon: Economic and Social Research Council.

Fainstein, S., Gordon, I. and Harloe, M. (1993) *Divided cities: Economic restructuring and social change in London and New York*, London: Blackwell.

Fieldhouse, E. (1999) 'Ethnic minority unemployment and spatial mismatch: the case of London', *Urban Studies*, vol 36, no 9, pp 1569-96.

Fieldhouse, E. and Tranmer, M. (2001) 'Concentration effects, spatial mismatch or neighbourhood selection? Exploring labour market and neighbourhood variation in male unemployment risk using Census microdata from Great Britain', *Geographical Analysis*, vol 33, no 4, pp 353-69.

Fieldhouse, E., Kalra, V. and Alam, S. (2002) 'How new is the New Deal? A qualitative study of the New Deal for Young People on minority ethnic groups in Oldham', *Local Economy*, vol 17, no 1, pp 50-64.

Finn, D. and Simmonds, D. (2003) *Intermediate labour markets in Britain and an international review of transitional employment programmes*, London: DWP.

Forrest, R. and Kearns, A. (1999) *Joined-up places? Social cohesion and neighbourhood regeneration*, York: York Publishing Services/Joseph Rowntree Foundation.

Forrest, R. and Kearns, A. (2001) 'Social cohesion, social capital and the neighbourhood', *Urban Studies*, vol 38, no 12, pp 2125-45.

Francis, L. and Thomas, H. (2006) 'Evaluating property-led initiatives in urban regeneration: tracing vacancy chains in Cardiff Bay', *Local Economy*, vol 21, no 1, pp 49-64.

Frankel, B. (1987) *The post-industrial utopians*, Cambridge: Polity Press.

Fuller, C., Bennett, R. and Ramsden, M. (2004) 'Local government and the changing institutional landscape of economic development in England and Wales', *Environment and Planning C: Government and Policy*, vol 22, pp 317-47.

Galster, G. (2001) 'On the nature of neighbourhood', *Urban Studies*, vol 38, no 12, pp 2111-24.

Galster, G., Quercia, R. and Cortes, A. (2000) 'Identifying neighbourhood thresholds: an empirical exploration', *Housing Policy Debate*, vol 11, no 3, pp 701-32.

Galster, G., Quercia, A. and Malega, R. (2003) 'The fortunes of poor neighbourhoods', *Urban Affairs Review*, vol 39, no 2, pp 205-27.

Garrahan, P. and Stewart, P. (1992) *The Nissan enigma: Flexibility at work in a local economy*, London: Mansell.

GHK (2004) *An evaluation of Phoenix Fund support for community development finance institutions*, London: Small Business Service.

Goodwin, M., Jones, M. and Jones, R. (2005) 'Devolution, constitutional change and economic development: explaining and understanding the new institutional geographies of the devolved UK territories', *Regional Studies*, vol 39, no 4, pp 421-36.

Goos, M. and Manning, A. (2004) 'McJobs and MacJobs: the growing polarisation of jobs in the UK', in R. Dickens, P. Gregg and J. Wadsworth (eds) *The labour market under New Labour: The state of working Britain*, London: Palgrave Macmillan.

Gordon, I. (1996) 'Family structure, educational achievement and the inner city', *Urban Studies*, vol 33, no 3, pp 407-23.

Gordon, I. (2003) 'Unemployment and spatial labour markets: strong adjustment and persistent concentration', in R. Martin and P. Morrison (eds) *Geographies of labour market inequality*, London: Routledge, pp 55-82.

Gordon, I. (2005) 'Integrating cities', in N. Buck, I. Gordon, A. Harding and I. Turok (eds) *Changing cities: Rethinking urban competitiveness, cohesion and governance*, Basingstoke: Palgrave Macmillan, pp 78-93.

Gordon, I. and Buck, N. (2005) 'Introduction: cities in the new conventional wisdom', in N. Buck, I. Gordon, A. Harding and I. Turok (eds) *Changing cities: Rethinking urban competitiveness, cohesion and governance*, Basingstoke: Palgrave Macmillan, pp 1-21.

Gordon, I. and Turok, I. (2005) 'How urban labour markets matter', in N. Buck, I. Gordon, A. Harding and I. Turok (eds) *Changing cities: Rethinking urban competitiveness, cohesion and governance*, Basingstoke: Palgrave Macmillan, pp 242-64.

Gordon, I., Travers, T. and Whitehead, C. (2007) *The impact of recent immigration on the London economy*, London: London School of Economics and Political Science and the City of London.

Gore, T. and Fothergill, S. (2007) 'Cities and their hinterlands: how much do governance structures really matter?' *People, Place and Policy*, vol 1, no 2, pp 55-68.

Gore, T., Fothergill, S., Hollywood, E., Lindsay, C., Morgan, K., Powell, R. and Upton, S. (2007) *Coalfields and neighbouring cities: Economic regeneration, labour markets and governance*, York: Joseph Rowntree Foundation.

Gorz, A. (1999) *Reclaiming work: Beyond the wage-based society*, Cambridge: Polity Press.

Gough, J. (2002) 'Neoliberalism and socialisation in the contemporary city: opposites, complements and instabilities', *Antipode*, vol 34, no 3, pp 405-26.

Grabiner, Lord (2000) *The informal economy: A report by Lord Grabiner*, London: The Stationery Office.

Gray, C. (1998) *Enterprise and culture*, London: Routledge.

Green, A. (1997) 'Exclusion, unemployment and non-employment', *Regional Studies*, vol 31, no 5, pp 505-20.

Green, A. (2007) 'Local action on labour market integration of new arrivals: issues and dilemmas for policy', *Local Economy*, vol 22, no 4, pp 349-61.

Green, A. and Owen, D. (1998) *Where are the jobless? Changing unemployment and non-employment in cities and regions*, Bristol: The Policy Press.

Green, A. and Owen, D. (2006) *The geography of poor skills and access to work*, York: Joseph Rowntree Foundation.

Green, A. and White, R. (2007) *Attachment to place: Social networks, mobility and prospects of young people*, York: Joseph Rowntree Foundation.

Green, A., Jones, P. and Owen, D. (2007) *Migrant workers in the East Midlands labour market*, Nottingham: East Midlands Development Agency.

Greene, F., Mole, K. and Storey, D. (2004) 'Does more mean worse? Three decades of enterprise policy in the Tees Valley', *Urban Studies*, vol 41, no 7, pp 1207-28.

Greene, F., Mole, K. and Storey, D. (2007) *Three decades of entrepreneurial culture? Entrepreneurship, economic regeneration and public policy*, Basingstoke: Palgrave Macmillan.

Gregg, P. and Machin, S. (1997) *Blighted lives: Disadvantaged children and adult unemployment*, Paper CEPCP021, London: Centre for Economic Performance, London School of Economics and Political Science.

Griggs, J., Whitworth, A., Walker, R., McLennan, D. and Noble, M. (2008) *Person or place-based policies to tackle disadvantage? Not knowing what works*, York: Joseph Rowntree Foundation.

Hales, J., Taylor, R., Mandy, W. and Miller, M. (2003) *Evaluation of Employment Zones: Report on a cohort survey of long-term unemployed people in the zones and a matched set of comparison areas*, Research Report No 176, Sheffield: DWP.

Harker, L. (2006) *Delivering on child poverty: What would it take?*, London: DWP.

Harloe, M. (2001) 'Social justice and the city: the new "liberal formulation"', *International Journal of Urban and Regional Research*, vol 25, no 4, pp 889-97.

Hartshorn, C. and Sear, L. (2005) 'Employability and enterprise: evidence from the North East', *Urban Studies*, vol 42, no 2, pp 271-83.

Harvey, D. (1985) *The urbanisation of capital*, Oxford: Blackwell.

Harvey, D. (1996) *Justice, nature and the geography of difference*, Oxford: Blackwell.

Harvey, D. (2000) *Spaces of hope*, Edinburgh: Edinburgh University Press.

Hasluck, C. (1999) *Employers, young people and the unemployed: A review of research*, Research Report ESR 12, Sheffield: Employment Service.

Hasluck, C. (2002) *The re-engineered New Deal 25 Plus: A summary of recent evaluation evidence*, Research Report WAE 137, Sheffield: DWP.

Hasluck, C., Elias, P. and Green, A. (2003) *The wider labour market impact of Employment Zones*, Research Report No 175, Sheffield: DWP.

Haughton, G. (ed) (1999) *Community economic development*, London: The Stationery Office/Regional Studies Association.

Haughton, G., Jones, M., Peck, J., Tickell, A. and While, A. (2000) 'Labour market policy as flexible welfare: prototype Employment Zones and the new workfarism', *Regional Studies*, vol 34, no 7, pp 669-80.

Henry, N., Medhurst, J. and Lyttle, J. (2005) *Review of the Social Enterprise Strategy*, Birmingham: GHK Consulting.

Hibbitt, K., Jones, P. and Meegan, R. (2001) 'Tackling social exclusion: the role of social capital in urban regeneration on Merseyside – from mistrust to trust?', *European Planning Studies*, vol 9, no 2, pp 141-6.

Hills, J. and Stewart, K. (eds) (2005) *A more equal society? New Labour, poverty, inequality and exclusion*, Bristol: The Policy Press.

Hirst, A., Tarling, R., Lefaucheux, M., Short, M., Rinne, S., MacGregor, A., Glass, A., Evans, M. and Simm, C. (2002) *Qualitative evaluation of Employment Zones: A study of local delivery agents and area case studies*, Research Report WAE 124, Sheffield: DWP.

HM Treasury (1999) *Enterprise and social exclusion*, Policy Action Team 3, National Strategy for Neighbourhood Renewal, London: HM Treasury.

HM Treasury (2001) *Productivity in the UK: 3 – the regional dimension*, London: HM Treasury.

HM Treasury (2002) *Enterprise Britain: A modern approach to meeting the enterprise challenge*, London: HM Treasury.

HM Treasury (2005a) *Enterprise and economic opportunity in deprived areas: A consultation for a Local Enterprise Growth Initiative*, London: HM Treasury.

HM Treasury (2005b) *Enterprising Britain: A competition to select the 2005 British capital of enterprise*, London: HM Treasury.

HM Treasury (2006a) *The future role of the third sector in social and economic regeneration: Interim report*, London: HM Treasury.

HM Treasury (2006b) *Prosperity for all in the global economy – world class skills*, Leitch Review of Skills, London: HM Treasury.

HM Treasury, Department of Trade and Industry and Office of the Deputy Prime Minister (2003) *A modern regional policy for the United Kingdom*, London: HM Treasury.

HM Treasury, Department for Business Enterprise and Regulatory Reform, Communities and Local Government (2007) *Review of sub-national economic development and regeneration*, London: HM Treasury.

Hogarth, T. and Wilson, R. (2003) *Skill shortages, vacancies and local unemployment: A synthesis of the exploring local areas, skills and unemployment analyses*, Sheffield: DES.

Home Office (2001) *Community cohesion: A report of the independent review team* (The Cantle Report), London: Home Office.

Home Office (2005) *Controlling our borders: Making migration work for Britain*, London: Home Office.

House of Commons (1988) *The employment effects of the Urban Development Corporations*, House of Commons Employment Committee, London: HMSO.

House of Commons (2000) *Employability and jobs: Is there a jobs gap?*, Fourth Report, Session 1999-2000, HC 60-1, House of Commons Education and Employment Committee, London: The Stationery Office.

House of Commons (2002a) *The government's employment strategy*, Third Report, Session 2001-02, HC 815, House of Commons Work and Pensions Committee, London: The Stationery Office.

House of Commons (2002b) *The New Deal for Young People*, Sixty-Second Report, Session 2001-02, HC 700, House of Commons Public Accounts Committee, London: The Stationery Office.

Hutton, W. (1995) 'The 30-30-40 society', *Regional Studies*, vol 29, no 8, pp 719-21.

IFF Research (2005) *A survey of social enterprises across the UK*, London: Small Business Service.

Imrie, R. and Raco, M. (eds) (2003) *Urban renaissance? New Labour, community and urban policy*, Bristol: The Policy Press.

Imrie, R. and Thomas, H. (eds) (1999) *British urban policy and the Urban Development Corporations*, London: Paul Chapman Publishing.

Jencks, C. and Mayer, S. (1990) 'The social consequences of growing up in a poor neighbourhood', in L. Lynn and M. McGeary (eds) *Inner city poverty in the United States*, Washington, DC: National Academic Press, pp 111-86.

Jones, M. and Ward, K. (2002) 'Excavating the logic of British urban policy: neo-liberalism, as the "crisis of crisis management"', *Antipode*, vol 34, no 3, pp 473-94.

Kasparova, D., Marsh, A., Vegeris, S. and Perry, J. (2003) *Families and children 2001: Work and childcare*, Research Report No 191, London: DWP.

Katungi, D., Neale, E. and Barbour, A. (2006) *Need not greed: Informal paid work*, York: Joseph Rowntree Foundation.

Kearns, A. and Parkinson, M. (2001) 'The significance of neighbourhood', *Urban Studies*, vol 38, no 12, pp 2103-10.

Kitson, M., Martin, R. and Wilkinson, F. (2000) 'Labour markets, social justice and economic efficiency', *Cambridge Journal of Economics*, vol 42, no 6, pp 631-41.

Kleinman, M. (1998) *Include me out? The new politics of place and poverty*, CASE Paper No 11, London: London School of Economics and Political Science.

Kloosterman, R., van der Leun, J. and Rath, J. (1999) 'Mixed embeddedness: immigrant entrepreneurship and informal economic activities', *International Journal of Urban and Regional Research*, vol 23, no 2, pp 253-67.

Lawless, P. (1995) 'Inner-city and suburban labour markets in a major English conurbation: processes and policy implications', *Urban Studies*, vol 32, no 7, pp 1097-125.

Lawless, P. (2007) 'Continuing dilemmas for area based urban regeneration: evidence from the New Deal for Communities Programme in England', *People, Place and Policy*, vol 1, no 1, pp 14-21.

Lees, L., Slater, T. and Wyly, E. (2007) *Gentrification*, New York: Routledge.

Lepine, E., Smith, I., Sullivan, H. and Taylor, M. (2007) 'Introduction: of neighbourhoods and governance', in I. Smith, E. Lepine and M. Taylor (eds) *Disadvantaged by where you live? Neighbourhood governance in contemporary urban policy*, Bristol: The Policy Press, pp 1-20.

Leyshon, A. and Thrift, N. (1995) 'Geographies of financial exclusion: financial abandonment in Britain and the United States', *Transactions of the Institute of British Geographers*, vol 20, no 3, pp 312-41.

Lindsay, C. and McQuaid, R. (2004) 'Avoiding the McJobs: unemployed job seekers and attitudes to service work', *Work, Employment and Society*, vol 18, no 2, pp 298-319.

Llanes, M. and Barbour, A. (2007) *Self-employed and micro-entrepreneurs: Informal trading and the journey towards formalisation*, London: Community Links.

London Assembly (2007) *London Olympic Games and Paralympic Games: The employment and skills legacy*, London: The Economic Development, Culture, Sport and Tourism Committee, London Assembly.

London Borough of Newham (2003) *Focus on Newham: Local people and local conditions*, London: London Borough of Newham.

Lupton, R. (2003) *Poverty street: The dynamics of neighbourhood decline and renewal*, Bristol: The Policy Press.

Lyon, F., Smallbone, D., Evans, M., Ekanem, I. and Smith, K. (2002) *Mapping the social economy in the rural East Midlands*, Report for the Countryside Agency by CEEDR, London: Middlesex University.

Lyon, F., Sepulveda, L. and Syrett, S. (2007) 'Enterprising refugees: contributions and challenges in deprived areas', *Local Economy*, vol 22, no 4, pp 363-76.

Macdonald, F. (1996) 'Welfare dependency, the enterprise culture and self-employed survival', *Work, Employment and Society*, vol 11, no 3, pp 431-47.

Maclennan, D. (2000) *Changing places, engaging people*, York: Joseph Rowntree Foundation/York Publishing Services.

Madanipour, A., Cars, G. and Allen, J. (1998) *Social exclusion in European cities: Processes, experiences, responses*, London: Jessica Kingsley Publishers/ Regional Studies Association.

Manski, C. (1993) 'The identification of endogenous social effects: the reflection problem', *Review of Economic Studies*, vol 60, no 3, pp 531-42.

Marcuse, P. and Van Kempen, R. (eds) (2000) *Globalizing cities: A new spatial order?*, Oxford: Blackwell.

Marsh, D., Richards, D. and Smith, M. (2003) 'Unequal plurality: towards an asymmetric power model of the British polity', *Government and Opposition*, vol 38, no 3, pp 306-32.

Martin, R. and Morrison, P. (2003) 'Thinking about the geographies of labour', in R. Martin and P. Morrison (eds) *Geographies of labour market inequality*, London: Routledge, pp 3-20.

Martin, R., Nativel, C. and Sunley, P. (2003) 'The local impact of the New Deal: does geography make a difference?', in R. Martin and P. Morrison (ed) *Geographies of labour market inequality*, London: Routledge, pp 175-207.

Massey, D. (1997) 'A global sense of place', in T. Barnes and D. Gregory (eds) *Reading human geography*, London: Arnold, pp 315-23.

Massey, D. (2005) *For space*, London: Sage Publications.

Massey, D. and Denton, N. (1993) *American apartheid: Segregation and the making of the underclass*, Cambridge, MA: Harvard University Press.

May, J., Wills, J., Datta, K., Evans, Y., Herbert, J. and McIlwaine, C. (2007) 'Keeping London working: global cities, the British state and London's new migrant division of labour', *Transactions of the Institute of British Geographers*, vol 32, no 2, pp 151-67.

Mayo, E. (1996) 'Dreaming of work', in P. Meadows (ed) *Work out or work in? Contributions to the debate on the future of work*, York: Joseph Rowntree Foundation, pp 143-64.

Mayo, M., Thake, S. and Gibson, T. (2003) *Taking power: An agenda for community economic renewal*, London: New Economics Foundation.

McCulloch, A. (2001) 'Ward level deprivation and individual social and economic outcomes in the British Household Panel Study', *Environment and Planning A*, vol 33, no 4, pp 667-84.

McGregor, A. and McConnachie, M. (1995) 'Social exclusion, urban regeneration and economic reintegration', *Urban Studies*, vol 32, no 10, pp 1587-600.

McGregor, A., Ferguson, Z., Fitzpatrick, I., McConnachie, M. and Richmond, K. (1997) *Bridging the jobs gap: An evaluation of the Wise Group and the intermediate labour market*, York: Joseph Rowntree Foundation.

McKay, S. (2003) *Working Families' Tax Credit in 2001*, Research Report No 181, London: DWP.

McQuaid, R. and Lindsay, C. (2002) 'The "employability gap": long-term unemployment and barriers to work in buoyant labour markets', *Environment and Planning C*, vol 20, no 4, pp 613-28.

McQuaid, R. and Lindsay, C. (2005) 'The concept of employability', *Urban Studies*, vol 42, no 2, pp 197-219.

Meadows, P. (2001) *Young men on the margins of work: An overview report*, York: Joseph Rowntree Foundation.

Meegan, R. (1999) 'Urban Development Corporations: urban entrepreneurialism and locality: the Merseyside Development Corporation', in R. Imrie and H.Thomas (eds) *Urban policy and locality*, London: Sage, pp 64-105.

Modood, T., Virdee, S. and Metcalf, H. (1995) *Asian self-employment in Britain: The interaction of culture and economics*, London: Policy Studies Institute.

Mole, K., Greene, F. and Storey, D. (2002) 'Entrepreneurship in three English counties', Paper presented at the ISBA 26th National Small Firms Policy and Research Conference, University of Brighton.

Moore, B. and Begg, I. (2004) 'Urban growth and competitiveness in Britain: a long-run perspective', in M. Boddy and M. Parkinson (eds) *City matters: Competitiveness, cohesion and urban governance*, Bristol: The Policy Press, pp 93-110.

Morris, L.D. (1993) 'Is there a British underclass?', *International Journal of Urban and Regional Research*, vol 17, no 3, pp 404-12.

Mumford, K. and Power, A. (2003) *East Enders: Family and community in East London*, Bristol: The Policy Press.

Murray, C. (1996) 'The emerging British underclass', in R. Lister (ed) *Charles Murray and the underclass: The developing debate*, London: Institute for Economic Affairs, pp 23-52.

Musson, S., Tickell, A. and John, P. (2005) 'A decade of decentralisation? Assessing the role of the Government Offices for the English regions', *Environment and Planning A*, vol 37, no 8, pp 1395-412.

National Audit Office (2007) *Helping people from workless households into work*, London: National Audit Office.

National Employment Panel (2005) *Enterprising people, enterprising places: Measures to increase ethnic minority employment and business growth*, London: National Employment Panel.

NEF (New Economics Foundation) (2002) *Plugging the leaks*, London: NEF.

NEF (2004) *The inner city 100: Impacts and influences*, London: NEF.

NEF (2005) *Clone town Britain*, London: NEF.

NEF (2008) *Hitting the target, missing the point: How government regeneration targets fail deprived areas*, London: NEF.

Nevin, B. (1998) 'Renewing the Black Country: an assessment of the employment impact of the Black Country UDC', *Local Economy*, vol 13, no 3, pp 239-54.

North, D. and Syrett, S. (2006) *The dynamics of local economies and deprived neighbourhoods*, London: DCLG.

North, D. and Syrett, S. (2008) 'Making the links: economic deprivation, neighbourhood renewal and scales of governance', *Regional Studies*, vol 42, no 1, pp 133-48.

North, D., Smallbone, D. and Leigh, R. (1994) 'Employment and labour process changes in manufacturing SMEs during the 1980s', in J. Atkinson and D. Storey (eds) *Employment, the small firm and the labour market*, London: Routledge, pp 206-55.

North, D., Stanworth, T. and Hotchkiss, G. (2002) *The use of the Single Regeneration Budget in London, 1994–2000: A mapping and classification of regeneration programmes*, London Regeneration Paper No 4, London: Middlesex University.

North, D., Syrett, S. and Etherington, D. (2007) *Devolution and regional governance: Tackling the economic needs of deprived areas*, York: Joseph Rowntree Foundation.

Oatley, N. (1998) 'Transitions in urban policy: explaining the emergence of the "Challenge Fund" model', in N. Oatley (ed) *Cities, economic competition and urban policy*, London: Paul Chapman, pp 21-37.

Oc, T. and Tiesdell, S. (1999) 'Supporting ethnic minority business: a review of business support for ethnic minorities in City Challenge areas', *Urban Studies*, vol 36, no 10, pp 1723-46.

ODPM (Office of the Deputy Prime Minister) (2004) *The English Indices of Deprivation 2004*, London: ODPM.

ODPM (2005) *National evaluation of Local Strategic Partnerships: LSPs, multi-level governance and economic development*, London: ODPM.

ODPM (2006) *An exploratory assessment of the economic case for regeneration investment from a national perspective*, London: ODPM.

OECD (Organisation for Economic Cooperation and Development) (2003) *Urban renaissance: Berlin. Towards an integrated strategy for social cohesion and economic development*, Paris: OECD.

Office for National Statistics (2005) *Annual population survey 2005*, London: Office for National Statistics.

One NorthEast (2006) *Leading the way: Regional economic strategy 2006–16*, Newcastle: One NorthEast Regional Development Agency.

Ostendorf, W., Musterd, S. and de Vos, S. (2001) 'Social mix and neighbourhood effect: policy ambitions and empirical evidence', *Housing Studies*, vol 16, no 3, pp 371-80.

Parkinson, M., Champion, T., Evans, R., Simmie, J., Turok, I., Crookston, M., Katz, B., Park, A., Berube, A., Coombes, M., Dorling, D., Glass, N., Hutchins, N., Kearns, A., Martin, R. and Wood, P. (2006) *The state of the English cities: Vols 1 and 2*, London: ODPM.

Peck, J. (1999) 'New labourers? Making a new deal for the "workless" class', *Environment and Planning C*, vol 17, no 3, pp 345-72.

Peck, J. (2001) *Workfare states*, New York: Guilford Press.

Peck, J. and Tickell, A. (2007) 'Conceptualising neoliberalism, thinking Thatcherism', in H. Leitner, J. Peck and E. S. Sheppard (eds) *Contesting neoliberalism*, New York: Guilford Press, pp 26-50.

Phizacklea, A. and Ram, M. (1995) 'Open for business? Ethnic entrepreneurship in comparative perspective', *Work, Employment and Society*, vol 10, no 2, pp 319-39.

Pike, A., Champion, T., Coombes, L., Humprey, L. and Tomaney, J. (2006a) *New Horizons programme: The economic viability and self-containment of geographical economies: A framework for analysis*, London: ODPM.

Pike, A., Rodriguez-Pose, A. and Tomaney, J. (2006b) *Local and regional development*, London: Routledge.

PMSU (Prime Minister's Strategy Unit) (2005) *Improving the prospects of people living in areas of multiple deprivation in England*, London: Cabinet Office.

Policy Research Institute (2007) *Towards skills for jobs: What works in tackling worklessness?*, Coventry: Learning and Skills Council.

Porter, M. (1995) 'The competitive advantage of the inner city', *Harvard Business Review*, May-June, pp 55-71.

Porter, M. (1997) 'New strategies for inner city economic development', *Economic Development Quarterly*, vol 11, no 1, pp 11-27.

Potter, J. and Moore, B. (2000) 'UK Enterprise Zones and the attraction of inward investment', *Urban Studies*, vol 37, no 8, pp 1279-312.

Potts, G. (2002) 'Competitiveness and the social-fabric: links and tensions in cities', in I. Begg (ed) *Urban competitiveness: policies for dynamic cities*, Bristol: The Policy Press, pp 55-80.

Power, A. (1996) 'Area-based poverty and resident empowerment', *Urban Studies*, vol 33, no 9, pp 1535-64.

Power, A. (1997) *Estates on the edge: The social consequences of mass housing in Northern Europe*, New York: St Martin's Press.

Power, A. (2000) 'Poor areas and social exclusion', in A. Power and W.J. Wilson (eds) *Social exclusion and the future of cities*, CASE Paper No. 35, London: Centre for Analysis of Social Exclusion, London School of Economics and Political Science.

Power, A. and Houghton, J. (2007) *Jigsaw cities: Big places, small spaces*, Bristol: The Policy Press.

Putnam, R. (2000) *Bowling alone: The collapse and revival of American community*, New York: Simon and Schuster.

Putnam, R. (2007) 'E Pluribus Unum: diversity and community in the twenty-first century: the 2006 Johan Skytte Prize Lecture', *Scandinavian Political Studies*, vol 30, no 2, pp 137-74.

Raco, M. (2005) 'Sustainable development, rolled-out neoliberalism and sustainabile communities', *Antipode*, vol 37, no 2, pp 324-47.

Ram, M. and Smallbone, D. (2001) *Ethnic minority enterprise: Policy in practice*, London: Small Business Service.

Ram, M. and Smallbone, D. (2003) 'Policies to support ethnic minority enterprise: the English experience', *Entrepreneurship and Regional Development*, vol 15, no 2, pp 151-66.

Ram, M., Abbas, B., Sanghera, B. and Hillin, G. (2000) 'Currying favour with the locals: Balti-owners and business enclaves', *International Journal of Entrepreneurial Behaviour and Research*, vol 6, no 1, pp 41-55.

Ram, M., Smallbone, D. and Deakins, D. (2002) *Ethnic minority businesses in the UK: Access to finance and business support*, London: British Bankers Association.

Renaisi Ltd and Ancer Spa (2003) *Workspace supply and demand in the City Fringe*, London: City Fringe Partnership.

Rhodes, J., Tyler, J. and Brennan, A. (2002) *Lessons and evaluation evidence from ten Single Regeneration Budget case studies: Mid term report*, London: DETR.

Rhodes, J., Tyler, P. and Brennan, A. (2007) *Evaluation of the Single Regeneration Budget: A partnership for regeneration*, Cambridge: Department for Land Economy, University of Cambridge.

Richardson, R. and Marshall, N. (1999) 'Teleservices, call centres and urban and regional development', *The Services Industries Journal*, vol 19, no 1, pp 96-116.

Ritchie, H., Casebourne, J. and Rick, J. (2005) *Understanding workless people and communities: A literature review*, Research Report DWPRR255, London: DWP.

Roberts, F. (1999) *Young people out of work in South West Newham*, Commentary Series No 83, London: Centre for Institutional Studies, University of East London.

Roberts, P. and Sykes, H. (2000) *Urban regeneration: A handbook*, London: Sage Publications.

Robson, B., Parkinson, M. and Robinson, F. (1994) *Assessing the impact of urban policy*, London: HMSO.

Robson, B., Bradford, M. and Deas, J. (1999) 'Beyond the boundaries: vacancy chains and the evaluation of Urban Development Corporations', *Environment and Planning A*, vol 31, no 4, pp 647-64.

Robson, B., Lymperopoulou, K. and Rae, A. (2008, forthcoming), 'People on the move: exploring the functional roles of deprived neighbourhoods', *Environment and Planning A*.

Robson, B., Peck, J. and Holden, A. (2000) *Regional agencies and area based regeneration*, Bristol: The Policy Press.

Rowthorn, R. and Webster, D. (2006) *Male worklessness and the rise of lone parenthood in Britain*, Working Paper No 30, Oxford: Oxford Centre for Population Research.

Sampson, R. (1988) 'Local friendship ties and community attachment in mass society', *American Sociological Review*, vol 55, no 5, pp 766-79.

Sampson, R. (1999) 'What "community" supplies', in R. Ferguson and W. Dickens (eds) *Urban problems and community development*, Washington, DC: Brookings Institution Press, pp 241-92.

Sampson, R. and Groves, W. B. (1989) 'Community structure and crime: testing social disorganisation theory', *American Journal of Sociology*, vol 94, no 4, pp 774-802.

Sanderson, I. (2006) *Worklessness in deprived neighbourhoods: A review of evidence*, Report to the Neighbourhood Renewal Unit, London: DCLG.

Sanderson, I., Walton, F. and Campbell, M. (1999) *Back to work: Local action on unemployment*, York: Joseph Rowntree Foundation.

Sassen, S. (2001) *The global city: New York, London, Tokyo* (2nd edition), Princeton, NJ, and London: Princeton University Press.

Scase, R. (1997) 'The role of small businesses in the economic transformation of Eastern Europe: real but relatively unimportant?', *International Small Business Journal*, vol 16, no 1, pp 13-21.

Sen, A. (1999) *Development as freedom*, Oxford: Oxford University Press.

Sepulveda, L. (2007) *Access to employment and enterprise opportunities for newly arrived Latin Americans in London: Assessing barriers, skills and needs*, Report for Celebrating Enterprise, City University and the *Carnaval del Pueblo* Association, London: CEEDR, Middlesex University.

Sepulveda, L. and Syrett, S. (2007) 'Out of the shadows? Formalisation approaches to informal economic activity', *Policy & Politics*, vol 35, no 1, pp 87–104.

Sepulveda, L., Lyon, F. and Syrett, S. (2006) *Refugees, new arrivals and enterprise: Their contributions and constraints*, London: Small Business Service and Business Link for London.

SEU (Social Exclusion Unit) (1999) *Policy Action Team 3: Enterprise and social exclusion: Final report*, London: SEU.

SEU (2000) *National strategy for neighbourhood renewal: A framework for consultation*, London: Cabinet Office.

SEU (2001) *A new commitment to neighbourhood renewal: National strategy action plan*, London: Cabinet Office.

SEU (2003) *Making the connections: Final report on transport and social exclusion*, London: SEU.

SEU (2004) *Jobs and enterprise in deprived areas*, London: ODPM.

Shuttleworth, I., Green, A. and Lavery, S. (2003) 'Young people, job search and local labour markets: the example of Belfast', Paper presented at the seminar 'Employability: Lessons for Labour Market Policy', University of Warwick, 13 May.

Sinclair, S. (2001) *Financial exclusion: An introductory survey*, Edinburgh: CRSIS Heriot Watt University.

Skifter-Anderson, H. (2003) *Urban sores: On the integration between segregation, urban decay and deprived neighbourhoods*, Aldershot: Ashgate.

Small Business Council (2004) *The informal economy: Making the transition to the formal economy*, London: Small Business Council.

Small Business Service (2004) *A government action plan for small business: The evidence base*, London: DTI.

Smallbone, D., Bertotti, M. and Ekanem, I. (2005) 'Diversification in ethnic minority business: the case of Asians in London's creative industries', *Journal of Small Business and Enterprise Development*, vol 12, no 1, pp 41-56.

Smith, A. (2006) 'Three district enterprise growth solutions prove a successful alternative to city-based approaches in the East Midlands', *Local Economy*, vol 21, no 3, pp 328-32.

Smith, D. (2000) 'Dealed out? Welfare to work and social exclusion', *Local Economy*, vol 15, no 4, pp 312-24.

Smith, D. and Wistrich, E. (2001) *Ethnic minority businesses and social capital: Contributions to regeneration?*, London Regeneration Paper No 2, London: Middlesex University.

Smith, I., Lepine, E. and Taylor, M. (eds) (2007) *Disadvantaged by where you live? Neighbourhood governance in contemporary urban policy*, Bristol: The Policy Press.

Smith, N. (1996) *The new urban frontier: Gentrification and revanchist city*, London: Routledge.

Song, M. (1999) *Helping out*, Philadelphia, PA: Temple University Press.

Speak, S. (2000) 'Barriers to lone parents' employment: looking beyond the obvious', *Local Economy*, vol 15, no 1, pp 32-44.

Speak, S. and Graham, S. (2000) *Service not included: Social implications of private sector restructuring in marginalised neighbourhoods*, Bristol: The Policy Press.

Stafford, B., Heaver, C., Ashworth, K., Bates, C., Walker, R., McKay, S. and Trickey, H. (1999) *Work and young men*, York: Joseph Rowntree Foundation.

Stedmen Jones, G. (1971) *Outcast London: A study in the relationship between classes in Victorian London*, Oxford: Clarendon Press.

Stewart, M. (1994) 'Between Whitehall and town hall: the realignment of urban regeneration policy in England', *Policy & Politics*, vol 22, no 2, pp 133-45.

Storey, D. (1994) *Understanding the small business sector*, London: Routledge.

Storper, M. (1995) 'The resurgence of regional economies, ten years later: the region as a nexus of untraded interdependencies', *European Urban and Regional Studies*, vol 2, no 3, pp 191-221.

Storper, M. (1997) *The regional world: Territorial development in a global economy*, London: Guilford Press.

Strategy Unit (2002) *Delivering for children and families*, Inter-Departmental Childcare Review, London: Strategy Unit.

Strugnell, C., Furey, S. and Farley, H. (2003) 'Food deserts – an example of social exclusion?, *Journal of Customer Studies*, vol 27, no 3, pp 229-30.

Sullivan, H. and Taylor, M. (2007) 'Theories of "neighbourhood" in urban policy', in I. Smith, E. Lepine and M. Taylor (eds) *Disadvantaged by where you live? Neighbourhood governance in contemporary urban policy*, Bristol: The Policy Press, pp 21-42.

Sunderland Partnership (2006) *International Strategy for Sunderland*, Consultative Draft.

Swash, T. (2007) 'Enterprise, diversity and inclusion: a new model of community-based enterprise development', *Local Economy*, vol 22, no 4, pp 395-401.

Swyngedouw, E., Moulaert, F. and Rodriguez, A. (2002) 'Neoliberal urbanization in Europe: large-scale urban development projects and the new urban policy', *Antipode*, vol 34, no 3, pp 542-77.

Syrett, S. (2006) 'Governing the global city: economic challenges and London's new institutional arrangements', *Local Government Studies*, vol 32, no 3, pp 293-309.

Syrett, S. and Lyons, M. (2007) 'Migration, new arrivals and local economies', *Local Economy*, vol 22, no 4, pp 325-34.

Taylor, M. (1999) 'Survival of the fittest? An analysis of self-employment duration in Britain', *Economic Journal*, vol 109, no 454, pp C140-55.

Taylor, M. (2002) 'Community and social exclusion', in V. Nash (ed) *Reclaiming community*, London: Institute for Public Policy Research.

Townsend, P. (1979) *Poverty in the United Kingdom*, Harmondsworth: Penguin.

TUC Commission on Vulnerable Employment (2008) *Hard work, hidden lives: The short report of the Commission on Vulnerable Employment*, London: Trade Union Congress.

Turok, I. (1992) 'Property-led urban regeneration: panacea or placebo?', *Environment and Planning A*, vol 24, no 3, pp 361-79.

Turok, I. (1993) 'Inward investment and local linkages: how deeply-embedded is Silicon Glen?', *Regional Studies*, vol 27, no 5, pp 401-17.

Turok, I. (1995) 'Multinational/supplier linkages in the Scottish electronics industry', in F. Chittenden, M. Robertson and I. Marshall (eds) *Small firms: Partnerships for growth*, London: Paul Chapman Publishing, pp 152-68.

Turok, I. and Edge, N. (1999) *The jobs gap in Britain's cities: Employment loss and labour market consequences*, Bristol: The Policy Press.

Turok, I., Bailey, N., Atkinson, R., Bramley, G., Docherty, I., Gibb, K., Goodlad, R., Hastings, A., Kintrea, K., Kirk, K., Leibovitz, J., Lever, W., Morgan, J. and Paddison, R. (2004) 'Sources of city prosperity and cohesion: the case of Glasgow and Edinburgh', in M. Boddy and M. Parkinson (eds) *City matters: Competitiveness, cohesion and urban governance*, Bristol: The Policy Press, pp 13-31.

Van Stel, A. and Storey, D. (2004) 'The link between firm births and job creation: is there a Upas tree effect?', *Regional Studies*, vol 38, no 8, pp 893-910.

Vertovec, S. (2006) *The emergence of super diversity in Britain*, Working Paper No 25, Oxford: Centre on Migration, Policy and Society, University of Oxford.

Wacquant, L.J.D. (1996) 'Red belt, black belt: racial division, class inequality and the state in the French urban periphery and the American ghetto', in E. Mingione (ed) *Urban poverty and the underclass: A reader*, Oxford: Blackwell, pp 234-74.

Watt, P. (2003) 'Urban marginality and labour market restructuring: local authority tenants and employment in an inner London Borough', *Urban Studies*, vol 40, no 9, pp 1769-89.

Webster, D. (1999) 'Targeted local jobs: the missing element in Labour's social inclusion policy', *New Economy*, vol 6, no 4, pp 193-8.

Webster, D. (2000) 'The geographical concentration of labour-market disadvantage', *Oxford Review of Economic Policy*, vol 16, no 1, pp 114-28.

Webster, D. (2006) 'Welfare reform: facing up to the geography of worklessness', *Local Economy*, vol 21, no 2, pp 107-16.

White, J. (2003) *Campbell Bunk: The worst street in North London between the wars*, London: Pimlico.

Wilkinson, D. (2003) *New Deal for People Aged 25 and Over: A synthesis report*, Research Report W161, Sheffield: DWP.

Williams, C.C. (2001) 'Tackling the participation of the unemployed in paid informal work: a critical evaluation of the deterrence approach', *Environment and Planning C: Government and Policy*, vol 19, no 5, pp 729-49.

Williams, C.C. (2004) 'Local initiatives to tackle informal employment: developing a formalisation support and advisory service', *Local Governance*, vol 39, no 2, pp 89-97.

Williams, C.C. and Windebank, J. (1998) *Informal employment in the advanced economies: Implications for work and welfare*, London: Routledge.

Williams, C.C. and Windebank, J. (2001) *Revitalising deprived urban neighbourhoods: An assisted self-help approach*, Aldershot: Ashgate.

Wilson, W. J. (1996) *When work disappears: The world of the new urban poor*, New York: Knopf.

Woodland, S., Miller, M. and Tipping, S. (2002) *Repeat study of parents' demand for childcare*, Research Report No 348, Sheffield: DfES.

Wrigley, N. (2002) '"Food deserts" in British cities: policy context and research priorities', *Urban Studies*, vol 39, no 11, pp 2029-40.

Wrigley, N., Warm, D. and Margetts, B. (2003) 'Deprivation, diet and food-retail access: findings from the Leeds "food deserts" study', *Environment and Planning A*, vol 35, no 1, pp 151-88.

Zacharakis, A., Bygrave, W. and Shepherd, D. (2000) *Global Entrepreneurship Monitor: National entrepreneurship assessment*, Kansas City: Kauffman Centre for Entrepreneurial Leadership.

Index

Note: Page numbers followed by *fig* or *tab* indicate that information is in a figure or a table respectively.

A

Action for Cities 22*tab*
Action Team for Jobs (ATJ) 126*tab*, 128, 129–30, 131
Action Zones 29, 30*tab*
Adams, J. 110
age and deprivation 71, 72
Amin, A. 164
area (neighbourhood) effects 10, 19, 75–7, 80, 92
Area-Based Grant (ABG) 31*tab*, 33, 214, 247
area-based initiatives (ABIs) 1, 2, 20–5, 23*tab*, 29, 137–8
  criticisms 20, 24, 91, 238
  enterprise policies 166–9, 186
  and worklessness 97, 125–6*tab*, 127–31
Ashfield LEGI 180, 181*tab*, 182–3
Audretsch, D. 143

B

Bailey, N. 72
Bank of England 160
Beatty, C. 96, 116
Beckton, Newham 59–60, 63, 71, 73, 74*tab*, 113*tab*
Begg, I. 25
benefits system 116, 121–2
  see also Incapacity Benefit
Berthoud, R. 110, 112
Birch, D. 154
Bizfizz initiative 239
black and minority ethnic businesses (BMEBs) 158–61, 164–5, 177*tab*
Blackaby, D. 110–11
Blackburn, R 159–60
Boddy, M. 6, 37
Bolsover LEGI 180, 181*tab*, 182–3
'bonding' social capital 51–2, 117
Brennan, A. 171
Brent and Harrow Business Support scheme 171
'bridging' social capital 52, 117
Bright, E. 51, 92
Brighton and Hove (case study area) 54–5, 56, 57*tab*, 60*tab*, 100–1
  enterprise and entrepreneurship 152, 172
  and ethnic diversity 74*tab*
  manufacturing decline 63, 64*tab*
  population structure 66, 71
  work and worklessness
    and educational attainment 113*tab*
    employment deprivation 101, 102, 105–6
    employment growth sectors 68*tab*
    employment rate 97–8, 99*tab*
    see also North Moulsecoomb; Saunders Park
British Household Panel Survey 119
Buck, N. 92, 111
Business Improvement Districts 248
business investment
  challenge to attract 248–9
  and enterprise 145–8, 174–6
  lacking in deprived neighbourhoods 50–1, 85, 87, 241
business start-ups *see* new business formation

C

call centres and inward investment 147–8
Carley, M. 86
case study local economies 53–61
  deprived areas 58–61
  and enterprise 151–2, 162–3, 172
  work and worklessness 97–102
    and educational attainment 113–14
    and policy initiatives 125–6*tab*, 127–8, 132–7
centralisation and coordination 224, 229
Chell, E. 145
Cheshire, P. 84–5, 91
childcare 122–3
cities
  and economic success 34–5
  and spatial concentration of deprivation 6–8, 12
  concentrations of worklessness 96
  see also urban policy
City Action Teams 22*tab*, 28